The Ipsalu Formula ~
A Method for
Tantra Bliss

The Ipsalu Formula ~
A Method for
Tantra Bliss

BODHI AVINASHA

Formatted by Sharon A. Dunn
Cover Art by Carol Flowers

DISCLAIMER:

Ipsalu Tantric Kriya Yoga is a system of practices promoting health and well-being. Caution and common sense should be used in following any of the suggestions about food, exercise, sexual activity, etc. This course is not meant to replace competent medical advice. Anyone suffering from venereal disease or any local illness of their sexual organs should consult a medical doctor before practicing the methods taught here.

ISBN: 0-929459-01-6
LCCN: 2002115906

IPSALU PUBLISHING
12115 Magnolia Blvd. #143
Valley Village, CA 91607
IpsaluTantra.com
info@IpsaluTantra.com
(800) 451-3704

Ipsalu Publishing

Special Thanks

To Sunyata Saraswati, my tantra teacher, for sharing with me the science of Kriya Yoga and many of the techniques presented here.

To Dick Asimus, whose dedicated efforts and great sensitivity have moved the work to the level of community. His assistance with the manuscript goes way beyond skillful editing. His clarity and integrity are reflected in every page.

To Teresa Johnston, Tom and Clare Vetter, Jean Paul Setlak, Nanji Cohran and Lexi Fisher for reading and commenting on the manuscript. Their input has been invaluable.

To Alston Anderson for many of the illustrations, and Lorraine Suzuki for helping in many ways. And to the people who have come into courses to transform their lives and to be teachers for me.

But most of all, to Babaji, my continual companion and inspiration.

ABOUT THE COVER

When a large metal plate is sprinkled with sand and vibrated by a sustained tone, the vibrations of the plate produce a pattern in the sand (see Chapter 4). The sound AH is the sound of the heart, the sound of orgasm. Of all the sounds in creation this is the sound that most strongly connects a person to the physical plane. That vibration creates on the metal plate two interlocking triangles, the ancient yogic symbol of the heart, representing the union of energies of male and female – heaven and earth – TantraBliss. The sand also produces perfect circles inside the triangles and outside. We have added the twelve petals traditionally associated with the heart chakra. The cover of *Jewel in the Lotus* depicts a couple in rapturous union, enfolded in a pink lotus. Here we see that same picture in symbolic form. Thanks to Carol Flowers for her lovely and inspired rendering of this symbol. Inquire about her collection of symbols as cards, etc. *(starflower@fuse.net)*.

Participants Speak of Their Experience

"Ipsalu Tantra is about opening wide the doorway to your soul. Connecting heart to heart with the pulse of the entire universe, found within each other. Seeing, feeling, touching, tasting, hearing the divinity of the present. It's like falling in love for the first time, over and over again. It's unsurpassed emotional healing."

  – Maureen Mueller (Hollywood, FL)

"Tantra International's work is to enable people to play. I've experienced and collapsed perimeters of old belief systems that held me away from my own inspiration, kept me at a distance from others and made intimacy taboo. The opening up of my life from first and second level Ipsalu Tantra courses has moved me into an unlimited place of joy and intimacy. Thank you."

  – Stan North (Hamilton, MT)

"Ipsalu is pure love. We learn to see the original innocence in each other and ourselves. By sharing our pain and our joys with each other, we come to see that we are all one and yet we also come to appreciate our uniqueness. It's the best process, by far, to heal sexual shame and unite the spiritual and the sexual."

  – Pat Sheehan (Indianapolis, IN)

"Ipsalu Tantra is more than the teaching of particular techniques or practice of ancient exercises. Ipsalu Tantra is about sensation, about leaving the mind aside for a while and allowing your true self, the self that just loves, to come to the surface. This sense of unity and self-love can only be experienced and not explained. Ipsalu Tantra is the blending of the physical and spiritual bodies to provide a sense of Bliss that you can carry wherever you go."

  – Iossy Medvinsky (Indianapolis, IN)

"My physical, sexual self is alive and beautiful. The awakening body has become my spiritual path to love and joy and immeasurable compassion for the world."

  – Clare Vetter (Maysville, KY)

"Ipsalu Tantra is an expression of love that bubbles up from the bottom of my soul. It's a feeling of companionship, as though two long-lost lovers are embracing after seeing each other again. It's a child in play, dancing to the beat of drums in full ecstasy. As the breath is inhaled, the light of the Gods enters my being, and on my exhalation I have a sensation of flying free on a breeze with nowhere to go."

– Jay Valinsky (Davie, FL)

"After more than twenty years of spiritual work and study, Ipsalu has been the most profound experience of my life. Barriers to our whole pure essence are removed. What's remaining is the experience of love. Imagine all of the work one does in the course of a lifetime to overcome barriers. What would be possible if those barriers were simply removed?"

– Megan Riley (Bloomington, IN)

"… Deeply and profoundly moving, and at the same time, ecstatic and joyous. The source of a behavior pattern that puzzled me for years became clear, and I know its hold on me is loosened, maybe even released!"

– Terri Maue (Cincinnati, OH)

"I'm learning to see who each person is and not what they look like, who they present themselves to be, or what I project onto them. Through learning to be present to the feelings I experience in any given moment, I am learning to experience the divine essence of other beings and to embody in my heart, mind, and soul the understanding that we are all one."

– Rad A. Drew (Indianapolis, IN)

"… An opportunity to go beyond, beyond the places I dared not go before, and then to emerge on the other side feeling a cleansing of the innermost depths of my body, mind, and spirit. The experience left me feeling like the miraculous being of divine light that my true self longs to be and share."

– Tracey Deiger (Cincinnati, OH)

FOREWORD:
FROM THE AUTHOR

The Ipsalu Formula ~ A Method for TantraBliss began as the follow-up materials for the weekend course "Living in Bliss." Materials introduced in that intensive are included and greatly expanded here.

The book can in no way replace the course. The awakening that happens there, the quantum leap of awareness, simply cannot be captured on paper. The group energy makes that magic happen. Being familiar with the conceptual basis in advance of the course allows one to go more deeply into that experience.

This is a companion piece to my earlier book *Jewel in the Lotus*. This book does stand alone but it presumes you have the background presented in *Jewel*. The basic practices, which we continue to recommend, are detailed there and not always repeated in this book. We refer frequently to material in *Jewel*, developing it more deeply, more scientifically, more practically.

Jewel in the Lotus was written shortly after I met my mentor and co-author, Sunyata Saraswati. Focusing more on techniques, it reflects the yogic perspective which he represented.

TantraBliss draws from seventeen years of experience, guiding thousands of people through that sometimes hazardous process. New methods have been added and refined. We have learned how to manage the process safely and efficiently.

The current approach is more feminine than the earlier work, recognizing the cosmic importance of feeling states and matters of the heart. Any technique, with a few modifications, can be used to draw either predominately masculine/Shiva energy into the body (the yogic preference), or feminine/Shakti energy (a more tantric approach.)

This book brings together materials from esoteric traditions (primarily Kriya Yoga), from state-of-the-art transpersonal psycho-therapy, from current scientific research in the physiology of mystical experiences and the mechanics of consciousness. The intention is to demonstrate in simple terms how this all fits together.

Dividing the material into topics has been somewhat arbitrary. It doesn't really fit into boxes and doesn't want to lay out in a linear way. It is more like working with a hologram where all of the understanding is included in every small piece. The better you understand each piece, the better you understand the whole. Therefore I have cross-referenced extensively.

This book is highly condensed. There are many topics presented here, any one of which could have been developed into an entire book. You will read it now and pick up certain information. When you reread it, you'll probably find something you didn't see before.

> The information is secondary to the spiritual
> practice and lifestyle. Reading about it points
> a direction. Diving in makes it real for you.

This book has come together magically. I have made it a point never to read a tantra book or attend a class. Bits of information and insights just show up, pieces of this cosmic jigsaw puzzle. During the several months of serious writing I would wake up in the middle of the night to write down ideas that were dancing in my mind. I would then take the morning to expand the ideas and fit them into the growing book. My astrologer says this book at this time is my destiny book, the integration and culmination of a lifetime of exploring.

The observations and interpretations offered here are presented as if they were the counsel and teachings of my Higher Self, speaking to my small self, the guidance and principles of which I need continual reminders. There seem to be a large number of people who also resonate to those reminders, and so I am happy to share them.

Hereafter, when I'm referring to my personal history, *the text will appear in italics*. Regular type will be used for the Higher Self discourse.

The Complete Ipsalu Tantra Method.

The two books, *Jewel in the Lotus* and *The Ipsalu Formula*, are the texts for Ipsalu classes and the TantraBliss Practicum, a process that takes one to two years to fully absorb.

- *Jewel in the Lotus* lays the foundation;
- The First Level course, "Living in Bliss," gives you the initial jump start and Cobra Breath, the essential technique which cannot be written;
- *The Ipsalu Formula* describes the tantric journey;
- The TantraBliss Practicum is a sequential personal program of insights and techniques, done alone or with the guidance of a mentor;
- The Second Level course, "Bliss in Relationships," provides a powerful opportunity for expanding your inter-personal and sexual life;
- The Third Level course, "Bliss in Cosmic Union," takes you beyond time and space, learning how to bring that transcendent dimension into everyday life; and
- The Fourth Level is available, but only to the very advanced tantrika.

The Tantrika International Community.

This work is supported by Tantrika International, a non-profit organization dedicated to transforming people's lives, offering to the world a real possibility of living in Bliss. See page 321 for more information.

CONTENTS

INTRODUCTION TO IPSALU TANTRA:
THE ART AND SCIENCE OF BLISS..1
A new paradigm is emerging, a way of being in the world that will allow you to discover TantraBliss. The Ipsalu Formula is a way of organizing your spiritual practice to find and maintain your attunement to that Bliss state.

CHAPTER 1. IPSALU TANTRIC KRIYA YOGA:
WHAT IT IS AND HOW IT CAME TO BE...13
Ipsalu is a tantric marriage between Osho's teachings and the spirit of Babaji, the deathless yogi. Cobra Breath is the key to this practice. Here is a look at the origins of tantra and forms of tantric practice. Ipsalu Tantra involves: liberation through expansion, interweaving of parts, balancing of polarities, recognizing divinity, the yoga of expanded sex, path of surrender and working with subtle energies.

CHAPTER 2. REMEMBERING YOUR MAGNIFICENCE:
BEING THE CREATOR OF YOUR LIFE...35
Explore the relationship between Ego and Soul, how they have co-created your life drama, how Ego has developed and how it can be transcended through Witness consciousness.

CHAPTER 3. FULFILLMENT AND EMPOWERMENT:
EGO'S DESIRES AND SOUL'S PURPOSE...61
Desires, when unfulfilled, bring pain and frustration, but can be used to discover your heart's desires, your life purpose, which is totally supported by Existence, and where true satisfaction lies.

CHAPTER 4. CREATING HEAVEN ON EARTH:
LEARN OF THE UNIVERSE BY STUDYING THE BODY........................77
Tantrikas seek enlightenment in physical form. Going deep inside the physical body allows discovery of the pranic body and subtle energies which can be used for healing and for exalted sexual experiences. Science and mysticism are meeting in this cutting-edge exploration.

CHAPTER 5. RETURNING ENERGY TO THE FLOW:
BALANCING MENTAL AND EMOTIONAL BODIES 101
Mental development gets far more attention than emotional maturity. This imbalance causes frustration and grief. Here are tools and efficient methods for coming into balance

CHAPTER 6. MYSTERIES OF THE HEART:
CREATING AND MAINTAINING THE STATE OF BLISS 123
The heart is far more than a pump. It has its own intelligence and connection to Universal energies. Its rhythms form the basis for blissful experience and mystical union.

CHAPTER 7. MALE/FEMALE POLARITY:
BALANCING THE INNER MAN AND WOMAN 147
The female essence has been repressed, but is now stepping forth to regain balance. Exploring this energy transforms both men and women, and certainly their relationships.

CHAPTER 8. AWAKENING KUNDALINI:
THE NEXT PLATEAU IN HUMAN DEVELOPMENT 175
Kundalini energy, the highest form of consciousness is the key to humanity's future. Learn how to safely bring it from its dormant state to free-flowing activation in the body.

CHAPTER 9. PREPARING THE BODY TEMPLE:
LIFESTYLE CHANGES TO NURTURE THE BODY 197
Obstructed flow of the materials, fluids, or subtle energies through the body are the cause of disease and aging and an obstacle to spiritual development. This also applies to sexual health considerations.

CHAPTER 10. BLISS IN RELATIONSHIP:
THE ULTIMATE CHALLENGE 217
Relationships are usually a primal therapy as couples work out their childhood issues. In tantric relationships issues are resolved much more quickly. Learn what your lover really wants and how to honor the divine in your mate. Here is insight on why/how you keep yourself single and how to attract a partner.

CHAPTER **11**. BEING ORGASMIC:
TANTRIC SEXUAL ATTITUDES AND PRACTICES 233
Sexuality is essential to spirituality. Learn to overcome conditioning that has held them separate. Learn how tantric lovemaking differs from "normal sex."

CHAPTER **12**. TANTRIC RITUAL:
A DOORWAY TO ECSTASY...261
Traditional tantric practice included rituals. More contemporary versions are suggested, including Seven Nights of Tantra and Tibetan Maithuna Ritual.

EPILOGUE: WHAT IS NEXT? 277

APPENDIX A. ENERGY PRACTICES
Exercises for Individuals and Couples 279

APPENDIX B. YOGA NIDRA: CONSCIOUS SLEEP 293

APPENDIX C. FIREBREATH: SEVEN-CHAKRA ORGASM....................299

APPENDIX D. NETWORK SPINAL ANALYSIS 315

INDEX OF TECHNIQUES..317

Introduction to

IPSALU TANTRA
The Art and Science of Bliss

*M*ost spiritual paths share the common goal of returning to the Source. You who follow any path are driven by a sense of incompleteness, an inner knowing that you are in separation, cut off from your true nature. You suffer a relentless longing for paradise lost. You hunger for re-connection to the universal heart and mind, for that supreme happiness of unconditional love, the Bliss State. You know deep within that what you experience and what you appear to be are but shadows of your truth.

"Normal life" offers many ways to numb yourself to the longings of your Soul. Your internal sub-conscious world is tormented by limiting beliefs, guilt, suppressed emotions, banished conflicts and stifled creativity. You use the external world to distract yourself with work, relationship dramas and health concerns, obsessing about image and position. You amuse yourself with sporting events, loud music, TV, movies, shopping, etc. You anesthetize yourself with comfort foods and chemicals. Most of these activities could be conducted in a blissful state, but as a rule the activities you use to fill your days are designed to stifle the cries of your heart.

Science is beginning to realize that every cell, every organ in your body requires an ecstatic energy flow if it is to perform its function. In that flow lies an information connection to the Source of existence. There are ways to create this required infusion of ecstasy, but most people tend to be spectators rather than participants in creating ecstatic energy, letting their favorite musicians or actors or preachers or sports stars do it for them.

This culture is impoverished. It doesn't offer ecstatic drumming or dancing or singing or ceremonies to provide for this need. These things are available in sub-cultures, but aren't mainstream. No wonder there is such a compelling draw toward sex and drugs which offer a temporary, though artificial, feeling of Bliss.

Perhaps you believe that Bliss may be for someone else and not available to you. This book is dedicated to showing you how you can learn to live in Bliss.

Mystics have tried to describe the Bliss State and most agree how difficult it is to capture in words. Even the word "Bliss" doesn't express the Ipsalu experience. For some Bliss connotes a heavenly, ungrounded state. Attaching the word Tantra to it makes it more clearly balanced. TantraBliss is heaven on earth.

Relate that to something you have known. Recall a moment in your life when you felt free, completely safe, totally loved, exalted, unbounded, connected to all existence, excited but deeply relaxed. The world was so beautiful you could hardly contain it. Perhaps it was a moment during orgasm or when you had just fallen in love.

Remember a moment that stands out from all others. Let this be the standard by which all the rest are measured. You know this is possible. Why settle for less?

> You can choose to live in Bliss
> every moment. The technology for
> transformation is available today. But you
> probably have more important things to do.

You entered this world as the embodiment of Bliss. The following chapters will discuss how you lost that sweet connection and why you are having such difficulty finding it. You will learn how to rediscover a Blissful state.

Discovering TantraBliss.

Ipsalu Tantra Kriya Yoga is a method for maintaining Bliss. It is not to be taken as a belief system, but rather as a point of view and a technology.

It is simple. 1) Study the Emerging Paradigm. Start looking at your life as if this paradigm were valid. 2) Do the practices according to the Ipsalu Formula. 3) See what happens. The simple techniques presented here are among the most powerful in the world. If practiced regularly they will rapidly attune you to the Universal Pulse of Love, the source of TantraBliss.

THE EMERGING PARADIGM

This paradigm is a way of looking at life, a way of being in the world, an invitation to explore.

It is based on experience rather than beliefs or borrowed knowledge.

It doesn't claim to be absolute truth, since understanding keeps expanding.

If you choose to live from this perspective, you will transform your life. You will discover Bliss.

• Self-Realization

Discover your true nature, realize your magnificence, look within for guidance and wisdom.

Identify more and more with the Soul, less and less with your history and personality.

Learn to stay present as a Soul in the body with whatever emerges from the shadows.

Honor the Divine in each other, in all around you.

Sense that all is in divine order, even when it appears otherwise.

Realize that all beings are connected, that separation is an illusion.

Looking within, find a fountain of unbounded love and acceptance for the way you are.

Thus there is no need to seek approval from others.

• Self-Responsibility

See how you create your own experiences, as others cooperate to play out your expectations.

You have chosen to learn lessons. They show up as "problems" and persist until the lesson is learned.

Understand that there are no victims, no accidents. **External events mirror your internal states.**

Take responsibility for creating your life drama. Then you are able to recreate it more consciously.

Nothing outside has to change. When you shift inside, everything else automatically changes.

Resolve your own issues, not waiting for someone else to handle them.

• Being Witness

Maintain non-judgemental Witness Consciousness, equally accepting of your light and your shadow.

Examine every subconscious process, and gradually free yourself from bondage to the past.

Disengage from self-defeating patterns and limiting beliefs (karma) by being a benevolent Witness.

Bring unexperienced feelings and outdated beliefs to completion. (Open chakras and energy channels.)

• Fulfillment/Empowerment

Realize that ego's desires can never be satisfied. (Ipsalu means "transcending desire.")

They are attempts to compensate for deep feelings of inadequacy and unworthiness.

Rather than trying to suppress ego's desires, provide yourself the love that has been missing.

Your Soul has desires, your life's purpose, which are totally supported by Existence.

Creative power comes through surrender of the ego to the Soul.

When your ego falls in love with your Soul, and becomes its devoted servant, you are then living in the cosmic flow. Your life becomes a magical series of synchronicities.

Existence provides for your needs with ease and grace. Your Heart's desires are realized.

• Earth/Body Centered

Come to understand the mysteries of the universe by studying the secrets and delights of the body.

Celebrate life on the earthly plane, and compassionately embrace all aspects of humanness.

Invite the God of your Heart to dwell in your body-temple, to play in physical reality, to have fun.

Enjoy the tantric arts: song, rhythm and movement, massage, aroma.

Learn to create Heaven on Earth.

• Balancing Polarities

Honor, empower, liberate, celebrate both the female energy (Shakti – the creative dynamic LifeForce) and the male energy (Shiva – clarity/stillness.) Bring them into balance and harmony.

Increased Shakti (orgasmic) energy in the body brings about physical cleansing, emotional activation/release and heightened intuitive awareness.

Increased Shiva energy brings higher consciousness and sweet Bliss.

By balancing these energies, you prepare your body for Kundalini awakening.

• Kundalini Awakening

The Ipsalu technology (based on Kriya Yoga/Cobra Breath) can safely awaken in your body a new level of consciousness, an extraordinary intelligence now lying dormant (Kundalini).

This higher vibration requires considerable preparation of mind and body through spiritual practice.

As Kundalini awakens, you will express increasingly these four qualities:

Living in a state of Bliss;

Opening to latent genius;

Absolute integrity; and

Access to inner knowledge, a constant stream of wisdom,
    always new, always appropriate.

These qualities will be the norm in the emerging new human.

• Health/Longevity

Once you learn to draw in greater amounts and higher vibrations of life-sustaining subtle energy, once your body's energies flow freely through their channels, unobstructed by emotional residue, your body can heal itself, and can maintain health and vitality for a much longer, healthier life.

Once you adjust your lifestyle to support the body's needs, the higher energies transform your body, reorganizing the DNA, creating a new advanced species.

• Service/Universal Love

For life to be satisfying, you must know that your efforts make a difference in the lives of others, that your Being inspires trust from others, and facilitates their journey toward self-discovery.

The greatest service is to love unconditionally, never losing sight of the divinity in all.

Bathed in the safety of that love, everything that is not love can come up to be healed.

Anyone can remember who they really are if someone loves them enough to remind them.

• Relationship

Tantric partnership brings deeper intimacy and much more satisfying sexual experience.

Reconnect love and sex, and **be really present** with your partner.

Initially you choose partners that recreate the primal family dynamic, picking the ones who push all your buttons to allow a healing of unresolved inner child issues.

Once that is accomplished, sharing polarized energies accelerates the evolution of both partners.

Give yourself and your partner space to dance in all your aspects, in all combinations: the parent, the child, the wise one, the beloved, the nurturer, the sensualist, etc.

Recognize the value of community with people who share a common vision, based on love.

Choices in alternate styles of relating (mono versus poly, hetero versus homo, etc.) are matters of personal preference and are not a part of this paradigm.

• Spiritual/Sexual Energy

Heal the encultured attitude that sexual energy compromises spiritual advancement.

Learn instead to use that powerful energy to accelerate your progress.

Become more sensitive to the subtle energies of other dimensions.

Discover greater creativity and psychic perceptions, for healing yourself and others.

7

Your sexual experience becomes a sharing of those energies and dimensions as two lovers merge into the Divine light.

• Tantra Bliss Formula

The frequent experience of Bliss is essential for the health of every human being.

That requires simultaneous activation/integration of mind, body and Soul.

By stilling the mind you bring yourself into the present moment, the only "time" when you can understand Truth, can feel love, can experience God.

By activating the sexual energies you enliven that stillness into dynamic Bliss.

By transmuting that arousal, you elevate its orientation from survival to service, from pleasure to creativity, from control to surrender.

Feeling gratitude in all things perpetuates the experience of Bliss.

The Emerging Paradigm, contains discoveries about reality available from within a blissful state, expressed in succinct form. Each point is explored in the chapters that follow. As each idea "dawns" for you and becomes your experience, you will draw nearer to an ongoing state of Bliss.

THE IPSALU FORMULA

There is a method, unique to Ipsalu Tantra, for attuning to Bliss. It is a formula that works in all circumstances, if you are willing to relax into it. It quickly brings groups of strangers into a loving blissful connection, as well as couples, especially when they combine the practice with their lovemaking. It brings an individual into Bliss at any time, in any place.

Initially it may take an hour or more of techniques to feel blissful. With a few months of regular practice you can reach Bliss in a few moments. This book clarifies why and how the formula works. These are simple but powerful techniques, taken from several spiritual traditions. They quickly open the body/mind to its highest potential.

Here is the essence of the formula to make the core of your daily practice. This is the sequence that creates the magic:

First: **Activate energies in the body.**
Second: **Still the mind.**
Third: **Arouse sexual energy.**
Fourth: **Transmute passion.**
Fifth: **Enjoy the TantraBliss.**

(Noticing that the first letters of the five steps seemed to make a word form, ASATE, I wondered if it might be a Sanskrit word. Consulting a dictionary I learned that indeed ASATE in Sanskrit means "uninterrupted sequence." An interesting synchronicity.)

Activate energies in the body. Enliven the body with practices designed to awaken the LifeForce within you, bringing an infusion of transformative, rejuvenating energy to awaken the body, mind and Soul. Experience the subtle energy flow in the physical body as it brings life-sustaining information to direct the cells' activities and an open connection to the infinite. (Techniques presented in this book are Bated Breath, 12-part Tension/Relaxation, Complete Breath, Rishi Isometrics, Inner Smile, Nauli. Additionally in *Jewel* are Rejuvenation Postures and Shakti Shake.)

<u>Still the mind.</u> A quiet mind allows the ego to step aside and cosmic energy/consciousness to enter the body. You come into the Eternal Now – the only way you can experience pure love and become the non-judgmental Witness. This is as far as many meditation practices go, and they do that with consciousness leaving the body. With the body freshly energized, you can go into deep meditative state without leaving the physical plane. (Techniques include Witnessing Thoughts, Watching the Breath, Hong Saw Breath Mantra, Khechari Mudra, and Trataka.)

Arouse sexual energy. Within this infinite stillness, the rhythm of the earth is called forth. In this context the juicy creative force takes on an extra-ordinary quality. You feel the primal energy which manifested the physical universe. (Techniques include Vajroli/ Sahajoli, Aswini, Moola Bandha and FireBreath. Additionally in *Jewel* are the Sexual Energizers.)

<u>Transmute passion.</u> You lift and refine that quintessential creative force and blend it with the heavenly consciousness. Your body, especially your heart, is the meeting place of heaven and earth. (In this book Transmutation Breath and FireBreath, in *Jewel* Prana Mudra, in Level 1 course Cobra Breath.)

<u>Enjoy the Bliss.</u> Sing, drum and dance, massage, heal and make love, speak to God and hear the reply. Share Bliss with a beloved or with friends. There are other "E" possibilities:

Express your Heart-song in new creative ways.

Earn a living doing what you love to do.

Experience the truth of Existence.

Exhibit extra-ordinary abilities.

Evoke your divine presence.

Expand your sense of Self.

Explore latent potentials.

Expect miracles.

With the thunder of Drums …
    in our Ears,
And the sparkle of the full Moon
      in our Eyes,
We danced all night …

You held me close,
    and my feet barely
        touched the ground …
The Wine we shared
    needed no cup,
It poured freely from
    the wine-bottle of Love …
Right into the mouths of
    those gathered.

Everyone was raised up
    and illuminated …
Like the Ocean,
    when the Ocean seems
      lit from within.
Night gave in to Day,
    and winter retreated …
Lucky flutes were heard,
    drawing us out to play …
Everything glimmered …

Time stood still …

            our Lips met …

Pyramidal temples spun

    in ecstatic Dance …

Mudra symbols were

    formed and acted

        as Keys to many locks.

We turned the Keys with

    our spiral steps …

Earth moved,

    and a subtle shift was felt.

Encouraged …

    We breathed open our Hearts …

                Ahhhh …

Written after a community celebration
by David Guy (*TheDavid@fuse.net*).

Chapter One

IPSALU TANTRIC KRIYA YOGA
What It Is and How It Came to Be

Raised in a fundamentalist religious culture, where "sexual sin is next to murder in the eyes of God," and the ideal for a young woman was to go to her marriage bed having never been kissed, I found adolescence and the awakening of sexuality a serious challenge. The hormones won out and several promiscuous years were followed by a decade of guilt and self-punishment.

I'd been taught that there was no forgiveness for sexual "sin," and my punishment was to be cut off from God forever. My relationship to "my Heavenly Father" was the center of my life, far more real than any human connections. My suffering was profound. I was resigned to an eternity of isolation and desperation. Looking back I'm grateful for this conflicted period. It prepared me to receive and to appreciate a more expanded and compassionate cosmology.

Years later, in a period of intense spiritual searching, I learned of two great tantra teachers, Osho (Rajneesh) and Babaji. There was no meeting in the physical plane, but in my initial encounter with each of them, I was powerfully struck by their energy. This was my first hint that I didn't have to choose between sexuality and spirituality, my first glimmer of the tantric path.

Ipsalu is a Tantric Marriage.

Babaji's Tantric Kriya Yoga and Osho's celebration of life are distinct paths. Some forms of Kriya are more mental, appealing to masculine, intellectual seekers who enjoy focused, disciplined, scientific practices. Other Kriya paths are devotional, seeking divine connection but avoiding sexual energies.

Osho's followers were body-oriented. They were encouraged to feel, to dance, to make love with abandon and to do very little thinking.

Kriya methods were powerful but quite dry. Osho's methods felt undisciplined but very juicy and alive. Each path, it seemed to me, could benefit greatly by incorporating the other.

The rest of this Ipsalu system has come mostly from Taoist and Tibetan sources, and from lessons in the school of life. All together they produce a synthesis that works well in the unique energies of our times.

Osho's Buddha Field.

For several years I was involved with Osho, one of the greatest modern tantrics. A most important learning for me was his admonition "Don't take yourself so seriously." Having always been terribly earnest, allowing myself not the slightest space for error or imperfection, torturing myself for any flaw, this teaching came as an enormous relief.

Another important teaching was "See life as a celebration." Once given that permission I experienced, on a number of occasions, new energies moving within me, waves of ecstasy flowing from my sex center to my heart, joy beyond description and love without bounds.

The teaching that most impacted my life was "You are already enlightened, pretending not to be." Previous to that, my life had been a race to achieve perfection before my earthly time ran out. I was told this was the only way to receive the highest eternal rewards. The pressure was intense. In light of Osho's teaching, I saw that perfection was already there, waiting to be recognized. I had but to notice what stood in the way of that recognition.

Osho spoke often of the Witness (more later) and emphasized the need for emotional release (not addressed in yoga). He delighted at poking fun at sacred cows, whether belief systems or holy persons, and challenging taboos, especially sexual. Most of the people drawn to this community in the early years came from severely repressed cultures and needed dynamite to break them loose from their rigid sexual rules. Initially it was wild. In time, that released energy matured.

Osho emphasized the heart rather than the mind. This orientation came after years of observing that most spiritual paths started at the mind, and none of them were very effective. Most of his followers were already so mental they needed to first get out of that mode and back to a more spontaneous way of being.

Toward the end of his life Osho was urging his followers back to the meditation discipline. In early discourses he had pointed out Kriya as the most authentic of the yogas. Had he lived longer he might well have performed this marriage himself.

Babaji, the Deathless Yogi.

The mortal-immortal avatar, whom we call Babaji, was born on the eastern coast of India in 203 AD as the boy Nagaraj. He is said to have been kidnapped by pirates as a child and sold into slavery. His owner soon recognized the boy's special gifts and released him to wander and study. Babaji gained eminence as a scholar and was initiated into Kundalini Yoga by the greatest teacher of that time. Still in his teens, he achieved immortality through the practice of Siddha Yoga and Siddha medicine, following a lineage that produced at least eighteen recognized immortal beings.

An avatar is a perfect manifestation of Divinity in human form. Avatars live in continual full consciousness of their Divine nature, an example of what is possible for humankind. Krishna and Gautama Buddha are well-known avatars.

Most avatars are mortal, leaving their bodies at the end of their earthly mission. A few achieve physical immortality (soruba samadhi). They are omnipresent at all times. They retain memory of all previous physical incarnations, yet their vision extends beyond time and space, beyond the origin of Creation. They appear when needed, otherwise remain hidden from the world.

Babaji has retained his form through the centuries, touching many, appearing to a few. He is called the MoolaGuru, expert on the energies of Mooladhara, the root chakra, the seat of Kundalini. He has taken responsibility for the yogic education of the souls incarnated on this planet and has served mankind since unrecorded time in this form or previous forms, encouraging and supporting anyone who wishes to become a Babaji.

Paramahansa Yogananda, in "Autobiography of a Yogi" relates accounts of Babaji and his disciples, including Lahiri Mahasaya, whom Babaji initiated into the complete science of Kriya Yoga. Through this lineage, Yogananda brought Kriya Yoga to America in the 1930s, but taught only the devotional aspect, since the tantric aspect was too potent for the people at that time. He instilled love for the Divine Mother, a nice balance for the Protestant patriarchal tone. He showed tens of thousands how the methods and teachings of East and West work together in harmony.

For many people the Babaji energy is an important connection. Students have reported vivid dreams of sitting at the feet of Babaji in a forest, learning from him. Stories are told of his remarkable abilities by students fortunate to experience him personally – tales of his ability to teleport, to be in several places at once, to know all things. His presence brings a great comfort, a sense that all is well, that you are protected and appreciated. It is the energy of unconditional love, profound and exquisite.

Babaji lives in an ashram high in the Himalayas, a shangri-la with meadows, waterfalls and perfect climate. He lives with his beautiful consort Mataji, who has also attained immortality. She is referred to in most Kriya systems as his sister but, acknowledging Babaji as a tantric master, we recognize her as his partner. She has been in the background for hundreds of years but recently has become more involved.

When Babaji wants to work with someone, s/he might experience him in remarkable ways. One couple in Australia was watching a brush fire on the hill near their home. The smoke from that fire seemed to form a face. At first they commented to each other that it looked like a man, and then it seemed to look like a woman. Then they heard, as clearly as if someone stood beside them speaking, "I will be with you soon." Several days later they came to a weekend intensive. When they saw Babaji's image on the altar there was instant recognition. Both experienced a major breakthrough in that weekend.

There have been so many stories of Babaji encounters that a whole book could be devoted just to that. Babaji is available and involved with the lives of those in his spiritual family.

"Babaji" is a title, meaning "honored father" a title used by many spiritual leaders. The immortal Babaji Nagaraj is unique, not to be confused with others.

Of my personal experiences of Babaji, the most wonderful happened during a weekend class in Australia. The group was advanced and the energy they generated was very high. By the end of Saturday I was so swept away I could barely verbalize enough to bring the class to a close. We chanted three OMs to finish but for several minutes nobody moved. We were transfixed. I found myself saying, "We are not alone. There is a Presence."

Wave after wave of orgasmic energy began coursing up my body, breaking at my heart. I was absolutely in rapture. This continued for about forty-five minutes. Several in the group who were attuned to Babaji said they saw him there. Certainly everyone there felt his energy.

From my earliest memories Jesus was the great love of my life. Initially it confused me to be experiencing the same profound love from another being. I eventually realized that the energy of unconditional love was the same, and attuning to that energy was the key to happiness. The Jesus image has been associated with pain and suffering for so long it makes it harder to find the underlying love. The Babaji image was clear, easier to access.

Invoking Babaji.

If you would like to attune yourself to Babaji you can do so, 1) by doing the Kriya practices; 2) by securing his image as an object of contemplation for your altar; 3) by gazing at the yantra that represents his energy; and 4) by repeating the mantra 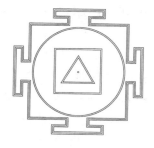 that invites that energy into your being: "Om Kriya Babaji Namah Aum." (The image and colored yantra are available through Tantrika International. When appropriate an advanced mantra, even more powerful, can be learned.)

Cobra Breath.

Ipsalu Tantra is based upon Kriya Yoga, a sacred science of ancient, proven techniques leading directly to cosmic consciousness and Self Realization within this lifetime. The key practice, the method for transmuting sexual energy, is the Cosmic Cobra Breath. This advanced and powerful method is Babaji's most precious gift to humanity.

Kriya masters have said that a million disease-free years of life on this planet are required to evolve a perfected brain capable of experiencing Cosmic Consciousness. Kriya practice enables one to move at a much faster pace, since each Cobra Breath produces one year of maturation. That's fourteen years per practice session, twenty-eight years per day, 10,220 evolution years per calendar year. Since most people drawn to this work have already invested countless lifetimes in spiritual development, they are on the final phase of this journey. It is easily within their grasp in this lifetime. (For more on reincarnation, see Chapter 5.)

The First Level Cobra Breath is a powerful method for quickly opening Ajna (the Third Eye). As this center is energized, you become able to perceive things as they are, rather than perceiving selectively only that which supports your ego positions. (The Second and Third Level Cobra Breaths will be described in Chapter 6.)

Receiving Cobra Breath.

Traditionally, methods as powerful as Cobra Breath were given only to very advanced students after long years of preparation, and then under close supervision of a master-teacher. It is now time to make these secret and profound methods more available, protected as they are by a self-selection process. Those who aren't ready for them usually aren't interested.

The protocol is still clear. This is an oral teaching. It is not to be written or recorded. If you go thumbing through this book or *Jewel* looking for it you won't find it. Anyone receiving this particular teaching must first promise not to reveal it to others. One needs to have a special context in order to appreciate it.

Cobra Breath is taught in Ipsalu weekend intensives. For those unable to attend a course, it is available through the TantraBliss Practicum (by correspondence).

There is a variety of styles and schools of Kriya, each with its own version of the advanced practices. Every teacher presents a version that works well for him/her. Each version produces a little different result. Students who resonate with that vibration are drawn to that teacher. The version we share produces results consistent with the values of this system, as stated in the Paradigm.

Some discussions and exercises refer to the Cobra Breath. If you have not yet received that, use the Transmutation Breath described in Appendix A.

Initiation and Lineage.

In times past, a hands-on initiation was considered essential to the spiritual process. Even earlier versions of *Jewel* recommended initiation. It provided an initial blast of energy, an experience that would later serve as a point of reference, something to work toward, but the receiver usually couldn't hold that charge. Only through consistent practice could one prepare the body to contain and maintain such a high energy.

The initiator then becomes an intermediary between you and your Soul. Like a priest administering sacraments, the initiator is an external means to an internal end. Some people still want that system and so it persists. You will find however that all the answers are within and no external intervention is required. When you are ready, the energy performs its own initiation. Rather than expecting a master to do it for you, do your practice and earn the initiation. You no longer depend on the grace of the guru. If needed, a guide will come, someone who has travelled your path of choice and knows the pitfalls and shortcuts.

In the yogic tradition one studied with a guru until the guru decided to authorize the student to teach. In the new energies of this time the age of the gurus is over. Each person can find the inner guru and learn to follow direction from within. The whole concept of lineage, therefore, has become an anachronism. Honor those who have attained through the old system, and at the same time see what incredible openings are occurring for those in the new system.

Many Forms of Yoga.

Babaji has been the source of inspiration leading to the foundation of many different yogic schools, styles and philosophies that have emerged over time. Since humans come in many temperaments, a path which appealed to one might not work for someone else. Therefore, he has provided many forms of yogic practice.

Some practices are more mental, emphasizing the knowledge and science. Some are more devotional and heart centered, interested in worship. Some are more physical, focused on perfecting the body. Most use similar techniques but with a different flavor or emphasis. You will find yourself drawn to a practice that suits you well.

Most yoga styles hold in common the goal of getting free from physical form. Tantra works within the form. It is more integrative, pulling together these and all the other dimensions of human nature. Ancient scriptures refer to tantra as the highest of the yogas.

ORIGINS OF TANTRA

Earliest Record.

Tantra has its origins in the earliest mother-goddess religions, still practiced today in southern India. It absorbed the yogic practices, using them for its own ends. Getting free of the body is a masculine predilection; enlightenment by means of the body is the feminine path to awakening.

Hindu legend has it that tantra was taught by Lord Shiva, King of the Yogis, to his consort Parvati (one of several names for the Divine Mother, Shakti). The original teaching is contained in a scripture called Maha-Nirvan-Tantra (The Scripture of Great Bliss). It deals with the three bodies: the gross physical body, the subtle energy body, and the cosmic spiritual body. The Tantric practice would liberate one from attachment to these bodies, freeing him to unite with pure Consciousness. This is done by working with cleansing vibrations of yantras (sacred symbols) and mantras (special syllables, which carry the Divine Vibration in condensed form.)

Tantra Transmission.

The Kriya tradition says that this tantric yoga teaching came to a highly advanced woman, born in Bengal of high caste. She travelled some 1,200 miles to the Himalayas, and there received directly from Babaji the Tantric art and science. This woman became famous as Brahmani (consort of Brahman, which means "he who knows Brahma, the Ultimate Self"). She also was known as Bhairavi (consort of Bairab, another name for Shiva). Under Babaji's direction she taught several great masters including Paramahansa Ramakrishna, one of the greatest saints of the 19th century. Much of what is now practiced as tantra comes from that transmission, particularly the work with mantras, yantras and the maithuna ritual. The work was incorporated into the Kriya tradition, the Cobra Breath being called the Bhairavi Breath.

Beyond Knowledge, Beyond Technique.

According to Osho, the Tantric path was discovered and formulated by a man named Saraha. He was born to a Brahmin family in a small kingdom in India around 500 AD. At an early age he displayed such brilliant scholarship that people flocked to him for spiritual instruction. The king was so impressed with his eloquence and great knowledge that he offered to Saraha his daughter's hand and succession to the throne.

Despite all the adulation, Saraha grew discontent. He startled his Hindu family by renouncing the life he had known and following a Buddhist master. That master's first instruction to him was to forget everything he had learned. It took him seven years to clear his mind of the burden of knowledge.

At that time he was attracted to a peasant woman in the marketplace. She was an arrowsmith woman, sitting in her stall making arrows; a woman who was enlightened. Saraha spoke to her, hoping to impress her with his wit. She laughed at him and told him he knew nothing.

Eventually they came together and lived near the crematorium. People coming to mourn their dead were caught up in the joyous dance and celebration of this tantric couple. Together they explored every aspect of sexual energy and relationship, and the art/science of Tantra took form. Through his surrender to the moment Saraha became enlightened. The path of tantra was developed by spiritually advanced women and their consorts.

In summary: Those following the yogic traditions strove to escape the physical body; those in the Kriya tradition become absorbed in devotions and practices; the Osho Sannyasins were interested mainly in dance and play.

FORMS OF
TANTRIC PRACTICE

Tantra has taken many forms of expression in virtually every culture in the history of this planet. If you are curious to know details of the history, mythology and practices, there are many books available. This knowledge will not, however, change the quality of your consciousness or allow you to share this experience. Here is a brief review of a few forms, for historical perspective.

• **Hindu Tantraism** revolved around worship of Shiva and Shakti, deification of the Male and Female principles. The male and female sexual organs (lingam and yoni) were honored and celebrated in art and ritual. Tantrikas believed that they could achieve release from the cycle of birth and death (Moksha) by using the power of sex in Tantric ritual. Tantra began gaining popularity in the early days of the Christian era. From 700 AD to 1300 AD it was widespread throughout Asia, engulfing Hinduism and Buddhism, as well as other religions. Its great appeal was that it promised liberation through enjoyable ritual, instead of requiring a lifetime of ascetic practice. This form has practically disappeared. People go to India in search of "authentic tantra" and can't find it. If it is happening, it is underground and not readily available to a visitor.

Note: Further references to Shiva and Shakti are only as archetypes, symbols of polarized energy and aspects of every individual. They are honored here, as are all cosmic principles, but not worshipped as personal deities.

• **Red Tantra.** Ancient tantric scripture encouraged rituals where all the rules were suspended, where all behaviors were considered holy. Maithunas and chakrapujas were held where people ate meat, drank wine, made love with wild abandon and indulged in the "soma" from the poppy. These were behaviors severely prohibited in that culture. In these earlier days, some communities dedicated to the Vama Marga, the left-handed path, took the scriptural injunctions very literally, their rituals often deteriorating into Bacchanalian feasts and orgies. This was common during the 18th century.

Modern attempts to replicate this practice fall embarrassingly short of the original intention. This is a vastly different culture, with different values and perspectives. What passes for red tantra today usually turns into an orgy without the redeeming spiritual values of yesteryear. These practices are not the focus of Ipsalu Tantra Yoga (more in Chapter 12).

• **White Tantra.** Some Tantrikas, dedicated to Dakshina Marga (the right-handed path) interpreted Tantric scripture as symbolic and their practice was more abstract and mental. Men and women meditated together, according to highly disciplined techniques, but maintained a celibate life. The Kundalini Yoga teachings of Yogi Bhajan are in this style and still prominent today.

• **Pink Tantra.** Ipsalu Tantra would strike a middle-point between the "red" and "white" orientations. It is less concerned with breaking the rules in order to break down one's conditioning, less intent on escaping from the temptations of life by rigorous solitary practice. It is more concerned with coming into the heart energy, surrendering to unconditional love (more in Chapter 2). A couple can make the journey together but the work also has incredible value for a single person.

• **Black Tantra – Sex Magic.** Tantric rituals in India often invoked the "dark" energies, the subconscious creative power that can be accessed during sexual arousal. Currently in India, tantra is considered synonymous with black magic since many practitioners there have become mired in the quest for power, seduced by the enormous creative force in sexual energy.

Some tantra teachers in the west are tapping into the potential of Sex Magic, which can be a great tool for personal growth. It can also easily be distorted into using sexual energies to control their environment, to manifest their wishes. This is unfortunate as it supports people in thinking small, rather than leading them toward true empowerment by remembering their magnificence.

• **Heart Magic – Synergy.** When you are in your heart, you want what is best for all, realizing that you are one with all. You make yourself available as an instrument by which changes can be wrought, in conformance to Divine Will. Then the real magic begins (more in Chapter 3).

> When you make yourself at one with Existence,
> it totally supports you. Then whatever
> you need flows effortlessly to you.

• **Sacred Sex** is currently the most popular version of tantric practice. Most Westerners are so damaged in expressing their sexuality that they require a great deal of healing: learning to overcome inhibitions, deal with guilt and abuse, activate the energies that have been turned off for a lifetime. These processes are merely a starting point to tantric practice. You might call these activities sexual healing or relationship therapy, rather than tantra. It is remedial work, prerequisite to the actual sacred practices.

Many Westerners are drawn to Tantra because they think it will improve their sexual satisfaction. It does that, beyond your wildest dreams, but not by bringing more of what you already know. It takes you into a whole new level of experience. In ancient times in India, tantric practice for hedonistic reasons was severely frowned upon. In modern America it is often as much as people can understand. It's a beginning. Don't get stuck there.

WHAT IS IPSALU TANTRA?

1) Tantra is Liberation through Expansion.

The roots of the word "Tantra" are two Sanskrit words meaning "liberation" and "expansion." This implies that you can be liberated by expanding your consciousness. You live in a very small reality. You define yourself in terms of your limitations: those imposed by society, those accepted during your early childhood conditioning, and decisions you made along the way. As you learn to identify with a larger truth, you begin to live more freely. In an expanded state you will find your true Self.

• **Free from shame.** Most personalities are built on a foundation of shame, a sense of unworthiness (see Chapter 2). In addition, you have been taught to be embarrassed about your body and its natural functions. This cuts you off from really knowing your body, experiencing it fully, and enjoying your physical nature. When you realize the body is a perfect manifestation of your self-concept, you come to see the body, and its every part and function, as an opportunity to learn about yourself, another holy expression of the Divine. Then you can simply enjoy your body and make a game of achieving body mastery.

• **Free from the fear of intimacy.** You haven't allowed yourself to be seen for fear that your inner self would be rejected. You won't even see yourself, perhaps because your magnificence is more than you can accept. You are afraid of being alone and yet fear the vulnerability required for real intimacy. You will come to realize that the sense of isolation and alienation that tortures most people is only an illusion. It persists only because they believe in it and find there a sense of safety. In your expanded moments you experience a unity with all beings.

• **Free from attachment to our "positive" attributes.** Even those can be a limitation because determining what is positive involves a judgement, and any judgement automatically excludes Soul. You can have preferences for one quality over another and make healthy choices, all without condemning the alternatives or feeling superior.

• **Free from social pressures.** You play out roles, doing what you think is expected, not being authentic. You have learned to be attached to others, looking to them for love and validation. As soon as you find the source of love within yourself, you no longer need approval from others. You come to follow your inner guidance. Other people's opinions and expectations become irrelevant. People don't actually see you anyway. What they see has been filtered through their projections. You are neither limited nor defined by your relationships.

• **Free from boundaries.** Eventually you will realize that you have a physical body, but are not limited to your body; you have feelings, but are not your feelings; you share a consensual reality, but are not confined to that viewpoint. In truth you have created your limits and you invest an enormous amount of energy holding them in place. Once that is clear you are in a position to release those artificial constructs. In the throes of sexual ecstasy you are as unbounded as Existence itself. You merge into the Divine and become one with All That Is. Eventually you can learn to come into that holy place outside the sexual arena.

2) Tantra is an Interweaving of Parts.

Another definition of the word Tantra is "a loom." A tantric orientation means an acceptance and celebration of your physical, emotional, spiritual and sexual aspects. Tantra is an interweaving of the energies of your many levels of consciousness, from the most mundane to the most erotic, to the most profound, into an intricate tapestry; reaching for the stars and then returning to the flow of life; tuning to the subtle cosmic energies while at the same time being deeply rooted in the earth. To accomplish this end you will learn to:

• **Stay present** with whatever aspect of your humanness or divinity is asking for expression in the moment, simply witnessing it without judgement.

• **Satisfy the senses.** Most yogas work to disconnect from the senses. Tantrikas arrive at that same goal by over-loading the senses, satisfying them to the point of satiation. They then go beyond their limits, expanding their range of perceptions to include what is normally unseen, unheard, unknown.

• **Honor sexuality.** You can reconnect love and sex, seeing sexual energy as one expression of higher consciousness (Kundalini). A sexual encounter is transformed when you see it as an opportunity for the Divine to experience life in a body. There are few moments in life when divinity is invited to participate.

Eventually you are no longer driven and obsessed by sexual appetite.

• **Experience repressed feelings.** You have learned to narrow your range of emotions, often losing contact with them entirely. As balancing progresses, you will learn to be aware of all feelings, honoring them, receiving and enjoying them. Feelings add a variety of colors to the palette from which you paint your life's picture. You will realize that your capacity for love and joy is much greater than your fear, or your pain, or your anger (more in Chapter 5).

• **Celebrate the body.** In Tantra the body is included in spiritual awakening. From the Tantric perspective, all the esoteric symbols can be interpreted as referring to body processes. There is nothing in creation that isn't represented in the body. A healthy attitude about your physical nature helps in completing your physical experience (more in Chapter 4).

> Osho has said, "A rose is an opportunity for beauty to happen. The physical body is an opportunity for love to happen. Tantra is an opportunity for Godliness to manifest through us, so that we, as limited beings, can share in the ecstasy of the Universe."

3) Tantra is Balancing of Polarities.

The "parts" mentioned above, (senses, sexuality, feelings, body) are often considered feminine aspects. Recognizing the duality of the universe, Tantra honors and empowers the female principle, operating in harmony and balance with the male principle (more in Chapter 7).

4) Tantra Acknowledges the Divinity in All People and All Paths.

Devotion and meditation are not separate from life. Every moment, every encounter, every experience is a unique jewel of great worth, to be fully savored and appreciated. "The Divine within me recognizes and honors the Divine within you. Namaste."

Many spiritual paths have become so steeped in forms, so institutionalized, that the main concern is maintaining an organization. This is often accomplished by convincing seekers that their particular path alone holds the key to regaining their true nature. Tantra honors all paths, even those that don't appear to be paths. Each Soul ultimately directs its own unfolding. When the time is right and you are willing, the optimal influences will be provided, sometimes in the most unlikely circumstances.

5) Tantra is the Yoga of Expanded Sex.

Sex is the beginning of this path, but not the end. Tantra is not an excuse for hedonism. It is a glorious way to enhance sexual pleasure and sense gratification, but is certainly not limited to that. Tantra is a form of meditation that uses sexual energy, the most powerful force available to beings at this stage of development. It becomes the fuel for a jet-path to self-realization and enlightenment (see Chapter 11).

6) Tantra is a Path of Surrender.

Rather than struggling to subdue the lower nature, Tantra provides the safety and love that allows Ego to surrender to its higher nature. Through self-acceptance and self-love, the lower nature is transformed, providing an instantaneous passageway into states of higher awareness.

7) Tantra is Working with Subtle Energies.

This is the heart of your tantric practice. Most other aspects of tantra represent a shift in attitude. These are changes brought about by practicing ancient techniques:

- Learning to generate and contain more energy in the body. (Chapter 4)
- Directing energies for rejuvenation, for healing self and others. (Chapter 4)
- Allowing energies to move within you by removing obstructions. (Chapter 4)
- Transmuting sexual energy into higher vibrations. (Chapter 8)
- Developing psychic abilities, trusting your impulses and inner knowingness. (Chapter 8)
- Purifying the subtle bodies, preparing to awaken Kundalini. (Chapter 8)

Value of Consistent Practice.

Everyone who wants to advance on their spiritual path must look at what is required. This generation is a bit spoiled by things coming so effortlessly. There is a bumper sticker proclaiming "Instant gratification is too slow!" You want instant enlightenment. You want some guru or savior to do it for you.

"I have seen the light" describes a great starting point, not an end result. All great traditions from all cultures – Greek, Roman, Hindu, Taoist – call this "the Holy Work" because it takes consistent practice of these simple techniques to awaken latent energy, to be fully conscious of your thoughts, actions and feelings every moment. This is the only "work" left. You've done everything else.

Enlightenment doesn't come from reading books. You can acquire the intellectual knowledge but your ability to hold energy is still limited. You can't do tantra in your mind. You must get into your body and prepare it for a new way of being. It's not enough to experiment with a technique a few times then set it aside.

> A regular practice changes your vibration frequency. Bliss is experienced at a certain vibration. As surely as you can turn a radio dial to a different frequency, you can learn to attune your body to the frequency of Bliss.

When you do any practice, your energy increases and sub-conscious material begins to bubble up to surface. Stay in the energy field, see how it feels, observe what shows up. Don't make excuses to back off your practice when you get uncomfortable. In tantra you go to the essence of the experience.

If you are already involved in other practices, you might consider setting them aside for a period of time and focus on this work for a few months. See if you like the results.

A student shared, "My personal practice provides most of my tantric experience. My sexual energy has been a door, a ladder, to my ecstatic connection to the Divine. These are very powerful, joyful blissful tools."

The technology of Kriya Yoga is remarkably diverse. In days past in the ashrams, an aspirant had to learn many postures and breathing techniques, working exhaustively for years before receiving tantric training. Technique can open doors to new expanded horizons, and in return the enhanced consciousness shapes and motivates your practice. It is an upward spiral. But ultimately it is the love and trust within your heart that draws to you the richness of life's possibilities.

Today the challenge is not to see how many techniques you can master but to see how deeply you are willing to go into your own sub-conscious. A few simple techniques will take you there. Those who are willing to stay present with whatever they discover in this inward look will eventually find themselves liberated into ecstatic consciousness.

Going Deeper

1. Review Lesson 1 of *Jewel* in the Lotus for additional background.
2. That's enough talking. It's time to explore. Begin to experience expansion and transcendence using the first two phases of the TantraBliss Formula. Set aside at least twenty minutes each day, ideally the same time each day, to practice the following experiments (also described at the end of Jewel, Lesson 1):

ACTIVATE THE BODY

- Bated Breath
- Kriya Energization

STILL THE MIND

- Witness Your Thoughts

3. Through the day, in all situations, continue to witness your thoughts.

Bated Breath – will let you feel increased LifeForce in your body's reservoir. This practice will lengthen your life and greatly enhance your vitality. That has been proven scientifically through extensive research by Guru Janardan Paramahansa.

Inhale deeply through the nose. As you exhale produce the whispered sound "SA, SA, ... , SA" quickly, repeatedly, until the air is gone. Each sound comes with a little contraction of the diaphragm. This gives you a gentle internal massage and wakes up the LifeForce in your belly.

As you continue the practice you will be able to refine the "SA" sound so it's almost inaudible, so the thrusting becomes more subtle.

After doing the technique, go through your body. Be aware of any sensations in your body. You will eventually feel a pulse. When you inhale you attract negative and positive ions in the air. Those go right into the Third Eye and automatically create a pulsing sensation. As you exhale with the "SA" sound you will produce a pulsing sensation in Manipura Chakra.

<u>Kriya Energization</u> – a powerful way to energize your body and also to sensitize yourself to subtle energy flow and practice directing its movement.

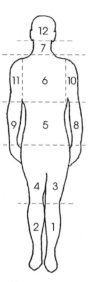

Consider your body to be divided into twelve parts:

1 left lower leg;	2 right lower leg;
3 left upper leg;	4 right upper leg;
5 mid section;	6 upper chest;
7 neck;	8 left lower arm;
9 right lower arm;	10 left upper arm;
11 right upper arm;	12 head.

Lie comfortably on your back with palms up. Tense and relax each body part in the order shown above. While tensing, breathe in through the nose, and while relaxing breathe out through the mouth, picturing energy flowing to that body part from the medulla oblongata (at the base of the skull where spinal cord meets brain.)

You can use tension-relaxation to heal yourself. Inhaling, tense an area that needs healing, exhaling relax and imagine prana flowing from the medulla to that spot. Increased energy enhances healing. Repeat as often as needed to heal the affected body part.

For a more dynamic result, inhale twice through the nose like two sniffs. Then exhale twice through the mouth with a non-vocal "who who" like a breathy, whistle. Move very rapidly from one body part to another. This can be done standing.

<u>Witness Your Thoughts</u> as if you were listening to an internal radio. Begin to detach from your thoughts and to see yourself as separate from them. Notice how the radio volume automatically goes down. Sometimes it turns off completely. How does it feel to sit in the silence?

Resources

Babaji and the 18 Siddha Kriya Yoga Tradition, M. Govindan. Available from Tantrika International.

Sex Matters, Osho (Bhagwan Shri Rajneesh), St. Martin's Press.

Autobiography of a Yogi, Paramahansa Yogananda.

Chapter Two

REMEMBERING YOUR MAGNIFICENCE

Being the Creator of Your Life

The most important results from spiritual practice are the awakening of consciousness and remembering who you really are. This chapter and the next examine the relationship between the physical body/mind and the Soul. Having this relationship well developed is the best preparation for a tantric relationship with another person and is the essence of living in TrantraBliss.

*B*uddha spoke of three bodies:

1) <u>The Material Body</u> – the ego, that with which you identify. It consists of your physical and emotional bodies, directed by the Limited Mind.

2) <u>The Bliss Body</u> – the Individual Soul, that aspect of God that is present with you as a unique being; the Higher Self, the infinite Unlimited Mind; the Inner Beloved; the Divine Presence, Existence, the Source.

3) <u>The Causal Body</u> – the Universal Soul, the undifferentiated One, the Tao, No Mind. You as an ego don't interact directly with the One. It is beyond mortal comprehension. Achieving God Realization comes later as the Individual Soul finally merges with the Universal Soul.

Ego prays to, and receives guidance from, the intermediary, the Bliss Body, but you see it as something separate and outside yourself.

> Achieving Self Realization means Ego identifies less and less with its history and beliefs, more and more with its Higher Self.

Ego – Limited Mind – Material Body.

"Ego" is Latin for "I am." It includes your body, your feelings and the part of you that thinks. It creates your self-definition which separates and distinguishes you from others. Ego is your interpretation of your history and environment, and how you fit in. It is the strategies you play out; the dramas in which you involve yourself. It includes your dreams and ambitions, your traumas and frustrations, and predispositions supplied by genetic code. It is what you think about, what you believe, and how you behave as an expression of those beliefs. Ego includes a Limited Mind, limited to the information programmed into it by parents and teachers, by social and religious belief systems and by its own experiences and the conclusions it draws. Ego exists because it created itself and persists because you give it energy. Ego could alternately be referred to as the identity, the small self, or the personality.

Ego also deals with predispositions from astrological influences and unfinished matters from previous lives (Karma), assuming that the qualities you develop during one life (skills, compassion and wisdom) factor in to your Soul-created predisposition in the next life cycle.

Soul – Unlimited Mind – Bliss Body.

The Higher Self is a part of God, eternal and infinite. Suppose that perfect Stillness (Universal Soul) divided itself into parts (Individual Souls) so the parts could play with each other to better understand and appreciate the Whole. In order to maintain the experience of separation and duality, the Souls had to temporarily forget their Source. The game was then to dance between light and shadow, to restore full Cosmic Consciousness, to eventually find their way back to the Stillness, to disappear into All That Is. "Enlightenment" is simply remembering how the game works and who you really are.

The Unlimited Mind is the intelligence that pervades all Existence, the fountain of all wisdom and knowledge. It is unconditional love of unfathomable depth; an awesome stillness; a profound and perfect peace beyond anything imaginable. It is your true essence, infinite and pure, beyond time and space, beyond the beyond.

Assume each ego is guided by a Soul. However, different souls express varying degrees of consciousness, different levels of access to the Infinite Wisdom, a spectrum ranging from the awareness of a stone through nature spirits, creatures and humans to Christ Consciousness. Anyone reading this material would be well progressed in the journey, approaching the home stretch.

Osho said most people haven't yet found their Soul. But most people have had glimpses. You recognize Soul expression as true artistry in music or any art form. When Soul reveals itself directly in a masterful performance it is thrilling and compelling, as when your tears begin to flow during the Hallelujah Chorus, or hairs stand up on your neck when a piece of poetry gets too close to Truth.

Your high-tech culture values the mind and encourages mental development far more than spiritual awakening, probably because the spiritual training of the past doesn't seem relevant today. Most of the problems in the world result from this imbalance. Many people have giant intellects with dwarf spiritual awareness.

Spiritual development has nothing to do with organized religion. It is achieving understanding of the Universe both objectively and subjectively. It is increasing refinement of the nervous system and expansion in the quality of consciousness to resonate with the higher levels of creation.

The Limited Mind can choose at any moment to invite its enlightened Essence to manifest through its physical form. The Soul waits patiently for that opportunity. Existence wants to make itself known to those who can comprehend its language. That language becomes more and more intelligible as spiritual awareness unfolds. Hosting the Divine Presence produces Bliss.

> Go sweep out the chambers of your heart.
> Make it ready. Make it ready
> To be the dwelling of the Beloved.
> When you depart, love will enter.
> In you, void of yourself,
> God will display His beauties.
>
> *(From the song of the 13th century Sufi Mystic, Shabistar)*

Transcending the Limited Mind.

Osho said that you are already enlightened, pretending not to be. Ego is unwilling to acknowledge its Soul's enlightenment and maintains separation from that light. Most psychotherapy is devoted to making the ego function more rationally, more effectively – a hopeless task, since it isn't real and its incongruities can only be healed by reconnecting to its enlightened Source.

In the Yogic approach, the personality is recognized as illusory, but as an adversary that must be subjugated, even "killed," in order for one to experience higher consciousness. This sets up an inner battle. The yogic emphasis is on developing will-power and self-discipline to overcome the lower nature. The physical body is whipped into submission by endless hours of exercise and ascetic practices, the emotional and sexual energies are stifled, suppressed, disowned.

The Tantric path differs from other spiritual paths by honoring and celebrating the "lower nature" – the physical body, the senses, the feelings, the sexual energies. By fully experiencing these aspects of your being you are able to complete them, to integrate them, to transcend their limitations. You can bring about a harmonious relationship between your lower and higher natures.

What stands in the way of Self Realization? Why are you stuck in this limited state? To rise above Ego's illusions you simply learn to separate your consciousness from the Ego. Realize that Ego is something you created. It is a great vehicle for experiencing humanness and it is not who you are.

The Limited Mind is like a computer which provides for your physical and emotional needs and security. Your Divine Essence needs a personality to function on the three-dimensional plane, to create a physical reality where the higher consciousness can dwell. Rather than subjugate Ego, Tantra invites Ego to fulfill its needs through loving acceptance. When Ego is nurtured and made to feel safe, it can relax its strategies and return to its undistorted childlike innocence. Safety only comes where love is unconditional.

How to Distinguish Ego from Soul.

Here are four inter-related qualities that will help to distinguish whether a particular thought or impulse is coming from the Ego or from the Soul. These are also Ego's primary methods of maintaining its illusory "reality," its sense of separation.

1) Criticism.

Ego is continually comparing itself, other people and situations to some standard. It constantly criticizes, judges, blames and complains. Observe your thoughts for an extended period and see how many of the thoughts are critical.

Soul simply observes what is so in the moment, not asking it to be different.

2) Guilt and Shame.

Ego harbors secret self-condemnation, guilt for things it's done or failed to do. It lives with a deep undercurrent of shame for being who it is. It longs for forgiveness, but won't forgive itself. It refuses the abundance of love and blessings available to it because it feels unworthy.

Soul sees a learning process, sees that all is in Divine Order. From the cosmic perspective, there was never a time when you were not forgiven.

3) Relationship to Time.

The dimensional doorway to transcend the Limited Mind is the Present Moment. Life is an illusion when lived through memory or fantasy.

Ego is absorbed in rehashing the past and fantasizing about the future. Assuming that the past predicts the future, Ego remembers pleasurable events and longs to recreate them. It remembers painful events and tries to avoid their recurrence. It cannot exist in present time. Sit a moment and notice the topics that stream through your mind. See their past and future orientation. But you have altered the dynamic. You are in present time, watching thoughts of past/future.

Soul has no sense of past or future, only the present moment. To come into the eternal now opens up a space beyond illusion and judgement. This space is always there, always has been there. Truth can be found only in the Eternal Now.

4) Stillness.

Ego persists in an ongoing mental discourse. The inner voice continues day and night speaking its opinions, justifying its positions and rehearsing its speeches. Notice how the chatter never stops.

Soul exists in profound silence, which can only be experienced when the Limited Mind is still. Sit for a while watching your breath go in and out. Notice how quiet your mind gets. An essential part of the daily practice is to come to that still point where you can access other dimensions.

Prayer, as usually practiced, is Ego's request for goods, services or information. When finished with its petition the Ego typically goes on about its business. Coming into stillness, where Ego no longer verbalizes, you are able to hear the answer to your question, receive the guidance you seek and return to the inner source of your creative power.

You will find several potent methods at the end of this chapter and in Appendix A to help still the mind.

SELF RESPONSIBILITY

Let's suppose that the Soul might have a certain plan for a life experience; that Soul could select two other souls to be the parents, based on their individual qualities and the dynamic between them; could fix the genetic pool to create a physical form appropriate for this character; could choose a birth time that would provide exactly the right astrological support; could generate a cultural climate as a base for the drama. Multiply this perfection by the number of people on the planet, all of whose dramas correlate perfectly. It's a stretch to imagine such immensity, such intelligence, such precision, but stretching is what Tantra is all about.

> As you become more closely identified with the Bliss Body, you realize that you, as a facet of the Divine Creator, designed your life drama. Soul set up the basic scenario. Ego then created a fictional character to survive in, to deal with, the situations it encountered. This co-creation continues moment by moment.

Your Life is a Movie.

You are the consummate movie maker. You have written a marvelous script, full of conflict and pathos, selected a perfect cast with heroes and villains. People are easily enrolled in your movie. If you want to play the victim, there are many who are happy to come in and victimize you. If you are really ready to give and receive love, someone will show up to share that with you. Whatever you wish to act out, there are supporting characters available.

The trick here is to keep remembering that you are setting this up. When you are aware of creating the movie, then it's really fun. When you are lost in the drama and think your life is happening to you, then it's an ordeal.

The hypothesis is that every major experience is something you, as a Soul, planned before embarking on this life; or something you agreed to do to support the drama of another Soul; or something

41

you have drawn to yourself, since like attracts like, so you can learn from it or play with it.

If you see the world as being objective, separation seems real and one person can victimize another. When you see that all are creators, and there is no separation, no one can be the victim. No one has ever done anything to you without your agreement. You can never be the victim of anything except your own unconsciousness. There are no accidents.

People are reluctant to admit they have set up their life drama and are very attached to the helpless victim role. Reclaiming your creative power is a giant step forward in awareness.

Taking responsibility for your life is not the same as assuming blame. When every incident is seen as an opportunity for growth, there's no place for blame.

Admittedly there is no way to prove that this point of view is "true." However, if you live life as though it were true, the quality of your life will be greatly enhanced. Rather than hold out for verifiable "truth" you might do well to accept a good working hypothesis.

Outside Reflects Inside.

There is a wonderful mantra to the Divine Mother as Quan Yin. "Om namo, Quan Shri Yin, pu sa." It translates as follows:

> I honor the noble Quan Yin, goddess of compassionate wisdom; she who hears the tears and laughter of the world; she who sees through the greatest illusion of all – the notion that outside is different from inside.

Your experiences out in the world are but a reflection of your inner world – your attitudes and expectations. Existence is attempting to draw your attention to what goes on covertly in your subconscious.

See the world as a mirror. When it seems as though someone is "doing it to you," figure out how you really do the same thing to yourself and to others.

After many years of working on emotions (in the old inefficient way) I thought myself pretty clear. Noticing some irritations buzzing around in my head, I decided to make a list of everyone toward whom I still harbored resentments. There were ninety-three people on the list!

I discovered that, in almost every case, they had made an agreement or promise that wasn't kept. Understanding the mirror principle I suddenly realized in that period of time I had probably promised myself ninety-three times to be more careful about diet, more diligent with exercise and spiritual practice, promises that were seldom kept. If I don't keep promises to myself, other people won't keep promises to me. Obviously I'm a slow learner, but Existence is a relentless teacher. Once I really "got it," the people in my life began to keep their promises much better, but still not completely.

Years later I see now the deeper level of this teaching. By carrying resentment toward people I dishonored them. But more importantly I judged myself for breaking my promises, for not accomplishing my goals, for not living up to my expectations. In that judgement I withheld from myself love and compassion. I dishonored myself. This is what the ninety-three people were reflecting back to me. All there is is Love, but when you withhold love from yourself, life treats you unlovingly.

The mirror principle allows a maturity and refinement of the more primitive idea of retribution. ("An eye for an eye;" or "As you sow, so shall you reap;" or "What goes around comes around.") It's not that you get what you deserve, but rather that you get from life what you are willing to give yourself.

MORE ABOUT EGO

• Your identity is absolutely fascinated with itself, its history, its concerns, its life-drama. Unfortunately, no one else is nearly as fascinated as you are, unless your character fits into their script.

• Your "history" is mostly bogus. You perceive a situation through your filters, and interpret it in the light of your experience. Your version of an event would be very different from someone else involved in the same situation.

• Your memory is creative. It retains selectively and makes adjustments. It's more important to look good than to recall an incident accurately.

• The mind is a problem-solving device. That's what it was designed to do. If there were no real problems to chew on, it would create some new ones just to stay busy. It's a matter of job security. The mind wants to stay in control.

• If you find your greatest joy in anticipating a future event, you miss the joy of all the present moments leading up to that one. If you torture yourself with dread of something that may happen, again you poison the moment. Love and joy only happen in present time. The rest is fantasy and illusion. Twelve step programs encourage people to take life one day at a time. Tantra says try one moment at a time.

• Ego's concerns include the major issues of the lower four chakras:

1st Chakra (root) Concerned with Survival.

Ego is a mechanism programmed to assure survival of the body and the Limited Mind with its attitudes, positions and strategies. It is concerned about safety.

2nd Chakra (sex center) Concerned with Seeking Pleasure/Avoiding Pain.

Ego finds pleasure in distorted love, having forgotten there was anything else. It prefers numbness to intense feeling, positive or negative.

3rd Chakra (power center) Concerned with Vanity and Power.

Ego is always trying to compensate for feeling unworthy, inadequate. It needs to be right, justifying its every thought, feeling and deed, making people wrong who have differing viewpoints. It would rather be right than happy. It wants to be accepted, getting approval by conforming to people's expectations. It wants to be special and superior, receiving admiration for outstanding accomplishments. It wants the power to control situations in order to fulfill its desires. Ego sees itself as <u>separate</u>, comparing itself to others, and judging itself and others for mistakes and shortcomings.

4th Chakra (heart) Concerned with Love.

4th Chakra (heart) Concerned with Love.

Ego is constantly looking for love and validation, usually not in a way that will work. Its history of love is built on a foundation of conditions and of withheld or <u>distorted love</u>.

Development of Limited Mind.

A woman had a new baby, and already had a four-year-old son. She noticed the little boy was hanging around the baby's crib and she was a little concerned. She asked the child why he spent so much time around the baby. The little fellow replied, "I'm asking him how it feels to live with God, because I'm starting to forget."

You came into this life knowing who you are. Look deeply into a baby's eyes and see a reflection of the Infinite. As an infant you received little support for your inborn awareness. Your parents didn't see you as a divine being. They only saw their fears and expectations and responsibilities. You depended totally on your parents for physical survival so, as the clarity of your vision faded, you came to believe the views of those around you. Like a hostage adopting the positions of his captors/caretakers, you accepted their ideas of what life is, who you are, how you fit in, how you should behave. Without consciousness, each generation adopts (by conforming to or rebelling against) the illusions of the generation before.

Parents unwittingly crush the spirit of their children in order to maintain control, as they were crushed by their parents. Having lived a lie, parents cannot bear to be reminded of the innocence they relinquished so long ago.

Conditioning.

The conditioning process is simple. Behavior A produces pleasurable reward B. Conclusion: Keep doing A. Behavior C produces painful result D. Conclusion: Don't do C any more. Many of your unconscious behaviors are the product of this process. It is a primitive but useful mechanism. Rats and chickens are trained to perform tricks in the same way. Interestingly, rats have enough sense to notice that a certain path in the maze doesn't lead to the cheese and they will stop going down that path. Humans seem to continue with the same ineffective strategies indefinitely.

Actually people sometimes do figure out there is no cheese. It seems you must continue to re-experience a non-rewarding path until you get totally bored with it. If you act unconsciously it takes a long time to get bored. If you bring consciousness into the process, if you start to watch it as a movie, boredom sets in much more quickly. How many times can you enjoy the same rerun?

Don't worry if deconditioning takes a while. You have time to complete this particular learning, however long it takes. Existence is not in a hurry, but it is efficient. If the learning could happen more quickly, it would. Once you are free from that ineffective strategy you can look for a way that leads to deeper satisfaction, a path based on unconditional love.

Conformity.

Here is a process that creates conformity. A child is told stories to make it conform. For example, the myth of Santa Claus is offered to children as truth. If you are good, Santa will bring you presents. If you are bad, you won't get anything, or worse yet, will be punished. The child wants to believe what he is told, because of the pleasures of the rewards. If he should challenge the myth, there is fear of losing the reward.

I taught many classes in Germany and noticed how diligent the students were, almost obsessed with meticulous accuracy and precision, no allowance for error. That made sense after I learned of an old German tradition about a black Santa that comes to take away disobedient children.

Soon the child will be told that he will go to Heaven if he does what the priest/minister says and go to Hell if he is "bad." Even though there's no immediate reward in sight, still his mind has been prepared to accept this myth. Later he will be told that it is his patriotic duty to go to war, and cowards are a disgrace. The church has him. The government has him.

Throughout history there has been a ruling class and an organized religion, determined to control the masses, to trap them in a limited world-view, to exploit their energies and resources. This continues now through the controlled media, which feeds the populace whatever stories the ruling powers dictate.

Society presents to you its unconscious view of reality, with severe penalties for being different. Those penalties serve to suppress any urge to question the accepted position.

> **No one can be a victim** without giving permission. When you give away your power for the comfort of fitting in with a group, you are easy prey for those who enjoy controlling.

Mystics have always talked about life being an illusion. Illusion is what you accept as being real without question. Tantra is the hero's path, for those with the courage to hold to their inner vision, even when society goes a different way. Many spiritual seekers are considered crazy by their families, sometimes even disowned. In each living moment you have a choice whether or not to continue supporting the collective illusion.

Belief Systems – Limiting Decisions.

From what you observe and experience, you draw some basic conclusions about yourself and your world. You accept (or adapt) your parents' belief systems about what's expected of you, and how to get what you need to survive. Once the beliefs are in place, filters in your mind allow you to perceive only that which supports your decisions and positions. The mind becomes rigid in defending its operating system. It finds security in a well defined world where it feels competent. That security comes with a heavy price. You no longer have access to the greater possibilities beyond your cozy box.

You create life situations that validate your position. For example, a father left his wife and young daughter. The child concludes "If you love a man, he'll leave you." She will later be involved in a series of relationships where the man invariably leaves. She attracts men with that propensity and then treats them in a way that drives them out. She is bored by men who could be loyal. She would rather be right and have her position validated than enjoy a loving relationship.

Parental Admonitions.

Most of your basic beliefs were formulated before age four. These early decisions were based on parents' instructions, but more importantly on parents' example. Children have wonderful psychic abilities. In the pre-verbal years a child knows exactly what's going on with parents emotionally without being told. The unspoken admonitions and emotional climate of the home are recorded as a reality very early in life.

> The response you get from your mother becomes the response you get from the world because that's what you expect and that's what you create.

Here are a few of the unspoken attitudes that hang in the atmosphere of many homes. See if any of these have a familiar ring to you. or bring on a tightness somewhere in your belly. See if your life is run by these, or similar, "rules."

Do things for people so they will like you.
Your ideas aren't worth anything.
When you are sick I will give you attention.
My life would be better without you.
Avoid close, intimate contact.
It's not OK to be happy.
You will be/are a failure.

Don't take chances.
Keep up appearances.
Don't trust people.
Don't follow your impulses.
You must earn my love.
Love is dangerous.
I don't want to live.

Duty before fun.

No one cares what you want

Your feelings are unimportant/ridiculous.

If you love me you will do as I say.

What will people think?

If you aren't successful, I will reject you.

No matter what you do, it is never enough.

Be what women/men want you to be.

That's man's/woman's work.

You have nothing important to say.

I do not have time for you.

Others are better than you .

I wish you had never been born.

Be like your friends.

You must make correct choices.

Don't outdo me.

Love me, don't leave me out.

Men don't cry.

Always obey authority.

Don't expect to be noticed.

Don't be closer to other men/women than you are to me.

Some admonitions are positive. The story is told of a Nobel prize winner who, as a small child, was trying to pour a glass of milk and dropped the milk bottle, spilling milk all over the kitchen. His mother came in to see what had happened. (Imagine here how your mother would have reacted.) This mother sat on the floor with her son and they played with the milk, splashing each other, laughing, "milking" the situation for its maximum pleasure.

After a while she said to her son "This milk needs to be cleaned up now. I see three possibilities. I can clean it up, or you can clean it up, or you and I can clean it up together. You choose." The son asked her to help him and they worked together. The incident was never mentioned again. How different your life would be if there had been that much room for error without fear of humiliation or punishment.

Distorted Love.

When you were very young, your love for your parents was absolute and unquestioning. You could not imagine that they had flaws or problems. If things were not going well at home, especially if mother was unhappy, the child invariably assumes that s/he is the cause of the problem. Your reality could be based on the idea that the people you love most are hurt by your presence in their lives, and they would be happier and better off if you weren't there.

If your parents hold an attitude that constrains their joy (I don't deserve any better) you as a child probably bought into that attitude, in support of the parent. This is another example of love distorted.

> Since no one ever receives enough love, you decide that there is something wrong with you, that you are not worthy of being loved.

It never occurs to the child that the parent is shut down to love, incapable of giving or receiving love. Your entire way of being in the world is based on the conclusions you drew in service to distorted love.

A fellow who came to a course in Australia was in a relationship with a lovely young woman. She was frustrated because he wouldn't make the commitment to live with her, even though he clearly loved her with all his heart. We explored his childhood and discovered that, when he was two, his mother gave birth to another child and then went into deep post-partum depression. It took a violent form, and she committed herself to a mental hospital, fearing for her children's safety. The child assumed that he had somehow caused her distress. He concluded that anyone he really loved would suffer a terrible fate. His current reluctance to go more deeply into a relationship was his way of protecting his beloved from the distress his presence would bring to her. Soon after he brought this into his consciousness and got clear that his mother's illness wasn't his fault, he and his lady married. At last report they were doing well.

> Only when you realize that you created a situation, do you have the power to change it.

Keep reminding yourself that you have collaborated in setting up your family dynamic. Perhaps you have chosen to deny yourself love so that you can discover what love is. If you were always surrounded by love, you wouldn't appreciate it. Would you ask the fish how he was enjoying the water? Having never been out of water, he couldn't have an opinion (if fish had opinions.)

Repeated Behavior Patterns.

Once your belief system is established, you develop strategies and behavior patterns that are repeated every time a trigger situation presents itself. These patterns are totally out of your control, because they come from the subconscious mind. They were developed without benefit of consciousness and play out like a reflex without consulting your logic.

• You establish a belief, based on your interpretation of your homelife.

• To cope with that "reality" and get what you need, you devise a strategy.

• From that strategy specific irrational behaviors emerge.

For example, there are many children and you don't get much attention.

Belief: Who you are doesn't bring the attention you want.

Strategy: When you're sick you get mother's full attention.

Behavior: Chronic illness, a series of illnesses, frequent injuries, acting out.

Come to recognize your patterns. Some are complex enough to deserve sub-personality status. Give them an affectionate name.

A friend tells about his partner doing her Cleopatra number – "Queen of Denial."

Remember the tale of Snow White and the seven little men who worked in the mines. Everyone has their underground sub-personalities. Get to know and recognize your own Grumpy, or Doc, Critic, Bitch, Victim, Peter Pan, Rescuer, Loser, Panderer, Martyr, Controller, Savior, Caretaker, Patient, Vamp, Fixer, etc.

The Esoteric Mind.

The esoteric mind is the last developmental stage of the Limited Mind and the most challenging. If transcendence isn't approached with unconditional love, Ego can become deceptive. It discourses in beautiful words, describing a reality that it doesn't know. Through

51

fantasy and imagination it learns to act as if Soul were present. It convinces itself and others that it has tapped into another dimension. Actually it is only Ego, asleep, dreaming that it is awake. This is true for many "spiritual teachers," particularly those who don't radiate love.

As Limited Mind develops, there is an intense longing for enlightenment, but if part of the mind feels threatened, it continues to sabotage the effort, creating diversions and imitations. Ego cooperates in spiritual growth up to a point, but it wants to survive and to remain in control, to continue its hidden agendas. It is not really convinced that its needs will best be satisfied by surrendering to Soul.

You might perform your practice diligently, all the while expecting to be rewarded in some way – to be acknowledged and admired as a holy person, to meet the perfect mate, to be supported in your material needs, etc. This is bartering, not surrender. If the rewards were withheld, the spiritual practice might be abandoned. Ego does things in order to attain a future goal. Ideally, the practice is its own reward, bringing you to the Bliss of the present moment.

Lacking love, Ego wants spiritual powers and healing powers to feel special. As chakras open, certain psychic abilities become available. It's a very seductive trap and you can easily become fascinated with your new-found powers. Sages have warned about this pitfall. Wanting to save the world (messiah complex), longing to achieve the perfect human manifestation, aspiring to be one of the special few who have attained enlightenment – this is all part of vanity.

Ego rejects love, because it believes itself to be unworthy. It continues to withhold love from itself. The Soul created that experience of separation and love withheld in order to see its magnificence more clearly. Ego will eventually come to realize, beyond all doubt, that:

> Love is available unconditionally from
> the Soul and worthiness is irrelevant.
> Love is all you really need.

WITNESS CONSCIOUSNESS

The only remedy for darkness is turning on the light. The only cure for memories recorded without the benefit of consciousness is to invite those images and feelings into awareness while you are fully conscious and present. Consciousness always has the choice of running away until the storm is over or staying present and observing the process as a Silent Witness. If you run away you miss the opportunity to learn an important lesson. Then Existence has to create another similar situation to give you yet another opportunity. If you stay present you begin the healing process. There simply is no other way. Every master has taught the principle of Witness Consciousness.

From the position of the Witness, you see the Limited Mind for what it is. You observe it in action and learn its patterns and agendas. Remember why you chose to experience this particular illusion. Let your compulsion to control give way to a deep surrender to Existence, trusting that everything is in Divine Order.

Be the Witness moment by moment. When you are watching a well-made film, you are transported into that reality and totally forget that there is any other reality. A badly made movie leaves you very aware that you are in a theater viewing images. You are such a clever film maker that the movie of your life is totally engrossing. Somehow you must stay aware that it is only a movie.

Witnessing is a knack, not difficult to learn and always transformative. Learn to pull back enough to get out of the illusion/drama, but not far enough to dissociate from it.

When emotions come to the surface,
experience them to the depths, with your
Higher Self fully present. When you can be
totally subjective and totally objective at the
same time, you are operating as a unified being.

Be wary of mind tricks. The mind can split itself, watch itself, pretending to be the Witness. If your Witness is judging or criticizing, it is an impostor. The true Witness has no opinions, no expectations, no standards, no judgements. It simply observes what is so in the moment.

Witness is a neutral position that moves you from the negative position of blame/complain/criticize/avoid to a neutral place of objective, but benevolent, observation. Eventually you will feel safe enough to move from neutral to a positive position of compassion and appreciation, even to real love and gratitude.

Going Deeper

1. Read *Jewel* Lessons 2 and 3.

2. For more about being present, read *The Power of Now* by Eckhart Tolle, available through Tantrika International.

3. Begin to examine your repeated patterns while maintaining Witness Consciousness. Keep a daily journal and record the high points and the upsets.

   • Are there certain situations in your life that trigger a predictable response? (Relationship is going well but I feel restless and break it off.)

   • In your internal commentary do you see a strategy that explains your behavior? (I better dump him before he has a chance to dump me.)

   • Can you track this back to an underlying belief that this experience validates (If you love someone he'll leave you.)

   • What patterns are complex enough to deserve sub-personality status? Describe them in your journal. Can you find affectionate names for them?

   • If one were to do an impression of you, what qualities would s/he imitate?

4. Outgrowing Conformity. Astrologists say that Saturn orbits in a twenty-nine-and-a-half year cycle. When it returns to the position it occupied at your birth, you receive a huge boost of energy for a major shift. Around age twenty-eight to thirty you might notice being less concerned about what family and friends want you to be, more interested in finding out what you want to be and to do with your life. Again at about age fifty-eight to sixty another opportunity is presented, another cosmic wake-up call. See if this corresponds to your personal history and that of your friends.

5. Come into stillness whenever you don't have to think. Try these methods:

Watching the Breath. This very simple technique is a perfect place to begin. You can quickly learn to be the Witness by sitting quietly and focusing on your breathing process. Observe the breath as it enters and leaves your body. Make no attempt to modify it. Have no opinion about how it should be. Give your full attention to watching the breath for several minutes.

Breath Mantra. As you observe the breath, you can also hear its cosmic sound. As you inhale, hear the sound "hong." As you exhale, hear the sound "saw." Hearing "Hong Saw" will still the mind and bring you into present time. Breath stops and enlightenment happens. Do Breath Mantra only during meditation. It takes you out of body.

Khechari Mudra. Holding the tongue tip to the roof of the mouth quiets the mind, among other benefits (see *Jewel*, page 109). Whenever the mind is chattering, you are saying all those words to yourself. If the tongue is immobilized so you can't "talk," the mind shuts down automatically.

6. Continue your daily practice routine. Be very aware of the sensations and feelings you experience during the practice. Your routine could now take this form (see below for instructions).

ACTIVATE THE BODY

- Complete Breath (alternative to Bated Breath)
- Rishi Isometrics (alternative to Kriya Energizer)

STILL THE MIND

- Watch the Breath (as described above, alternative to Witness Your Thoughts)

Complete Breath

The Complete Breath is the basis for breath mastery as you learn to increase your lung capacity and to breathe very slowly. In yogic breathing the lungs are filled completely and emptied completely. This exercise will leave you very relaxed and calm, and yet revitalized. Use it during the day when you feel tension in your body. Don't rush through the practice or do it mechanically. Stand tall with your spine straight, head erect and eyes closed. Perform the breath three times.

1) Firmly tense the arms, legs and buttocks as you inhale through the nose to the count of eight. Fill the lower lungs as the belly expands (like a balloon being inflated.) Then fill the middle and upper parts of the lungs. Fill the lungs but without strain.

2) Hold your breath as long as is comfortable. (If you have high blood pressure, don't hold the breath.)

3) Vigorously exhale through pursed lips (as if you were about to whistle) to the count of eight. Relax the body but draw in the abdomen, lifting it upwards to squeeze out every bit of air.

4) Relax completely.

Rishi Isometrics

Read about these wonderful movements in *Jewel*, Lesson 3, to appreciate their great value. Use them before meditation to relax, stimulate and prepare the body. Be present and conscious of each breath. Keep your mind focused on the movement, the stretch, the breath and the energy produced. Move slowly and gracefully. Perform each part three times. Inhale through the nose, exhale through the mouth. If you have high blood pressure, don't hold your breath. Feet are parallel, jaws relaxed.

Part A. Stretching Up

1) To open the front of the lungs: As you inhale (nose), sweep the arms to the sides and then overhead. Stretch up, lifting onto the balls of your feet, stimulating the Bubbling Spring, entry point in the body for earth energy. Elongate the spine. Press the palms together to create dynamic tension in the arms and underarms. (Eventually learn to tighten every muscle in the body with the twelve-body-part tension.) Hold the breath, hold the tension for a few seconds. Exhale (mouth), lower the arms and relax. Perform three or more repetitions.

57

2) To open the back of the lungs: Inhale, stretch up as before, this time pressing the backs of the hands together overhead. Feel tension in the shoulders. Exhale and relax the arms back to the sides. Repeat.

3) Relax and feel the streaming sensations in your arms and shoulders.

Part B. <u>Side Bend</u>

1) Stretch left side: Take a little wider stance. Inhaling, stretch arms overhead and lock the thumbs, pulling one thumb against the other to create dynamic tension.Exhaling (mouth), bend slowly to the right side, keeping the elbows in line with the ears. Drop the head to the side. Feel the line of tension from the side of your foot to the tips of your fingers. Hold the breath out, hold the tension, for a few seconds. As you inhale (nose), return to upright position, arms overhead, holding tension. Repeat twice or more.

2) Stretch right side: Reverse the thumbs. Pull to create tension. Exhale as you bend slowly to the left. Continue as above.

3) At the end, relax arms to your sides and focus on the movement of energy.

Part C. <u>Forward Bend</u>

1) Clasp thumbs behind your back, pulling one thumb against the other. Step out with your left foot. Inhale deeply. On the exhale (mouth), bend forward keeping the back straight and lifting the arms as high as possible. Lift the chin to feel tension in the throat. Feel tension in the groin. Bend the knee if necessary. Feel the pull from sacrum to medulla. Hold the tension for a few seconds. As

you inhale (nose), return to upright posture, thumbs still clasped, relaxing tension. Repeat twice more. Then return arms to sides, feet together, relax completely.

2) Switch the thumbs and pull to create tension. Step out with the right foot. Continue as above.

3) Relax and feel the energy streaming in your body.

Part D. <u>Back Bend</u>

1) Feet together. On the inhale, press your palms together in front and raise the arms overhead. Holding the breath, lean back. Drop the head back, arching the spine as much as possible, with tension in the arms. Tense the entire body and focus on the sacrum. Hold the breath, hold the tension.

2) Begin to exhale (mouth) as you return to an upright position, relaxing tensions, arms still extended overhead. As you complete the exhalation bend forward until torso and arms are parallel to the earth. Stretch the arms, stretch the spine. You might feel the energy shoot up your spine. Repeat twice more.

3) During the last exhale, drop the body forward like a rag doll. After a moment, on the inhale, slowly come upright.

4) Feel the energy.

Part E. <u>Spinal Twist</u>

1) Stand with feet shoulder width apart, hands at waist level, palms toward the body. On the exhale, twist the torso and head slowly to the right. Press the right palm toward the earth and the left palm toward the heavens, pressing up and to the right side, across the body. Hold the breath out and stretch for four counts.

2) On the inhale, slowly return to center position, relaxing all tensions, with hands at waist level.

3) Twisting to the left on the exhale, right palm to the heavens, left to the earth. Hold and tense, then return, relaxed, to center on the inhale.

4) Repeat steps 1 to 3 twice more. Then relax and notice the movement of energy.

Chapter Three

FULFILLMENT AND EMPOWERMENT
Ego's Desires and Soul's Purpose

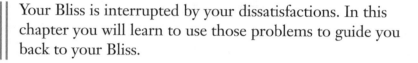

Your Bliss is interrupted by your dissatisfactions. In this chapter you will learn to use those problems to guide you back to your Bliss.

The name given for this "new" transmission of Tantra was "Ipsalu," which turned out to be a Sanskrit word that means "overcoming desire." When this word first came, through a pendulum, it felt like a declaration of war on the body and its essential energies. Did this mean that, as a candidate for enlightenment, one should never again feel that fire in the loins, or find rapture in a touch or a kiss or orgasm? And what about desires for things/experiences outside the sexual arena?

"Desire" is defined as "a wish or longing, a yearning," all activities of the mind that have little to do with the body. Wishing for something you imagine to be pleasurable; longing for something you anticipate happening; yearning for a repeat of something that happened before; these are all mental exercises based on the past and future. "Hope" is yet another snare that ties you to the belief that happiness depends on something that's not currently available. These mental games keep you out of the Eternal Now. True passion occurs in present time, in the energy flow of the body when the mind is still.

"Overcoming desire" doesn't mean stifling your sexuality. It simply means surrendering to the moment, the only time that is real. When sexual energy overtakes you, enjoy it. If the energy is present and there is no partner to share it, then learn to enjoy it by yourself rather than fantasizing about a lover. Put your mind on hold and be totally present with the energy. Eventually it will be there when you want it, but will no longer dominate you.

Desires for Other than Sex.

Desires are based on Ego's assumption that you will be happy as soon as you have ___, or as soon as you are rid of ___, or as soon as you can do ___. Ego's main concerns are survival (safety), pleasure (being happy), and vanity (being right.) Your desires are the means by which you expect to accomplish those ends. The converse, of course, is that you can't feel safe, happy or right until you have those desires realized. Ego clings to this fallacy to justify its agenda.

Ego values possessions, image, accomplishments, position, power, approval, etc. It expects satisfactions from attaining these goals. The gap between what you want and what you actually have creates great tension and anxiety. To relieve that pressure you could either feel driven to work harder toward the goal or you could give it up with a defeated resignation.

Ironically, even if the objects of desire are attained, they usually don't bring lasting satisfaction. So Ego sets new goals, bigger desires. It doesn't "get" the futility of this whole process. (Want to make God laugh? Tell Him your plan.)

> Ego desires are usually attempts to compensate for subconscious feelings of unworthiness and inadequacy, core beliefs adopted in early childhood

The only source of true satisfaction is re-connecting to your Inner Beloved. Then you are filled with a sense that all is in Divine Order, that nothing needs to be altered or added. Your reality is changing, is in a dynamic flux, but where it is at any given moment is perfectly acceptable. Enfolded by Soul you feel totally protected, blissfully happy, and profoundly appropriate in your actions. To find this lovely place, the only thing that needs to change is your attitude. Then the whole game of desire is finished.

Buddha taught that desire was the cause of mankind's suffering. He advised that letting go of desire, not being invested in the outcome, was the key to tranquillity. With the greatest respect for this masterful teaching, perhaps you are now mature enough to consider additional possibilities. You can use the ego's desire as a clue to track down what is really troubling you, what you are really crying out for. You will soon learn just how to accomplish this.

Soul's Purpose.

The last chapter suggested that your Soul created the major influences in your life – the challenges for you to work through, puzzles for you to solve, a treasure hunt with clues at key points.

> Your Soul has intentions in this plan – what you are to learn, what you might create, what you can experience. This is your Dharma, your destiny. This plan is totally supported by Existence.

You are fully empowered to accomplish these aims. Whatever is required to assist you will be provided. Manifesting Soul's purpose brings a profound sense of completion and fulfillment. This is very different from Ego's futile attempts to find satisfaction through its compensatory desires.

When asked what they most desire, meditative people usually share their longing for deep relationship, abundance, spiritual openings, discovering their life's purpose, profound sex, health and vitality, more fun, or productivity in creative ventures like art or writing. Any of these could be part of Soul's purpose. If these experiences are not manifesting, you can discover why.

There is an old conundrum – If God is all powerful, can He build a rock so big He can't lift it? The answer – "Yes. The ego." What follows describes how you as an ego thwart your divine destiny.

• You have a pattern of recurring **self-sabotaging behaviors** – abrasive or retiring ways that keep people at a distance, food or drug choices that anesthetize you, deflecting feedback rather than letting people tell you what is amiss, denial of the obvious, messing up on the brink of success, in other word, **whatever it takes to maintain safety, numbness and separation.**

• These behaviors grow out of your **self-limiting beliefs** – It won't be good enough. They won't like me anyway. It works for other people but not for me. It's not safe. I will make a fool of myself.

• The beliefs are cemented in place by emotionally charged memories stored in body tissue and energy channels, obstructing the flow of energy, serving as **emotional blocks** – fear of rejection/humiliation, pain from losing a beloved friend, anger because earlier attempts were unsuccessful. Each of these assumes that past predicts future and previous trauma must not be repeated. (More in Chapter 5.)

You can analyze a "problem" in this way and understand its complexities but the healing doesn't begin until you go to the quick, to the place in the body where the frozen emotion lives. You must re-experience that old fear, pain or anger, this time consciously. You must admit your attachment to the current situation and the pleasure or comfort it gives you, even if it seems irrational.

There are an infinite number of ways to set the program in place. Some people create horrendous childhood experiences. Others seem to have an idyllic childhood, but even in the most perfect family scene there is at least one uncharacteristic moment when a parent creates enough trauma to wound the child for life. That is the job they signed on for. This is the wound that will take a lifetime to heal, and in the process fulfill the major learning for this lifetime.

Spock Syndrome.

Many people born in the '40s through '60s, millions of baby-boomers (myself included) were raised according to the dictates of the popular baby book written by Dr. Benjamin Spock. I will share my own experiences because they are common to so many others of my generation. Among other directions, Dr. Spock cautioned mothers to feed a baby and pick it up only on schedule. (He recanted this position late in his life after countless lives had been skewed.)

My infant metabolism was a little faster than average and the need for food came earlier than the scheduled time. I was left screaming in terror, feeling I was going to die from hunger, while my well-intentioned mother stood by and anxiously watched the clock.

My baby self might have felt a need for comfort or nurturing and asked to be held (by crying, since that was the only communication available). My mother, wanting to do what's "right" for the baby, not to "spoil" it, would let me cry without responding.

Several belief systems were generated for me out of this situation, systems around feeling unsupported and helpless, systems of compulsion around food and sex. See how my later life desires, even Soul purpose, have been affected by those beliefs. See how you can use an inner dialogue to explore those beliefs that paralyze you, and begin to transcend their limitations.

INTENTION DIALOGUE

Life Problem – Feeling Unsupported

What is your <u>current desire</u>, something you want very much but aren't able to produce?

I want to establish an organization to help me spread the tantric teaching. It feels like my Soul's purpose.

What is <u>actually manifesting</u> in your life?

People get excited for a while and want to help, but that doesn't last long. Usually they make a mess of whatever they try to do and I have to redo it.

Are you <u>willing to take responsibility</u> to see how you create and perpetuate this situation rather than seeing yourself as the victim?

I'm not convinced but OK for the sake of argument.

What <u>behaviors</u> do you find yourself doing automatically?

> *When an assistant does something well, I take it for granted. That's his job. More often I find fault in some way, sometimes even get really upset.*

You probably attract people whose mother always told them "No matter what you do it is never good enough." They would be perfect for this role.

So what is your <u>strategy</u> for dealing with the situation?

> *To get anything done right I'll have to do it myself.*

Say this mantra a few times: I love feeling superior to everyone.

> *I love feeling superior. I love feeling superior. I really do love that feeling.*

Say your strategies and behaviors were stems and leaves. What <u>belief</u> would lie at the root?

> *Those who are supposed to be helping me can't be trusted.*

Go very young. How is that feeling in your body?

> *I feel angry at being ignored when I need help. I'm sad that nobody loves me enough to notice what I need and take care of me. I'm afraid I'm going to die.*

Your mind is saying these things. Go deeper and speak from the place in your body where these feelings live, where they are still happening in this moment.

> *There's tension all over my belly.*

Say it again from that place.

(Repeat until the voice quavers, until you reach the frozen emotion.)

The dialogue continues long enough to reveal the truth that produces <u>transformation</u>.

> • *It was important for me to feel superior. That's what mother required, and I felt compelled to carry on that charade to please her, to hold her interest and support. I forgave my mother for trying to live out her ambitions through me.*

> • *I learned to allow space for her and others to make errors without judgement or penalty. Obviously that reflected my internal process, so I had to*

allow myself to make errors. Very soon people began showing up with extraordinary abilities, world-class talent, eager to help out.

A friend, reading this, resonated with the situation but identified his personal belief – When you love someone, they don't take care of your needs. Love equals unmet needs. And his strategy – Choose a partner who doesn't meet your needs. If someone does take care of you, question the validity of their love.

Each process clarifies a <u>lesson</u>. Because nobody is ever a victim and the Spock syndrome was chosen by so many souls, you must assume it had great potential for learning.

For me part of the value was learning tolerance and compassion, on the way to learning unconditional love. Judging the performance of others simply reflected judgements I have of myself, based on the notion that love has to be earned by superior performance.

I realized how much my own "stuff" got in the way of my Soul purpose manifesting, and how being present to that stuff enhanced my own aware-ness. Seeing what was not effective helped me appreciate what was effective. The work I was destined to do is now moving forward much better.

The Spock syndrome uncertainty around food and touch created for me, and for countless others, major life challenges around food addiction (binge/purge cycles) and sex addiction (promiscuity/celibacy cycles). The strategy for me was "Get it while you can. No telling when you will get another chance."

The lesson was about bringing consciousness and love to the physical processes of food and sex. In earlier times vows of poverty, chastity and obedience governed the lives of spiritual seekers. Avoidance was the strategy. In these times you can use conscious-ness to make the best choices without such limitations.

To Summarize.

The intention dialogue helps to identify several essential elements:
Desire – what do you want?
Current manifestation – what do you have?

Willingness to take responsibility. – what have you created?

Recurrent behaviors – what are you doing?

Underlying strategies – what do you hope to accomplish by these behaviors?

Core beliefs – what decisions have you made?

Frozen feeling – where does it live in your body and how does it feel?

Value of the limiting position; how it supports you – maintains separation/safety/numbness, relieves pressure, creates adventure without too much risk.

Lesson – what did you intend to learn or experience in this situation?

Transformation – what attitude needs to shift for you to release this pattern?

Dialoguing your issues is very revealing. Anyone would benefit greatly from this exercise. Different people have different issues. Whatever their source, the issues can be explored by probing deeply to find the reasons underlying your unfulfilled desires.

The responses in this dialogue may not come quickly, since strategies and core beliefs are deeply buried in the subconscious and well protected. A daily practice tends to bring the issues into consciousness to be acknowledged, completed and released. The old feelings are frozen in time, still happening in the present. When you come into the moment, this is what you will be facing. Opportunities are provided in Ipsalu courses for release work with guidance, and private sessions are available with a skilled facilitator.

> Transformation comes from telling
> the truth, admitting how much you love,
> enjoy and depend on the situation you are
> protesting. See how beautifully it serves you,
> even though your mind might object

Ineffective Ways to Formulate Desires.

• in order to – If the object desired is expected to produce another result, it is an ego manipulation. "I desire a fancy car in order to attract women."

• past or future – If the goal involves something outside the present moment, it loses power. You can only influence the present moment and let that influence moments to come. "I desire a thirty-pound weight loss by a certain date. But for now, pass the ice cream."

• dependence – If someone or something outside you has to change for your desire to be realized, you are out of bounds. When something shifts inside you, everything around you will shift automatically, but going at it directly doesn't work. "I desire my wife to be less critical."

• fixing – If you are motivated by a sense that something is wrong, there is an implied judgement which precludes the Presence. "I desire to be more confident."

• don't want – Focus on what you want rather than what you don't want. "I desire to stop getting involved with unavailable men."

Divine Guidance or Neurotic Compulsion?

To realize your desires or intentions, you have to make certain choices, perform certain actions. An idea pops into your mind and you wonder whether to follow that prompting. How can you tell whether the idea is a direction from your Higher Self or the Ego's urging to pursue one of its futile strategies?

Life is Hell when you know it's just a matter of time before you find yourself into another serious mess (not realizing how you got yourself there). Life is Heaven when you are in the divine flow and every move is filled with ease and grace, bringing peace and harmony.

Almost every action of a person who has not entered into self-examination is driven by an ego strategy. As you become familiar with these patterns, you can learn to recognize a habitual trigger and choose to not react.

As you progress there are more and more moments when a sweet impulse comes that clearly is an expression of selflessness and love. You learn to recognize that inner voice, to follow your heart, to trust those impulses, even when they don't seem rational. They have an intelligence that goes beyond rationality. You begin tapping the body's wisdom and eventually the cosmic wisdom.

There are moments when it's not at all clear what is driving you. Refer again to the list in the preceding section. Here are a few more criteria to consider in deciding whether to act on an impulse:

- Do you get to be right or superior while making someone wrong or lesser?

- Does the action make you feel more separate or more connected?

- Do you truly honor the other people involved, without any hidden agendas?

- Do you honor yourself, unconditionally, with such an action?

- Take a moment to still the mind (per Chapter 2.) Let your heart be filled with gratitude. Ask for clarity. You don't usually get to see the whole picture, just one step at a time. If that step feels right give it your all, then see where you are and wait to see what comes next.

Latihan (BodyFlow).

Latihan is a lovely process that teaches you to recognize and follow inner promptings. It was considered by Osho to be a MahaMudra, the greatest energy-enhancing movement. The name BodyFlow is more contemporary, more descriptive. Consider it a moving meditation that invites inspiration and guidance to come through.

Simply come to a still point (quiet mind) and then wait for an impulse to move or make a sound. If unsure about an impulse, wait a little longer for it to come again. The movement or sound is not volitional, not something you decide to do. It seems to happen outside your doingness, coming from your beingness.

In a natural setting, by yourself, this process becomes an exquisite dance with the elementals. As part of your lovemaking it brings spontaneity and freshness. Done in a group setting it often sets up healing situations. Eventually it could become a lifestyle. Try it!

Tools to Assist in Manifesting Desires.

Sometimes Existence is just waiting for you to decide what you want and ask for it. Assume the wish is clean, not a compensation, not something you want "in order to" get something else. It is just something you want for the pleasure of having or doing it. If you have no game plan, no direction, the wish probably won't materialize.

Perhaps the idea is a co-creation of a conscious Ego and divine guidance. Something inside you wants to be given birth. Don't be attached to your plan. It may need to be modified along the way.

Here are several potent yogic methods for directing unfocused creative energy toward manifesting. None of these methods will work, however, if you have a belief system that prohibits success or satisfaction. Your beliefs are stronger than your desires. If the methods don't work, look deeper to see what stands in the way, as in the preceding intention dialogue.

The Yoga Nidra process is a powerful tool for reprogramming your Ego beliefs. It creates a state of lucid dreaming, a highly suggestible place where you can plant resolves into the subconscious. This goes much deeper than self-hypnosis (see Appendix B).

The Hindu deity Ganesh is known as the Remover of Obstacles. Millions of devout Hindus pray and offer gifts to this deity in hope of enlisting his aid in solving their problems. He is pictured as a plump man with an elephant's head. The mantra that evokes his assistance is "Om Gam Ganapataye Namaha," pronounced om gahm gah-nah-pah-tah-yay nah-mah-hah.

Each vowel sound stimulates a certain chakra and the "ah" sound is most effective on the Heart Chakra. Notice how many "ah" sounds are present in this mantra. If you were to chant it for an extended period, you would find your heart opening. In the heart space, obstacles disappear. It probably has nothing to do with a mythical image, but the mythology is charming and it touches the subconscious. For some people it's easier to love and trust a deity than it is to love and trust yourself.

A yantra represents a mantra visually. Ganesh's yantra is based on a 6-pointed star, symbol of the heart (Anahata – dwelling place of the Soul), surrounded and supported by a triangle, symbol of the solar plexus (Manipura – center of the ego). This says that when Ego surrenders itself in service to the Soul, there are no more obstacles. (Yantra and image available through Tantrika International.)

Sex Magic in Orgasm. One advanced technique uses sex magic visualizations. Approaching an orgasm, bring into your mind a picture of what you desire and use the orgasmic energy to empower the vision. See the image on the screen of your imagination, in full color, much bigger than life, accurate to the finest detail. Then breathe life into it from this torrent of highly charged energy and release the image to the Cosmos at the moment of orgasm. Your vision will surely manifest (see FireBreath in Appendix C). Don't get so caught up in making magic that you lose sight of lovemaking as an expression of love.

Cautions about Sex Magic.

Magic is defined by Alister Crowley as a science for causing change in conformity to one's will. Magical tantric ritual is goal-oriented and comes from 3rd chakra energy of personal power. According to these practices, it's not necessary to feel any love for your ritual partner. More sophisticated magicians would try to justify using magical means for attaining spiritual ends. Ironically, if the goal you are trying to conjure up is enlightenment, that goal can't be attained until you lose interest in control and reach a state of surrender. The effectiveness of true tantric ritual does depend on the love you feel for your partner, as a symbol of the Divine. At that point magic simply doesn't apply.

Sex magic is probably the most potent form of self-hypnosis. It is effective because of the extremely sensitive and suggestible state that occurs around orgasm. You can use those magical moments to visualize something you want to manifest or you can use that same power to surrender in love to your union with the Divine. You always have that choice.

It's all right to use an affirmation with an orgasm to clear your internal resistances. It's fine to create something just because you want to create it. But not so fine for one person to manipulate other people or situations to their own advantage. Take care that your vision doesn't impinge on someone else's self-direction, even when you are trying to help them. You are likely to create unpleasant consequences.

Heart Magic.

When you are in your heart, your desires are not for personal gratification. You want what is best for all, realizing that you are one with all. You make yourself available as an instrument by which changes can be wrought, in service to the greatest good. True satisfaction comes only when Ego subordinates its agenda to Soul.

When Ego is in a state of surrender, when your heart is attuned to the Infinite, you automatically find yourself in a magical place. On many occasions your thoughts manifest, almost instantly. You think of someone and they call you, or you encounter them in an unlikely place. You become aware of the need for some item, and someone offers it to you. Small miracles happen so frequently, you begin to take them for granted. The "magic" happens not because you are efforting to impose your will on Existence, but rather because you have made yourself at one with Existence and it totally supports you.

> Surrender requires enormous trust,
> a surety that Existence will always give
> you what is in your best interests, even if
> it isn't what you thought was needed.

Going Deeper

1. Begin to look deeply at the forces that drive you. Identify your desires. Make a list of what you want to happen in your life which isn't happening.

2. Look at each desire to see if you are holding the idea that you cannot, will not, be happy until that desire is realized. See if it might be possible to be happy anyway. Realize that what you resist will persist. Making peace with that situation may be the only way to change it.

3. Admit to the fact that if you really wanted that desire, you would have it.

4. Find out what's in the way. Take yourself through a dialogue like the one in this chapter. Have a friend assist you or write it in your journal.

   What is your current desire, something you want, but aren't able to produce?

   What is actually manifesting in your life?

   Are you willing to take responsibility, to see how you create and perpetuate this situation rather than seeing yourself as its victim?

   What behaviors do you find yourself repeating?

   What is your underlying strategy for dealing with the situation?

   What core belief is at the root?

   How is that feeling in your body?

5. Continue with the daily practice:

ACTIVATE THE BODY

- Complete Breath/Rishi Isometrics

STILL THE MIND

- Watching the Breath

AROUSE SEXUAL ENERGY

- Aswini Mudra (below)

6. Read about Yoga Nidra in Appendix B. You can get the audio course (booklet and tape or CD) from Tantrika International to guide you into learning this method. Then make it a part of your daily waking up and/or going to sleep ritual.

7. Look into FireBreath in Appendix C. This is a technique to build energy for sex magic.

8. Explore the BodyFlow (Latihan) experience described earlier either alone, with a partner or with a small group.

Aswini Mudra.

1) Sit comfortably, breath naturally, relax and close your eyes.

2) Contract and relax the anal sphincter muscle, about one contraction/second.

3) Bring your attention to the lower end of the spine. Feel pressure waves being generated (in the first chakra) and moving up a few inches (to the second chakra.)

4) Continue a few minutes until you feel some excitement or heat. Another version, more complicated, appears in *Jewel*. This is a good starter.

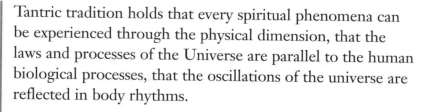

Chapter Four

CREATING HEAVEN ON EARTH

Learn of the Universe by Studying the Body

Tantric tradition holds that every spiritual phenomena can be experienced through the physical dimension, that the laws and processes of the Universe are parallel to the human biological processes, that the oscillations of the universe are reflected in body rhythms.

"He who realizes the truth of the body can then come to know the truth of the Universe." (Ratnasara Tantra)

Attitudes about the Body.

The body offers a wonderful opportunity to gain many levels of knowledge and experience, but most spiritual paths don't take advantage of this possibility. Early in the Christian tradition, body and Soul were declared antagonists. Overcoming the flesh became a serious endeavor. The body was denigrated and punished, even whipped and scourged as a spiritual practice.

Other forms of yoga vilify the body and encourage meditations that offer escape from the physical world. Earlier in this book an ancient source is quoted, saying that the original purpose for Tantra was to escape from attachment from the physical and subtle bodies. Ancient Tantrikas were motivated by their wish for liberation from the cycle of birth and death.

Consider the irony in the possibility that liberation only comes when you no longer yearn for it, when you are so delighted with the life process that you aren't eager to leave. This delight can only happen when you live in the moment, fully present to both the temporal and eternal dimensions, at the stillpoint.

Ipsalu Tantra encourages you to stay connected to form. Many people seriously work on their physical bodies, but they don't stay present there. They live in their mental body – in their thoughts and their dramas. The mental and physical bodies are out of alignment. Most body-mind relationships are abusive, with the mind passing heavy judgment on the body's "flaws." Most people aren't happy with their body and few are willing to be present with it.

Tantra has been defined as the path for saving the body. The first step is rescuing the body from neglect and disrespect, learning to truly honor this awesome vehicle. Focus on the millions of things it does to serve you rather than on its "imperfections," which are actually outpicturings of your hidden attitudes.

In many spiritual paths, people look forward to dying so they can go to Heaven to live with God. Modern Tantrikas prefer to see that Heaven is here, wherever you are, and now, in the present moment. You prepare yourself to experience divine Presence in your body, your physical temple. Preparation includes cleansing of the physical, etheric/emotional and mental dimensions. It includes bringing consciousness to the details of maintaining the body-temple, even celebrating it through ceremonies around food, bathing, touching, making love and sleeping (more in Chapter 9).

Enlightenment in Physical Form.

The stated goal of some spiritual paths is to unify, the body and Soul, but body and Soul are not separate. The body is part of the Soul, the part that you can touch. You know that is true because the body always tells the truth and it lives in present time. Body is that aspect of Soul that conveys experiences through the senses. Soul is that aspect of body that is initially beyond the perceptive range of the five senses. Soul has always been present and available, but kept out of consciousness by the Ego's barriers – unacknowledged attitudes, suppressed feelings, controlling strategies.

Many beings have achieved some degree of enlightenment while out of body and deep in meditation. Most spiritual practices are designed to reach that goal. Some of these beings have chosen to come back and achieve more complete enlightenment while present in the body and involved in earthly matters.

When meditation makes people "spacy," that indicates consciousness has detached from the physical plane. Grounding practices are very important to maintain physical presence and should precede and follow every experience of altered consciousness. Walking, dancing and hugging bring you into your body.

A simple set of movements, one of the most effective for grounding, uses a 10" piece of turned wood called the Tai Chi ruler or the Immortals' Wand. The system is an ancient and noble legacy, a lazy man's guide to vibrant health. (Wand, instructions and video, Innergetics, are available through Tantrika International.)

The Avatars, those blessed ones who have achieved the highest state possible for humans, are considered perfect embodiments in whom the Divine Essence has been completely realized in physical form. They have demonstrated what is possible for you. The mortal immortal, Babaji Nagaraj, set the example and offers encouragement to anyone who wishes to become a Babaji.

The Physical and Pranic Bodies.

Ordinary people recognize only flesh, blood and bone. But through thousands of years of study and practice the yogis have observed a greater force behind the physical elements – the pranic body. Let your personal exploration be guided by the yogis' research.

The prana which animates a human body is more subtle than the nucleus of an atom. In various cultures this LifeForce energy has been called Spirit, Prana, Chi, Ki, rLung, etc. Yogis have discerned at least seven dimensions of bodies with increasing subtlety. Your main concern is with the first two dimensions – the physical and the pranic (etheric) – although you tend to hang out in the third level, the mental, and occasionally escape to higher spiritual levels. You could start noticing when you do that. Other dimensions are discussed in *Jewel*.

The physical body is in close communication with the pranic body. Focusing on the physical allows one to easily access the pranic. The physical body expresses and externalizes emotional states. Sensitivity to the pranic body helps you discover subconscious attitudes and feelings, which live someplace within that subtle system, which obstruct the free flow of pranic energy.

Scientists are discovering the energy link between physical and nonphysical bodies. They now realize that all forms of matter are permeated with a subtle energy and that this energy (pranic force) and matter convert back and forth from one to the other.

Each drop within the infinite ocean of energy is like a hologram of the whole ocean. Every cell in every body contains all the knowledge there is. (See Bentov's book, *Stalking the Wild Pendulum*, to understand how cosmic holograms work.)

In each human body there is a reservoir and a dynamic flow of prana, which is in constant interchange with the universal prana which permeates all space. A pebble dropped in your corner of the universe creates waves that are felt throughout the system.

> Every being is in subtle communication
> with all beings and with all creation.
> Anything one person does, thinks or
> feels affects everyone and everything else.

There are several forms of prana, but two major types. First the individual prana, Shakti, related to the physical and etheric bodies, which is more gross and more tangible. It is often equated to oxygen. Breathing is the principle means of absorbing this prana into the body. The prana carries information that directs the bodies' many

activities, instructs the DNA when to open and close its genetic direc-
tives. Since prana maintains life and consciousness in every creature
that breathes, individual prana manifests as individual existence on
the physical level. Carrying an unusual amount of this magnetic force
produces a charismatic presence – a star quality.

In its higher sense, "prana" refers to Cosmic Prana, also called
Spirit, Universal Energy, Shiva. It is a much faster vibration which is
very subtle and can only be perceived by the Unlimited Mind. In the
order of creation, prana emanates from the unmanifest reality. The
Bible documents how God formed man from the dust and "breathing
into his nostrils the breath of life, he became a living Soul." By
becoming sensitive to the prana in your own body, you can learn to
discern its subtler aspects. Thus, breathing not only maintains the
physical and pranic bodies, but is the key to accessing the immensity
of cosmic consciousness.

Pranic energy in every life form emits an aura of light. Some
people are able to easily discern this light. Anyone can learn to see
it when they become sensitized to the energy. Using a Kirlian camera
you can photograph your aura. It is an electro-magnetic field,
manifesting in ever-changing frequencies and colors. Throughout life
it expands and contracts, reflecting your state of body, mind and
emotion. Negative thoughts lower the pranic vibration, while positive
thoughts enhance it. Through tantric practice you become aware of
interaction between prana, emotions, body and mind. You learn to
maintain harmony among those energies (see Chapters 5 to 8).

At the moment of death, the spirit or pranic body (together with
the other more subtle bodies) leaves the physical. People who are
able to perceive prana might see that as a ghost. This is nothing
supernatural, but rather very natural and inevitable.

Osho said that the pranic body disintegrates within thirteen days of
death, leaving the higher bodies to go on to other dimensions. Many
people have reported feeling the presence of a newly deceased loved

one, come to say goodbye during that window of time while the more perceptible energies were still intact.

Playing with Pranic Energy.

You come into a new relationship with the physical body when you begin cultivating this subtle energy source. The yogis have developed, over centuries of study, methods of charging the mind and body with prana through techniques of pranayama (life-giving breath.) They devised practices that enable you to increase the pranic capacity, to expand the aura, and to perceive the subtlety of your existence in relation to the universe. As you perform your recommended physical practices – the Rishi Isometrics and the Rejuvenation Postures – pay attention to the energy that is activated. It is an easy step from awareness of the physical body to awareness of the energy body. (Rishis are described in Chapter 2; Rejuvenation Postures are described in *Jewel,* Chapter 7.)

Yogis have emphasized the power of attention while directing and discharging energy. They described a controlled upward movement of prana through the chakras which, after some practice, brings about a state of conscious Bliss and peace. This is the universal aim and the highest necessity of life, because in that state you are conscious of the Infinite and feel the expanded state of your real Self. The more this is experienced, the more your limitations and conditioning fall away, and the state of universality is realized. The body is crying out for this connection. This is the true purpose of spiritual practice.

A Tantric master is one who, by use of consciousness, is able to direct the movement of subtle energy through matter. By practicing the techniques presented in this course, you are moving toward such mastery. You can use your limited consciousness to intensify the energy so it propels you into higher states of awareness. You are gradually learning to perceive and manipulate more and more subtle frequencies until you enter the realm of pure consciousness.

It is easy to fall into the trap of wanting to be "in control" of the energy. The Ego enjoys that illusion of power. However this work leads to its highest possible result only when entered with an attitude of devotion and surrender.

The Inner Smile.

This is an easy method to draw Universal Energy into your being. Begin with a smile on your lips and gradually relax those muscles as you draw the smile feeling back toward the base of your skull. You may feel the skull plates as they shift a bit. You use the muscles similarly to wiggle your ears.

> The Inner Smile opens the Mouth of God at the base of your skull, the entry point for blissful Universal Energy. When this door is closed (during a neutral or frowning expression) that energy simply cannot enter.

This is the Mona Lisa smile, the smile of the Divine Christ child. Smiling in this way allows the clarity of consciousness and the Bliss associated with Universal Energy to enter your body. Use this smile any time, especially when you feel overwhelmed by situations in your life. Smiling in this subtle way also stimulates production of endorphins, the hormones that make you feel good.

This energy portal at the medulla, (base of the skull) the entry point for Shiva energy, is the female pole of Ajna chakra (the Third Eye.) It is symbolized by a crescent. The same yantra form is used to symbolize the 2nd chakra, center of sexual energy, the Shakti force. This suggests the close connection between the throat center and sexual energy.

Nadis and Pranic Flow.

Nadis are the etheric paths through which pranic currents flow They form a vast network of subtle fibers conducting LifeForce to every cell of the body. This LifeForce is essential in maintaining physical health and vitality. Yogic tradition speaks of 72,000 nadis, centered in the etheric body at Manipura chakra (at the belly) in much the same way as the cardio-vascular system is centered at the physical heart. Manipura serves as a reservoir for the body's LifeForce and also directs the pranic flow throughout the various bodies. Prana is like a tiny stream of light particles passing along the nadis. As you work with these energies and become more sensitive, you can learn to see these light particles as well as to feel them in your own body and in others.

Nadis are related to the nerves but they work at different levels. Nerves carry electrical impulses within the physical body. Nadis carry higher vibrational energies to the subtle bodies. Prana is required by all of your bodies, providing information/stimulation and sustaining each body's correct relationship to the other bodies in higher dimensions.

There are usually areas of a body – physical and subtle – where the flow of prana is out of balance or blocked by repressed emotional material, unresolved trauma, or negative attitudes. The tissue or organ of the physical body which is receiving too little or too much pranic flow is subject to disease and degeneration. Every discomfort or disease is a signal from the body that something needs your conscious attention. A typical medical response is to stifle the signals.

Energy blockage results from inability or unwillingness to stay present with repressed attitudes and unexperienced feelings. It is sometimes expressed in the physical body as muscular armoring (chronic tension.) It can be held in place by toxicity from environment and inappropriate food and drug choices. Every subconscious pattern also lives in the pranic (etheric) body, which is the archive for all karma (i.e. memories encoded in moments of unconsciousness). In order to keep the pattern subconscious, Ego must block the energy (consciousness) from passing through that body part. Each unfinished experience creates an obstruction in the pranic energy flow. Clearing at the pranic level is simply bringing consciousness to these memories, replacing obstructive emotional residue with harmonious emotions and thereby restoring the free flow of prana through the nadis.

Clearing on a mental or pranic level automatically brings about cleansing on the physical level. People often report flu symptoms in the first few days of breathing practices. The converse also is true. For example, a physical clearing in an herbal liver cleanse can bring up old repressed anger.

Yogis have designed special exercises for clearing the nadis. At the end of this chapter are three techniques that will assist you: 1) Nadi Purifier, 2) Nadi Stimulator and 3) Nadi Vibrator. Even more powerful are the Tibetan Lama Breaths presented in the Practicum.

These techniques don't replace or bypass actually experiencing the repressed material. With a quiet mind and willingness to pay attention, you can employ the breath to bring more prana into the blocked area, inviting banished memories back into consciousness to be experienced, accepted, witnessed, the lesson learned, the attachment released.

Directing Prana for Healing.

As the body becomes more purified, it can tolerate a higher quality and quantity of energy. It often becomes less tolerant of chaotic energies. Environments that used to feel OK might become uncomfortable. You can learn to consciously draw higher energy into your body through concentration and intention, based on some knowledge. As you become more sensitive, you can learn to direct the pranic energy through the nadis into your body parts and organs where it is needed for strengthening or healing.

One simple example of this is dispersing a headache. Often the pressure of excess energy in the head creates discomfort. When that energy is redistributed through the body, the headache disappears.

Lower back pain is often associated with repressed sexual energy. Just holding a clear consciousness, increasing the energy, and staying present with the feelings often makes healing possible. The body is probably notifying you of some distress, chemical or emotional, and wants your attention.

You can also learn to direct that energy toward another person's body. Sometimes that transmitted energy can be seen as flashes of light jumping from the healer's body to the receiving body. This is the practice of Pranic Healing.

Many systems of pranic healing are currently being taught – Reiki, Radiance, Seichim, etc. All are based on these same principles – accessing and transmitting prana. Taken to their depth, all are one system. They all came out of Tibet to open up the ancient hidden knowledge, to allow people to serve each other.

In sickness, the energy levels of the body drop. Pranic healing can restore the body to its normal energy level. Healing can be facilitated by the infusion of energy from another person. No one can actually heal another. The energy does the healing. But you can provide additional energy to someone who is temporarily unable to generate what they need.

Sharing energy should happen only at the recipient's request, and even then with some discretion. A healer might take on the client's energy pattern and begin to experience their problems. If you assume the role of someone's healer, you can prevent them from learning the lesson represented by the disease. You don't want to interfere with their process. If they are healed without a shift in consciousness, their disease process will simply take a different form.

Beyond Reiki.

Most of the popular healing forms draw only from the higher vibrational frequencies – Universal energy. Reiki originally used Shakti force to produce balanced energy, but the practitioners discovered that activating Shakti opened Pandora's box and their karma came up to consciousness. Training and purification took many months, even years. Most Reiki teachers and practitioners eliminated that aspect of the healing, greatly compromising their effectiveness as healers. The popular version can be learned in a weekend. It certainly is easier to market.

For healing energy to be maximally effective, Shakti Prana (earth energy) must be drawn up to Anahata (the heart chakra), blended with Shiva Prana (solar energy), and then directed toward the receiver, usually through the hands. (You could call this Tantreiki.) After that connection is established, the energy for the treatment can flow freely to the patient without draining the healer. In advanced work it is not even necessary for the healer to be in the same room as the receiver.

Jesus invited you to be reborn as little children, to return to the innocence of childhood. Innocence produces pure energy, unfiltered through the ego. When the energy comes into your body, let it flow. Mother Nature knows where that energy is needed. True healing comes through when you get out of the way and become the Witness.

Network.

A healing system fully compatible with the Ipsalu approach is Network Spinal Analysis. Subconscious patterns are stored in the spine as distortions. The subtle interventions of a NSA practitioner assist greatly in freeing up the energy flow. This system has identified the same levels/sequence of healing as Ipsalu. If you wish to work with a hands-on practitioner, check Resources at the end of this chapter and Appendix D for more detail.

The Meeting of Science and Mysticism.

It is exciting to discover how much scientific conjecture and research is now focused on esoteric principles, validating the ancient teachings. Researchers are demonstrating mathematically and graphically the vibration patterns that define consciousness, how energy is woven into matter, how spirit works through the power of love. These processes can be explained in terms of wave mechanics and unified field theory. This is a bit mind-boggling to those untrained in theoretical physics, but you can at least get the feeling that a great bridge is being built between the scientific and esoteric worlds.

Mysticism is no longer so mysterious and science can produce images on a computer screen that were once only available in mystical vision. This is the sort of breakthrough, long predicted by Nostradamus and others, for the dawning of the New Age.

What follows is simplistic, but might provide some appreciation for the principles that govern both the microcosm and macrocosm.

Vibration as the Basis of Reality.

A few basic ideas about the mechanics of consciousness will be introduced here for better understanding of how the Bliss vibration works. For more in-depth treatment, see Resources.

Yogis have known from ancient times that matter was simply a dense form of energy. As modern physicists are just realizing, the energy which makes up matter, when reduced to its essence, is simply consciousness. The entire universe consists of waveforms/ matter/energy/consciousness, one continuum of the LifeForce, from its most dense expression to the most subtle.

The lower levels form our physical world. Higher frequency vibrations form the etheric dimension. Even higher levels constitute the Bliss Body, Divine Presence. In tantric cosmology, God is the Absolute, pure consciousness, a static state beyond substance or movement. Without movement there is no objective or subjective reality. In stillness it all disappears back into infinite Essence.

All of creation consists of vibrations, based on a sine wave, a simple oscillation between pressure and relaxation, between movement (Shakti) and stillness (Shiva), occurring in a vast spectrum of frequencies (vibrations per second = Hertz = Hz).

The graph above shows a vibration moving through time, as in a seismograph where the pen vibrates back and forth while paper moves underneath, showing frequency along the horizontal line and intensity along the vertical scale.

Among the lowest frequencies, 0 to 40 Hz are signature vibrations for each emotion, for each level of human brain activity, for the planet and most important, for the heart vibration of love, the basis of physical life. These ultra low frequencies also contain the range for whale songs that ring through the oceans, and for the purr of a cat, which has an amazing healing capacity – hence 9 lives. Frequencies in the range of 40 to 25,000 Hz are audible as sound. A higher range of frequencies carry radio and TV signals, then the visible spectrum, then matter, x-rays, and various dimensions of subtle energy and finally pure consciousness.

S H A K T I	Hz levels:							S H I V A
	0–40	40–25,000	10^4–10^{12}	10^{12}–10^{16}	10^{15}	10^{16}–10^{18}	*	*	
	earth heart brain emotion love	sound	radio-TV shortwave	infra-red visible light ultra-violet	matter	X-rays	pranic energies	consciousness (Kundalini)	

(Matter at 10^{15} Hz is 10,000,000,000,000,000 vibrations per second!!)
*The higher energies haven't been measured yet.

Cosmic Communication.

Information is stored and transmitted in the vibrations. This idea may have been a stretch a century ago, but now, with cell-phones and satellite TVs everywhere, the atmosphere is a soup of information waves. The clarity of this communication is hampered by interference, noise in the system, lack of coherence.

There is a direct connection to the Source, an umbilical cord through which flows the Supreme Intelligence that manages the universal life process. This information and energy is the key to health, mental and emotional stability, and expanding consciousness. It is the owner's manual for the physical body.

Ipsalu techniques teach you how to tune in to that frequency.

Analogy to Sound.

The language, in its wisdom, is rich with metaphors about sound in reference to human interaction. "We work in harmony."; "He rings my bells."; "I'm tuned in to her."; "You are singing my song."; "That remark struck a sour note."; "It has a good vibe."; "I can resonate to that."; etc. Other references deal with cosmic phenomenon in terms of sound: "the music of the spheres," "my soul song," etc.

These are far more than figures of speech. They are descriptive of the actual vibrations present within an individual or in an interaction with another person. Many of the principles that apply to sound vibrations also apply to the whole of reality, since everything is a vibratory system.

Sound as Noise, Pure Tones, or Music.

- Sound that has a chaotic, irregular vibration pattern is perceived as noise.
- A regular wave creates a pure tone.
- Musical sounds are composites of many harmonious frequencies, complex curves that recur in an orderly way.

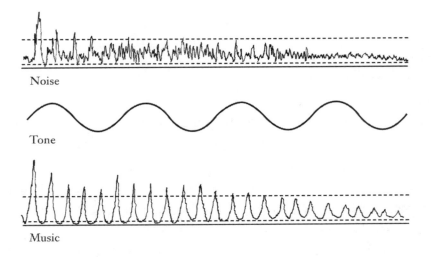

Noise

Tone

Music

The word "cosmic" is defined as "orderly." Its opposite would be "chaotic." Cosmic Consciousness must then be an awareness of the

Divine Order of the universe and the perfection of the life process. The ability of waves to transmit information and energy depends on how orderly they are, how coherent.

The harmful effects of noise and the healing effects of tones and music are being researched. Healing by sound vibration is coming to be acknowledged as a powerful science. Yogis and monastics have always known that, chanting their mantras and prayers, enjoying the physical benefits as well as spiritual.

Positive Interference.

Look now at two pure tones, say from tuning forks. As the waves interact they alter each other, creating an interference pattern. When the wave fronts are going the same direction they reinforce each other. They are in phase so there is a positive interference.

Below, curve A and curve B enhance each other so the interference is positive. To chart the wave created by these two vibrations, you would add together the distance above (+) or below (-) the

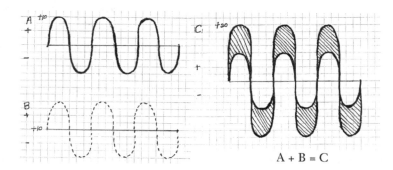

A + B = C

horizontal line for each wave at each point. Adding them together, the resulting wave C has higher peaks and lower valleys. Complex wave forms of music are the sum of the various frequencies of their component overtones.

View of several wave forms, some longer, some shorter, whose energies are phase-locked so their effect on each other is constructive.

Negative Interference.

Striking simultaneously the middle C and the black key just above it, C sharp, produces an unpleasant sound. The two vibrations are dissonant. The patterns fight each other. Adding the horizontal distances together, the waves don't meet at the base line. In the box see waves out of phase, causing destructive interference.

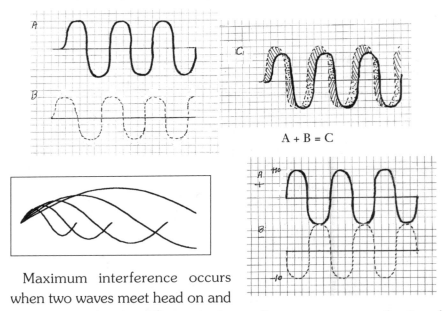

A + B = C

Maximum interference occurs when two waves meet head on and neutralize each other. This is the least efficient way to use vibrational energy. The principle is used in noise dampening systems.

Harmonics.

Some tones sound very pleasant when played together. They are considered harmonious or consonant (sound together) or coherent (stick together). Striking middle C on the piano and the same key eight notes (an octave) higher and an octave lower would produce three fundamental vibrations. The middle C vibrates twice as fast as the lower C, and the higher note vibrates twice as fast as the middle C. They all fit together as if it were just one sound. The lower, slower vibration provides a carrier wave in which the faster vibrations can nest. Any faster vibration that divides the fundamental (slowest wave) into equal parts (1/2, 1/3, 1/4, etc.) could appear naturally as an overtone or harmonic. All the vibrations come to a still point at the same time. That stillpoint is where matter connects to the divine.

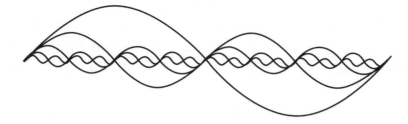

Standing Wave.

If you pluck a guitar string the entire string
vibrates. Lightly touch the center and the string vibrates both at full length and also at half length.

A higher sound is produced by the shorter segment and the sound will continue as a standing wave. For the standing wave to persist, the faster vibrations must divide the string length into equal segments.

A standing wave could happen in the pipe of a great organ. Imagine a sound vibration at one end. The wave front travels down the pipe and bounces back from the far end. If both the original wave and the rebounding wave are synchronized there is no interference. They phase lock and a stable system is formed. The standing wave, with minimum interference, is the most efficient use of vibrational energy.

You will see in Chapter 6 how a loving heart can produce in the aorta a standing wave that that transforms many other body energies.

Physical matter is composed of a very stable system of standing waves, creating the illusion of being solid. The vibrations take on spins which create sub-atomic "particles," electrons in orbits around a nucleus. The same process is reflected in the solar system and again in the galaxy.

Modulation – Nodes.

When a metal plate sprinkled with sand is vibrated by a sustained tone, the vibrations of the plate produce a pattern as the sand moves towards the stationary points, the nodes. This outlines the standing wave which the plate is holding.

The sound AH is the sound that stimulates the heart, the sound of orgasm. Of all the sounds a voice can make, AH most strongly connects a person to the physical plane. It creates on the metal plate two interlocking triangles, the ancient yogic symbol for the heart, representing the union of energies of heaven and earth.

The sound OM is the seed sound of creation (more in Chapter 7). When vibrated on a metal plate, this sound creates a Shri Yantra, the most revered form in sacred geometry.

AH Sound   OM Sound

If one tone vibrates at 50 Hz and another at 60 Hz, the combined waves will meet at the still point (the point of rest, the node) ten times each second. This creates a modulation, a new vibration of 10 Hz.

This is a device used in nature to convert higher frequency vibrations to lower, to bring information from higher dimensions to the physical realm.

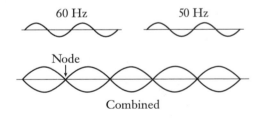

60 Hz   50 Hz

Node

Combined

Coherence.

Sun light contains a full spectrum of colors, representing the range of visible vibrations. The waves move randomly in all directions. If a device produces a single vibration, a mono-chromatic light, and the wave fronts of that vibration line up to reinforce each other, that is coherent vibration, a laser beam.

The amount of light produced by a normal light bulb, when brought into coherence, is powerful enough to cut through steel.

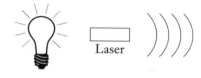

Witness consciousness, in terms of vibration, equals coherence. The random and chaotic normal thought stream becomes quiet and mind attunes itself to vibration of spirit. Brain wave coherence is the key to communication between dimensions.

Other body frequencies can be brought into coherence, profoundly affecting your health, your emotions, your consciousness (see Chapters 5 to 8). This is the source of power that will transform your life.

The orderly relationships between wave lengths establishes a connection between frequencies and fields which can only persist when it resonates with all frequencies and fields. This harmonic cascade establishes a cosmic holography, which we experience as ecstasy.

Resonance and Sympathetic Vibration.

The guitar string mentioned earlier would normally be attached to an instrument, which vibrates in response to the string. The size and shape of the body of that instrument determines how the vibrations ricochet around inside, producing higher frequencies – harmonics – which determine the quality of the sound, the frequency of the standing wave it supports. This is resonance. A similar thing happens when you sing in the shower.

If you play one open string on a violin, the same string on a second violin begins to vibrate, absorbing the energy of the first sound. This is sympathetic vibration, another form of resonance. The resonating string has its own natural frequency and responds only to that particular vibration.

You'll see in Chapter 6 how the heart, when its vibration is coherent, sets up vital resonances in your body.

Entrainment.

When several vibrations are at the same or similar frequency, they soon entrain, coming into synchronized movement at the faster vibration. Several pendulum clocks placed in the same room will initially be at different places in their swing at any moment, but soon all of them will line up and swing together. This makes up a vibrating system. The more members there are in the system, the more stable it is.

This is why people sit at the feet of a master, allowing the frequency of their mind and body to be entrained to that higher frequency, and why it is easier to hold that vibration in a group than it is to maintain it alone.

Golden Mean.

The musical spectrum is divided into octaves, each higher octave repeating the notes of the octave below at a higher frequency, each note twice as fast as its lower counterpart. Similarly the subtle energies define higher dimensions, each a replica of the one before but at higher frequencies, again at a specific ratio – The Golden Mean.

This magical ratio (proportion) is found throughout nature's designs in plants and animals, including many parts of the human body. It is used extensively in our greatest art and architecture. The Golden Mean is the basis for much of sacred geometry, which explains natural phenomena in mathematical terms. It is also called Phi for the Greek letter.

The circle represents matter and the vertical line represents divine energy passing through.

The ratio is 1 to 1.618... . This ratio occurs when a line segment is divided into two unequal parts, such that the smaller portion is in the same proportion to the longer portion as the larger piece is to the whole line. Say the short piece is 0.618 units long, the longer piece would be 1 unit, (0.618 times 1.618 = 1) Adding the two pieces together, the total segment would be 1.618. (arithmetic) It is also true that 1 unit (the larger segment) times 1.618 = 1.618 (geometric).

When successive segments of a line are in the Golden Mean ratio, the line forms a spiral. When rotating, this forms a figure that looks like a cup within a cup within a cup no matter how deeply you go into it. Perhaps this figure was the legendary Holy Grail, symbol of consciousness.

When two waves intersect at a point (node) they create new wave lengths, by addition and multiplication. If those new waves don't fit in the nest, destructive interference sets in. So the Golden Mean creates the least resistance. It is the most efficient means for information to be transmitted unaltered from one octave or dimension of Existence to the next, connecting the material world to the divine. It is the tunnel of light we pass through in transition from this life to the next.

Technical Terms that are Now Familiar:
> Coherence
> Entrainment
> Golden Mean – Phi Ratio
> Harmonics
> Interference
> Nodes
> Resonance
> Standing Waves
> Sympathetic Vibration

Wilhelm Reich asserted, "Once we open to the flow of the energy within our own body, we also open up to the flow of energy in the universe." The workings of the body reveal the secrets of the Universe. As above, so below.

Continue in your daily practice and become ever more sensitive to this truth.

Going Deeper

1. Review material on subtle energies in *Jewel*, Lesson 2.
2. Continue your daily practice, expanding to thirty minutes.

ACTIVATE THE BODY

- Complete Breath
- Rishi Isometrics, or Nadi Kriyas (below)

STILL THE MIND

- Breath Mantra (Hong Saw)

AROUSE SEXUAL ENERGY

- FireBreath at 1st and 2nd chakras

TRANSMUTE

- FireBreath to 6th chakra

ENJOY THE ENERGY

- Meditation

3. Become more aware of subtle energies. During your practice, take a moment at the end of every set of movements to witness the flow of energies in your body.

4. The Inner Smile (Drawing in Universal Energy)

   As described earlier in this chapter, use this practice any time you wish to come into a blissful state.

5. The FireBreath (Drawing in Earth Energy)

   Here is a great practice to do by yourself for learning to feel your energy flow. It is a Kriya breath that consciously pulls sexual (earth) energy into the body and directs it through the chakra system. People who have had trouble feeling prana or sensing the aura often feel it in this process.

   The pranic energy becomes very thick for three to four inches around you and a foot above. You may need to practice several times before you have a real energetic experience. If you are open and have done a lot of pranayam and consciousness-expanding work, it will happen more quickly. If you are a beginner, be patient with yourself and it will come. Eventually you will feel the tingling in your body and an ecstatic state of mind (see FireBreath, Appendix C).

FireBreath produces many benefits:

- It works well for waking up pre-orgasmic women.
- It cleanses the nadis and opens up the chakras.
- It sensitizes you to subtle energy.
- It generates sexual energy in foreplay.

6. Eventually you can combine the Inner Smile and FireBreath, bringing in both Shiva and Shakti energy to dance within your body.

The Nadi Kriyas (extracted from *Jewel*, page 102) are a simple and powerful method for clearing the psychic channels, to allow more life to flow through you.

Perform each Kriya seven times. Breathe in through the nose and blow out through pursed lips (as if about to whistle). With each inhalation, contract the anal sphincter muscle and rock the anus forward slightly. With each exhalation, relax the anal sphincter and rock the anus back slightly.

Part A. Nadi Cleanser unblocks the nadi channels so energy can flow freely.

1) Sit in the easy pose, or on a chair.

2) Inhale, rock pelvis forward, and contract anal sphincter for six counts.

3) Hold the breath and contraction for three counts.

4) Blow out with a powerful and steady force for six counts, rocking back and releasing the contraction.

Part B. Nadi Activator stimulates the nervous system with a rush of energy.

1) Standing with head and back straight, throw your shoulders back, rock the pelvis forward, tense your abdomen, anus/cervix, legs and knees.

2) Inhale a complete breath.

3) Holding the breath, extend both arms out in front of you shoulder high. Slowly clench your fists as you draw them back to your shoulders, tensing every muscle. Hold as long as possible.

4) Blow out explosively, drop the arms abruptly and relax the tension.

Part C. <u>Nadi Energizer</u> vibrates all the systems (nadi, nervous, and vascular). Use when you feel sluggish.

1) Sit in the easy pose.

2) Inhale in six vigorous sniffs, rocking the pelvis forward, contracting the anus/cervix.

3) Hold the breath as long as possible.

4) Blow out with a long slow sigh, relaxing contraction and rocking pelvis back.

Resources

Stalking the Wild Pendulum: On the Mechanics of Consciousness, Itzhak Bentov with more details on how this all works, for those who wish to know.

Healing Myths, Healing Magic, Dr. Donald Epstein, Amber/Allen Publishers. (303) 678-8086 for Network practitioner list or *www.inateintelligence.com*.

Alphabet of the Heart, Dan Winter (available at *spirals.eternite.com*) and his video *Sacred Geometry: The Unified Field Theory*. *www.DanWinter.com*.

The Tao of Physics, Fritz Kapra.

Dancing Wu Li Masters, Gary Zuckov.

Quantum Mind – the Edge Between Physics and Psychology, Arnold Mindell.

Innergetics video and Tai Chi Ruler available through Tantrika International.

Chapter Five

RETURNING ENERGY
TO THE FLOW

Balancing Mental and Emotional Bodies

To experience Bliss you must be in present time. But coming present, you often confront old emotional patterns, frozen in time. Clearing those patterns allows you to enjoy the Bliss.

*Y*our emotional (pranic) body contains fragmented memories of traumatic experiences and emotions too intense to deal with at the time they happened. Lacking the awareness, tools, support or confidence to integrate the experience, you stored it to be assimilated later. These memories were suppressed into the subconscious, together with your interpretation, a conclusion you drew about how things work and what you must do to survive or to fit in. You probably discovered early on that your expressions of love and joy weren't welcome and so you closed them down similarly.

Each memory fragment has developed its own strategies and agenda, behavior patterns which operate autonomously, outside of rationality, often contrary to your conscious intentions. You have certainly experienced your mental and emotional selves at odds with each other, your intentions and resolutions sabotaged by these dissident elements. Emotional outbursts that the mind later regrets clearly are not a balanced expression. Your mind may seek goals, including spiritual growth, but if the emotions have a different agenda, the emotions usually win out.

Integrating the Emotions.

As you do the Ipsalu practice, increasing the energy flow in your body, every dissociated fragment from the shadows and dark places of the subconscious will eventually come into the light. When love is present, all that is not love comes up to be healed. Enlightenment simply means that all the shadows have been explored. The memories have been re-experienced in the light of consciousness. Then there is no longer a subconscious. Through the practice of Ipsalu Tantra you can bring these banished aspects of your being into alignment, balance and harmony. You can heal the nervous system so your feeling states are a response to the present moment rather than a replay of past experiences.

First Tantric Marriage.

The most familiar part of the mind is the intellect. It is linear, logical and problem solving. It has been measured by IQ tests, and researchers concluded that IQ doesn't increase with education. Intellectual activity takes place mostly in the left hemisphere of the brain. The right brain hemisphere activity is intuitive, inductive, with a direct knowing, accessing universal wisdom and truth. This part of the mind, less under control, uses emotional intelligence which also takes place throughout the body. (You will see later that there is a brain – mass of neurons – in the heart, and an even bigger one in the belly.) With conscious attention, these aspects can be developed. You are learning to build a partnership between the intellectual and intuitive functions.

You can think of the fragments in the emotional body as unconscious expressions of female energy. You can see the intellect as an unconscious expression of male energy, struggling to justify the inconsistencies among the emotional fragments so it appears to be in control.

You can tell which part predominates at any moment by the position of your head. Like a Balinese dancer, with shoulders unmoving and head remaining vertical, move your head forward and back. The forward position, chin jutting forward, represents leading with the intellect. Is that how you sit at your computer? The back position reflects alignment between intellect and emotions. Bowing your head in prayer also produces this effect.

Once the emotional side has integrity, it can enter totally into partnership with the mental side, giving its creative energies in support of the mind's ideas and dreams, to manifest them and give them substance, to complete and fulfill the mind. The female adds intensity and passion, the male adds stability and rationality. From that point forward you have the richness of a full emotional expression and confidence that your feelings will be expressed appropriately.

Surrender to Soul.

Once integrated, this mental/emotional entity (ego) is able to offer its small self in service to the Higher Self, able to outgrow its compulsive need for control and separateness, to transcend its limiting agendas.

You might be more highly advanced spiritually than mentally because emotional immaturity has bogged down mental development. Once the emotional/mental complex is unified and untethered, it rises rapidly to match the spiritual awareness.

Mental Development.

Scientists discovered early in this century that everyone radiates a unique vibration from their mental activity. It is possible to measure the vibrational frequency of this ultra-violet radiation, and to assign a numerical score to a person's mental function. That score was observed to be consistent, waking or sleeping, healthy or ill, irrespective of education. (It is not clear whether these numbers are actual frequencies or just a scale for comparison.)

This research continued, with many thousands of people being measured and assessed. From this huge sample it was possible to establish a correspondence between one's vibratory rate and his ability to function mentally. Those in the lower vibratory rates were best suited for repetitive jobs, were most interested in possessions, pleasure and prestige. Those in the higher ranges showed increasing clarity of thought, breadth of vision, creativity and concern about serving humanity. This has all been charted and validated through decades of research. (Detailed chart is included with the Practicum.)

These ratings are not at all like the IQ scores which test only intellectual capacity These ratings include other forms of intelligence – the intuitive and inductive capabilities.

The vibratory rates ranged from 200 to 800 cycles, with nearly 98% of mankind operating below the 400 mark. In the 200 to 400 range, every point gained reflected a predictable change in ability and aptitude. The details about this lower group are irrelevant here since those drawn to this material are almost invariably at the 400 level and above.

One characteristic of those at the 400 level is motivation to bring their personality fragments into a unified whole, to seek higher levels of wisdom and intuition. They can't rise above the 400 level until emotional integration occurs. People at the 400 level usually feel out of step with their friends and family, finding it difficult to share their inner longings with those who don't understand. They may even be ridiculed for being different and may shut down their inner voice and doubt their intuitive perceptions.

If they have the courage to stand fast and follow their guidance, these advanced people are led into situations and experiences which are out of the ordinary. They need time alone to process their experiences. Sometimes this is hard for their associates to understand.

> There are a few people whose minds and feelings are naturally balanced. They are rare. When such people do show up, they make contributions that alter the course of history.

The following list shows ratings ascribed to some famous creative geniuses. These could be measured, even on people long deceased, because, strange as it may seem, the frequency that radiates from the brain also emanates from the thumb. Anything a person touched during his life is imprinted with his vibration and it can be measured even hundreds of years later.

Leonardo de Vinci	725	Lord Byron	522
Michelangelo	678	Noel Coward	520
Madam Blavatsky	660	Nehru	520
Titian	660	George Washington	512
Frederic the Great	657	Admiral Nelson	510
Raphael	649	Ralph Waldo Emerson	500
Sir Francis Bacon	640	Garibaldi	493
Rembrandt	638	Mme. Curie	492
Reubens	625	Edgar Allen Poe	489
Napoleon	598	Herbert Hoover	473
Tschaikovsky	567	Thomas Edison	470
Johann Strauss	561	Abraham Lincoln	462
Chopin	550	Gandhi	462
Charles Dickens	540	Albert Einstein	462
Richard Wagner	538	A. Conan Doyle	431
Elizabeth Barrett Browning	529	Sigmund Freud	426
Greta Garbo	528	Rudolf Steiner	426
Lord Tennyson	525	Tolstoy	422

The researchers concluded that one was born with a certain fixed capacity, and the number wouldn't change more than a point or two in a lifetime. This is true only for those who are not on the spiritual path.

In the last decade that limitation has been disproved as hundreds of people, using the Ipsalu methods, are making enormous jumps in their mental capacity once their emotions are brought into balance.

Limitations from Emotional Immaturity.

Western man has long identified with his mental activity. "I think, therefore I am." Our culture gives great attention to developing the mental faculties. As a result, virtually everyone on the spiritual path has matured mentally far more than emotionally, which causes great internal tension.

People who measured high on the mental scores displayed a wide variation in their effectiveness. After some deliberation, researchers determined that emotional development was what differentiated the successful people from the unsuccessful.

The emotional body operates at a lower vibrational frequency than the mental, stepping down the energy of abstract conceptualization (masculine) into energy of action and manifestation (feminine). When the mental and emotional bodies are well balanced and aligned, action and conceptual energy support one another, allowing them to operate at highest capacity. An idea is generated on the mental plane, then nurtured and given form on the material plane by the emotional energy. The faster informational vibrations literally are nested within the slower emotional vibration. It is a coherent system which operates efficiently.

When these bodies are out of balance, (vibrations are out of sync) ideas are generated, but simply flounder. Dreams are never realized; understandings never make a difference in the quality of life; creativity remains unexpressed. For the people who live in this imbalance, life is terribly frustrating. They see how things might be but are unable to make their lives work or get what they need. The greater the disparity the greater is their pain and dissatisfaction. They can't live up to their own expectations and they tend to be hyper-critical of themselves. They may have an inner sense of their purpose in life but are unable to realize that purpose.

The tension created by this imbalance drives bright people to try many spiritual or self-help methods to remedy the problem. They sometimes find momentary relief, but seldom anything that holds up over time. They often find themselves trapped in dull, meaningless jobs and unsatisfying relationships. Many seek escape in drugs, food and alcohol or they manifest physical or mental illness.

The Emotional Plane.

Suppose that this planet is the place where souls come to experience and learn about emotions and love. Suppose that the earth energy supports the vibrational range associated with feelings. All emotions can be experienced here, particularly love, made more poignant when mixed with pain or fear or anger, feelings usually considered negative. You often have to lose something before you come to appreciate it. By experiencing withdrawal of love, you realize how precious it is, how essential it is to your well-being.

Mental activity and meditation can be conducted on higher planes and love is the essence of all creation, but only in the physical dimension can you have feelings. The more aware you are of your uncomfortable feelings, moment by moment, and the more willing you are to be present with them, the more quickly the discomfort will pass and the better life will work for you.

Supposing it is true that souls incarnate on this planet to experience emotions, it's interesting to note that many seekers continue to focus on the mental and meditational aspects of spiritual practice, doing everything possible to avoid their emotions! Most paths, most techniques, are carefully constructed to stay within the abstract comfort zone, to avoid contact with emotions, especially love and sexuality (which are all closely related.)

Those drawn to the Tantric path have probably already explored every diversion possible, and now realize that emotional/sexual mastery is the only thing left to accomplish. It is the final challenge. That's why you can talk boldly about enlightenment being close.

You will probably encounter massive internal resistance to this healing process. Ego is comfortable with the familiar and resistant to change. There are memories of trusting and being betrayed, of the humiliation of trying and failing. Some personalities are unwilling to acknowledge the possibility of growth. They prefer to maintain the image of already being healed.

Bringing Feelings Out of the Shadows.

Unconscious emotions and patterns rule your life. As you perform the daily practices, you will find yourself becoming aware of old emotional patterns, beliefs and survival strategies developed during early childhood. You will begin to see how those old patterns have served you, but don't serve you any more. As you observe these oft-repeated behaviors from this new perspective, they will begin to lose their power, allowing you to respond to life in a more appropriate way. You are making room for more joy and satisfaction, for the free flow of energies in your body-temple and for the flowering of transcendent, unconditional love.

Emotions are triggered by situations in your life, and seem to have a life of their own, quite independent of your rational control. Many people have spent years in psychoanalysis and understand their neuroses perfectly, but still lack the ability to change their self-destructive behaviors. Locked in to the assumption that "past predicts future," it seems that once the button is pushed you must play out this old program, as you have done many times before. It seems you can't stop yourself.

These emotional programs come out of experiences that were encoded in memory without benefit of consciousness. Your higher self was simply not present when the experiences were happening.

Most people have been conditioned to fear sexual energies, to feel guilty and ashamed about expressing those energies. Soul cannot be present where there is judgement. For their entire lives, many people have carried out their sexual activity without Consciousness present. They are locked in past/future, plagued by performance anxiety (resulting in impotence and frigidity) and fear of rejection (reject them before they can reject me). They are guarded, uncommunicative and minimally available. They tend to recreate past disappointments, personalize their partner's defensive strategies ("If you loved me, you wouldn't act that way.") and look for validation of their self-dishonoring positions ("No one loves me.").

Emotions in Trauma.

The crucial events might have been fairly mild experiences, in a somewhat supportive environment. These are relatively easy to access and process. The more intense, the more life threatening an experience was, the more challenging it is to recreate with consciousness.

Imagine a wild-life program with a herd of gazelles stampeding across the African plain, pursued by a lioness. The slowest and weakest of the herd falls behind and is overtaken by its predator. The unfortunate animal struggles for a moment and then movement stops as the lioness rips its body apart.

This scene is not as cruel as it appears. Nature, in her wisdom, has provided that an animal struggle to survive as long as there is a possibility of escaping, but once it is clear that there is no escape, the spirit of the animal withdraws. At the moment when the flesh is torn, no one is there to feel pain.

Mankind has retained this ability to escape from both physical and emotional pain, as higher consciousness is often unwilling to stay present during moments of trauma. Woody Allen said it best, "I'm not afraid of dying. I just don't want to be there when it happens." Often Soul withdraws when life is threatened; or when fear, anger or grief become unbearable; or when there is a burden of guilt or judgement.

There are many reports of people watching from overhead as doctors struggle to revive their bodies during near-death experiences. Masters have taught that the moment of death can bring enlightenment if consciousness is willing to stay present in that experience. When Gandhi was assassinated, he chanted one of the names of God (Ram, Ram Ram) as he died. He believed, through his Hindu training, that staying conscious at the moment of death would free him from having to come back for another incarnation. A more life-affirming view would be that dying consciously allows you to return in your next life with a much higher state of awareness.

Emotional trauma triggers this same flight of consciousness. Some years back, a school bus full of children was kidnapped in Chowchilla, California. The abductors had prepared an underground tank to hold their captives while the villains negotiated for ransom. The imprisoned children were terrified, giving up the struggle to survive, becoming whimpering and helpless. One of the older children managed to retain his wits. He rigged a ladder and opened the trapdoor, allowing the children to escape. Many of the children had so completely given up that they had to be dragged to freedom.

Psychologists were called in to study the children and their families, to assess the emotional damage done by this experience. They found that in almost every case the children were crippled psychologically and their families with them. The children were acting out in disruptive ways or retreating into their own world. The single exception was the one child who had not given up but stayed conscious and continued to work with the situation. He suffered minimal ill effects.

Everyone experiences emotional trauma, although it is usually not as dramatic as being taken hostage. Every child feels it is being abused at some point. Any trauma suffered before age eight, when consciousness fully attaches to the body, has probably happened in an unconscious state. The feeling/event is programmed into memory without consciousness and virtually has a life of its own, demanding occasional expression. This is your dark side, the "shadow" spoken of by Carl Jung. The subconscious has a strong need to keep recreating those events until they are healed. Being the Witness allows you to quickly accomplish the healing.

Any subsequent event that reminds you of that old experience will produce the same response that was programmed at the time of trauma. Feelings of helplessness, outbursts of rage, "shutting down" or other inappropriate responses are simply replays of tapes which were recorded during the trauma.

Many people use alcohol, drugs, or food to relieve the pressures that build up around repressed emotions. During drunken rages or crying jags, consciousness is totally absent. Any attempt to deal rationally with someone who is intoxicated is wasted effort, since no one is home. The emotional outburst simply vents energy, but the energy will build up again and the whole scene will be replayed, often word for word. No lasting benefits ever occur in that unconscious state.

Many people have done cathartic therapies, with session after session of screaming, crying and raging. At the next session the feelings would still be there undiminished. If those sessions were performed with Consciousness (the non-judgemental Witness) it would only take a few times for the memory to heal.

Reenacting a trauma without the Witness burns it deeper into memory, making it harder to heal. Therapists who encourage unconscious trauma work do a huge disservice to their clients.

Withdrawal of consciousness, especially during drunkenness or a drug "trip," makes room in the vacated body/temple for other entities to move in and take charge in that moment. From then on whenever consciousness leaves, that alien spirit is in control. Possession is a real phenomenon, not as portrayed by Hollywood, but as the sharing of a body by two distinctly different personalities.

I lived for a while with a man who was seriously alcoholic. A veteran of Viet Nam, he suffered post-battle stress syndrome. Consciousness had taken flight during atrocities he couldn't bear. Whenever he got drunk, his commanding officer and his whole unit came to visit. This went on for years – the voices commanding him to go out and shoot someone. Learning to stay present in that situation, to hold my center and demand that these visitors leave (with the help of certain powerful mantra) was the most empowering spiritual training of my life.

Because no one is ever the victim, this sharing has to be a collusion, an agreement between an entity and a host. Exorcism simply means renegotiating the agreement. Sometimes what appears to be possession is just a part of one's own psyche taking on a separate identity. Mental illness is simply a device for not dealing with the issues.

Emotions as Interrupted Flow.

As you have three primary colors – red, blue, and yellow – with various blends producing every other color, so you have three primary emotions, normally considered negative: Anger, Sadness, and Fear. Other emotions are blends of two, or even all three.

• Fear.

Fear produces a burst of adrenaline/energy to deal with a dangerous situation. This feeling is associated with the 1st chakra, the closest connection to your animal ancestry. Your survival instinct tells you that danger is imminent and you must either face it or run away. When you are free to use that energy in either fight or flight, it turns into exhilaration. In ancient times this burst of energy saved mankind from predators or marauding tribes. Some segments of our society are still working at that level.

In modern times, most threats have become more subtle – mostly fear of not being adequate, or not living up to expectations with the resulting rejection and humiliation. Fight and flight are not useful options. A third possibility – freeze – is more common. Chronic fear debilitates you when you dare not react. It creates mistrust of your impulses. When locked in fear, you won't receive those inner promptings and won't take them into action.

The most frightening thing is the unknown. You doubt your ability to handle an unfamiliar situation. Coming into a new relationship with the unknown is a huge step forward. The secret is simple: stay present and breathe.

(Fear/Anxiety) + oxygen = (Excitement/Adventure)

• Pain/Sadness.

Sadness, especially with weeping, is the means by which you adjust to painful change (loss or gain). This essential function allows the body to re-orient to a new situation. As the tears sweep through the body/mind, they wash away your connection with something that is no more and allow you to deal with what is now present. However when your grief is unexpressed, the body/mind continues to believe that loss/change is still happening and still hurting.

Sadness is sometimes used as a cover for anger, particularly by women. Society doesn't encourage women to express anger directly but is comfortable with a woman weeping. For healing to occur you must address the authentic feeling state.

The body is an extension of the Soul so it only experiences the present moment. But if it gets stuck in time it continues to experience a past moment over and over as if it were present time. You return to a painful memory and it feels like it's still happening.

Pain/sadness and ecstasy are not opposite ends of a continuum, but rather come together in a circle. If you go deep enough into your pain you will hit bottom and come up into ecstasy.

Pain and sadness are associated with the 2nd chakra, the water element, symbolic of flow. You experience chronic sadness when you don't allow the energy to flow through to closure.

• Anger.

Anger is energy that wants to express into the world but has been blocked. It's the same energy you generate to accomplish anything. You only call it anger when you encounter an obstacle and can't complete your intention. Only under extreme or repeated conditions of powerlessness, or when an individual is seen as the obstacle, is it distorted into violence or a desire to do harm.

Anger is often used as a cover for other feelings. For a man it is more socially acceptable to be angry than to admit to fear or sadness. His anger can come from an inability to resolve those other feelings.

Anger is distorted when you want to change something in the past or future, rather than the present. These situations no longer exist in the "real" world, but are stuck in your mind/body as if they were still happening.

Anger is at its most destructive when turned inward with self-judgement. That is the cause of depression. Often that is energy that wants to create change within you. Some internal program blocks its creative process.

Anger is associated with the 3rd chakra, the personal power energy, the energy by which you make your mark in the world. Chinese healing traditions associate anger with the liver, which is located in the 3rd chakra area. Liver disease often results from years of unresolved, unexpressed anger.

In Terms of Vibration.

Sentics (pioneered by Manfred Clyne) is the study of wave forms describing emotions. It's been shown that each emotion has a characteristic frequency, a simple long-wave vibration, consistent in every culture.

Emotional blockage occurs when wave forms interact with negative interference. Emotion waves unassimilated stand alone, out of phase. They are not coherent. Intentional relaxation, as in meditation or breathing practices, brings order by reducing destructive interference. It also causes cross-hemispheric coherence in the brain.

Fear is a choice to be non-conductive, to resist the energy flow in body tissue, not allowing that flow to cascade from the higher octaves where information and guidance is available.

The emotion with the most destructive interference is hatred – for another or for yourself in the form of shame. You've heard that Soul cannot abide where there is judgement. This is literally true as the love vibration is cancelled out by negative interference from the hatred vibration.

Frozen emotions are stored in the body by crystallizing the liquid crystal of muscle tissue. This is the nature of muscular armoring. It creates a layer of stored electrical incoherence in the muscle which separates you from the world. Cut off from the information flow that tells them how to function, the membranes that surround each cell become distorted. The receptor site on the cell wall designed to receive endorphins (pleasure hormones) becomes so twisted that those hormones cannot park there. The cell is deprived of feeling good.

The cell membrane is a standing wave system which holds the memory of every emotion which was integrated, a tapestry of woven memory. Fear, pain and anger that have been assimilated (experienced consciously) become part of the cell membrane tapestry. Long waves of emotion make a nest or home for short waves of light and information that drives cell metabolism.

Vibrations rendered incoherent by unassimilated emotions are not nested in the basic vibration. The unassimilated emotions continue to disrupt the flow of the carrier wave bearing life-sustaining energies.

Incoherent emotions dump destructive hormones directly from the glands. The effects are worse than cigarettes. This hastens the aging process and stresses the immune system. Teens tending to anger and hostility have ten times as much chance of cardiac death as their more coherent friends.

The carrier wave that delivers life-sustaining energy and information is a vibration we experience as love. Some emotions (joy, pleasure) nest naturally in that carrier wave with no interference. They are coherent feelings.

Other emotions, considered negative, can be experienced at the same time as love. In many species, fear of a mother protecting her young gives her a fierce strength. Fear for survival coupled with your love of life makes you resourceful in avoiding danger. Movie audiences love it when the hero outwits his attacker.

Pain is usually felt at the loss of someone or something you love. As long as the love component is present, that pain becomes poignant and beautiful.

Anger is usually toward someone you love, especially if they appear to be the obstacle to your self-expression. Most violence is domestic against loved ones. Keeping the focus on the love, you can rage for your love. It's great drama.

Re-experiencing the frozen feelings with Witness Consciousness is equivalent to nesting the vibrations into the carrier wave of Divine Mother, pure love.

Getting Unstuck.

The methods Ipsalu uses to transform stagnant energy into flowing energy involve movement, breath, sound and consciousness. As you come into present time, you discover where the body/mind is stuck in something from the past, thinking it is still present. When that frozen memory/belief is re-experienced in the light of consciousness, its energy is returned to the flow.

Any chakra that is blocked indicates memories, attitudes and conditioned patterns you refuse to look at. When a chakra opens, that means you no longer resist that part of your personality, that you have accepted it and reclaimed it.

A Healing Conversation.

This dialogue is a little easier to do than the one presented in an earlier chapter. You can do this process alone or ask a loving friend to guide you. The emotional, mental and spiritual aspects of your being could be seen as the child, adult, and wise one. Let the child and adult enter into a dialogue, while the wise one watches benevolently. Give each of them voice, and even move from one chair to another when changing roles. Let them speak their positions. Search within your body for the unhappy elements.

1) Close your eyes and relax. Speak about something that is troubling you.

2) Scan your body. Find a point of discomfort or trembling, the place where the memory lives. Put your hand there and be fully present in that place.

3) Breathe into that space. Consciousness enters on the breath.

4) Be clear what the feeling is and allow that feeling to expand.

5) A picture related to the feeling may form – a primal or past life memory.

6) Let yourself speak, cry out, scream, or rage, expressing fully whatever you feel, Witnessing all the while.

7) Love yourself for having that feeling. Come to love the feeling.

8) Let there be no judgement whatsoever.

9) Recall the limiting decision you made during this event (see Chapter 2).

10) Acknowledge yourself as the creator of the event. Rise above the tendency to see yourself as the victim, or to feel guilty. Blame and guilt exclude the Soul.

11) Remember the lesson you wanted to learn, or what you wanted to experience.

12) Be clear that the lesson is learned and doesn't need to be re-experienced.

13) Feel gratitude to the other parties for providing this opportunity. Appreciate how perfectly each has played their role.

Emotional Cycles.

As an emotional fragment is consciously experienced, energy begins to flow through it. It loses its power and autonomy. You are less driven by that emotional response pattern. The issue will recur, the button will be pushed again, and the same response will start to happen. It may seem you have gone around a circle and are back where you started.

More accurately, you are on a spiral. This recurrence can be observed from a higher vantage point. You are more able to put it in perspective, to recognize it as just an old pattern, an old friend, nothing to be concerned about.

Each time you come to this point on your spiral, the issue will be resolved more quickly. What took thirty years to work through initially can be handled in a matter of hours or minutes after several rounds of experiencing/Witnessing. It may never go away completely, but it won't run you any more.

Karma.

The emotional fragments you are working with have been called Karma. They are the consequences of unfinished actions and feelings not experienced with full consciousness. Many people think that Karmic law requires every misdeed to produce a punitive backlash. Karma is not a system of retribution. The paradigm of sin and punishment is a fallacy introduced in earlier times to control the barbaric populace by fear of God's reprisal. You have outgrown the need for such manipulation.

"Sin" is from a Greek archery term for "missing the mark." You have misinterpreted situations in your life, drawn conclusions that aren't accurate. You have defined yourself by these limiting decisions. Rather than thinking in terms of "sin and punishment," rethink those beliefs and positions. Look for greater accuracy in realizing who you are.

The process of confessing your "sins" and being "absolved" may relieve guilt momentarily, but unless a shift in consciousness occurs, until you've released the pattern at an energy level, you will feel compelled to repeat the same behavior. God/Existence never judged you. That's a human activity. You judge yourself and that judgement keeps you separate from God.

Let us consider, as an alternative paradigm, that every situation we find ourselves in was co-created and choreographed by all the participants, at their enlightened level. Each chooses to be involved because the situation provides a lesson, a demonstration of a principle, an experience the Soul wishes to have or a game it wishes to play. Maybe one plays a role just to assist another.

Suppose the entity has been a plundering soldier for many lives and wishes to rise from a 3rd chakra aggressive nature to a 4th chakra level of compassion. He might go into a battle situation where unspeakable atrocities are being committed (with the consent of all concerned, each for their own reasons) so that he might be sickened with violence and warfare and be finished forever.

If, in that situation, he kills one hundred people, the laws of Karma do not require him to live another one hundred lives so each of his victims has the opportunity to kill him. In this paradigm there are no victims. Rather, he has the opportunity to learn the lesson and be finished with warfare.

Don't waste time thinking about past lives. Any unfinished business will be recreated in the formative years of your current life. If the idea of reincarnation doesn't appeal to you, you can ignore this whole line of thought without taking away from the rest of this paradigm. Just deal with what is up at present.

To heal any trauma or subconscious wound, one must go through the healing steps presented earlier. At that point Karma is satisfied. In the example above, even if there have been countless bully lives, all are healed in the same moment. As soon as all your repressed material has been so handled, you become complete with this level of Existence.

Sometimes when their personal work is completed, beings can continue the processing, handling global karma, cleaning up attitudes that have been left hanging in the atmosphere as part of the collective consciousness. Some souls choose to come back repeatedly to assist in cleansing the planet.

Certain characteristics are typical of people at lower and higher emotional maturity scale. Rate yourself now and have someone who knows you well do a rating also. One score per item. After several months of practice rate yourself again: 1 point for each item in the left column that describes you, 3 points for the right column. If you are in between, or vacillate back and forth, score 2 points.

At lower levels you would feel:	At higher levels you would feel:
Low physical energy. Easily exhausted. High stress and resulting ailments.	Increased stamina and improved health. Much lower levels of stress.
Unable to complete a project or hold a job. Scattered. Short attention span.	Able to stay focused on a task to completion, be in the moment, not daydreaming.
Dependent on someone to take care of you, and at the same time resentful of your caretaker.	Independent. Having a sense of what needs to be done, and the ability to handle problems as they arise.
An ongoing state of nameless anxiety and self-doubt. Lacking confidence, feeling inferiority, guilt, unworthiness.	Sense of inner peace and confidence. Feeling on an even keel with peers. Letting go of fears, guilt and doubts.
Being overly meticulous to compensate or fear of being inadequate.	Being more relaxed in your work, allowing the space to make mistakes.
Afraid to express an opinion or make a decision.	A clear sense of your own truth, and the courage to speak that truth.
Wanting a special relationship, but unable to develop or sustain one. Jealous and possessive of friends.	Deepened relationships. Able to open up to give and receive respect, realizing that people come and go in our lives.
Sensitive to criticism, yet highly critical of others. Avoiding responsibility for your actions. Blaming others for your inability to perform.	Able to accept constructive criticism, allowing undeserved criticism to roll off. Taking responsibility for your errors. Accepting others as they are.
Reflecting the mood of your peer group.	Distinguishing your feelings from others.
Constantly trying to improve yourself, apologizing for the way you are.	Sense of purpose and delight in your process of unfolding.
Reliving past events trying to imagine what you should have said or done.	Trusting in Existence, not feeling a need to be in control. Living in present time.
Rationalization of your position, attempting to always be right.	Let go of self-delusions, not playing the victim or manipulation games.
Mood swings. Impatience, resentments. Restlessness.	Quickly resolving emotional issues as they emerge.
Perception clouded by feelings. Feelings affect actions disproportionately. Self-destructive patterns are repeated.	Clarity of perception and thought. Response to a situation is appropriate, coming from a loving, nurturing place.
Looking for someone to tell you what to do, not trusting inner guidance.	Listening to inner direction. Secure in guidance from your Higher Self.
Sense of separateness, alienation. Personality is in conflict with the Higher Self.	Feeling yourself more as Presence than personality, with increasing consistency.

Going Deeper

1. Continue your daily practice, varying the techniques in each phase of the Formula:

ACTIVATING THE BODY

- Bated Breath, Kriya Energization, Complete Breath, Rishi Isometrics

STILLING THE MIND

- Khechari Mudra, Witness Thoughts, Watching the Breath, Alternate Nostril Breath, Hong Saw, Trataka

AROUSING SEXUAL ENERGY.

- Aswini Mudra, FireBreath

TRANSMUTING

- Cobra Breath, Transmutation Breath, FireBreath

2. Pay attention to your jaw and head position throughout the day.

   A relaxed jaw promotes the free flow of sexual energy. Tension in the jaw impedes that flow. It also reveals suppressed anger.

   The head held back aligns the physical and spiritual bodies. When your chin juts forward, you are using only the intellect, not the body wisdom.

3. Personal Inventory.

   Continue to look at your "personal" life, being the Witness without judgement. "Persona" is the Greek word for masks worn on stage. Begin to detach from this role you have been playing, the fictional character you portray.

   Study the behaviors and moods listed on the previous page. As suggested there, rate yourself at this point and again after three months of regular practice.

   At the end of each day record in your journal your behaviors that reflect items on that list.

   Continue to examine your basic beliefs, the roots from which those behaviors grew, beliefs which you have taken for granted as "the way it is."

FireBreath for Energy Flow.

The FireBreath (see Appendix C) is one of the most powerful methods for bringing repressed psychological trauma into consciousness and invoking emotional release. When you do strong breathing, you bring more energy into the system and break through repression.

Every time you do the FireBreath you will feel different feelings. Sometimes you might cry and feel sad. Sometimes anger may surface. Sometimes you may feel laughter and great joy. That is to be expected. Simply experience the emotion, be the Witness and keep the breath and movement going. You are purifying and clearing the chakras.

Initially you might be working through heavy emotional material that has been buried a long time in the lower chakras. In time, the expressions will become more subtle, more gentle. Eventually the feelings become sublime. You will discover the full range of feelings available to you.

Resources

Acknowledging Dr. Bovis for discovering how to measure brain waves and Dr. Oscar Brunler for measuring thousands of people and creating a scale of correspondence between vibration frequency and mental function.

The Brain Scale of Dr. Brunler, by Arthur M. Young, (1980) Mill Valley, CA: Robert Briggs Associates.

The Brunler-Bovis Biometer and its Uses, by A.L. Swanholm (1963) Los Angeles: DeVorss.

Waking the Tiger, by Peter Levine, PhD, pioneering work in treating trauma patients.

The Touch of Emotions, by Manfred Clyne.

Chapter Six

MYSTERIES OF THE HEART
Creating and Maintaining the State of Bliss

This chapter examines the physiology of love and emotions to see the impact of your spiritual practices on the physical body and the benefits to health and cosmic awareness. Only when you fully open to the heart energies are you are able to live in a state of Bliss.

Nearly every religion and culture have recognized the heart as a very special place. It is the source of higher wisdom and great love, of elevating thoughts and feelings. The yogis considered the heart to be the point of perfect balance between the higher and lower worlds, a meeting place for heaven and earth, for divinity and humanness. It is where the Soul dwells within the physical body.

Processing Emotions.

Research shows that emotions are governed by a brain center called the amygdala. It continually receives information from the senses about the environment and compares it to memories of past hazards and trauma to see if there is any threat present. If so, it sends signals to the sympathetic nervous system to spring into activity (adrenaline rush, etc.) to meet the threat with a fight or flight response. It activates the emotions designated appropriate according to past experience. This happens instantaneously before the higher brain functions have a chance to reason it all out. The system was designed to help you survive in a dangerous world.

Threats to your emotional defenses, the strategies you use to preserve your sense of safety, are taken as seriously by the mind as are real threats of physical danger. When a situation "pushes your buttons" and you react irrationally, this is the mechanism that triggers that reaction.

You are subjected to an ongoing barrage of "threatening" situations besides environmental hazards – pressures on the job, tensions in relationships, internal emotional battles. Probably the greatest stress comes from identifying with the smaller self and its limited capabilities. Most people live in a constant state of high stress, with their fight-or-flight mechanism chronically locked in. This produces serious health consequences.

Stress is one of the major factors in almost every physical and mental disease. Some 90% of visits to doctors are for stress related conditions. A recent study looked at people suffering from stress-induced disorders such as high blood pressure, sleeplessness, indigestion, fatigue, body aches, arrhythmia, auto-immune disorders and hormone imbalances. Those who learned to deal consciously with their distressing emotions experienced dramatic improvement. Similar benefits came to emotional problems such as post-trauma stress disorder, anxiety and depression. Many other conditions will yet be discovered in larger studies.

Benefits of the Witness.

You've been introduced to a method for consciously dealing with emotions by: 1) being aware of the emotional reaction; 2) standing back a bit, observing without judgement; 3) admitting that you have created the drama; and 4) still experiencing it but not getting swept away.

This is a core practice in Ipsalu Tantra. Thousands of people have worked miracles in their lives with this method. It is exciting to discover scientific validation of this principle and to learn in detail what happens in the body during this process.

Intelligence of the Heart.

The heart is able to think. Everyone intuitively knows that to be true.

Look in the language: "Follow your heart." ... "You're thinking with your heart." ... "I trust him because he speaks from his heart."

HEART FACTS

The Heart-Brain.

The heart actually has its own brain. (This may come as a surprise.)

- It has a complete nervous system made up of some 40,000 neurons, the same type of cells that make up the brain.

- It is capable of sensing and feeling, of learning and remembering, of deciding and communicating.

- The heart receives direction from the brain but doesn't necessarily act on that direction. It makes its own determination whether or not to comply.

- Heart beat is independent of the brain. Nerve connections from the brain are severed during a heart transplant and yet the heart continues to beat.

- In a developing fetus the heart (emotional brain) is beating long before the logical brain has developed.

- Communication goes both ways. The heart continually sends information to the brain, with every pulse. In many cases the brain follows the heart's instructions which can make a huge difference in the quality of your life.

Heart Communications.

The heart communicates with the brain and the rest of the body in several ways:

- Neurologically – through nerve impulses transmitted with every heart beat;

- Biochemically – through hormones and neurotransmitters it produces (The medical establishment recently added the heart to the list of endocrine glands);

- Biophysically – through pressure waves, standing waves in the main vessels;

- Rhythmically – by variability of heart rhythms in response to moment-to-moment changes in feeling states;

- Energetically – through an electromagnetic field generated around the heart, 3,000 times more powerful than the field around the brain. It is a measurable field which permeates every body cell and extends out ten feet from the physical body, affecting everyone and everything in its environment. It is strongly influenced by feeling states.

Look in the songs: *These Foolish Things* – "... stumbling words that tell you what my heart meant;" *My Funny Valentine* – "... you made me smile with my heart."

Look in Broadway shows: *Greasepaint* – "Who can I run to? My heart wants to know;" and *Guys and Dolls* – "I'll know when my love comes along, I'll know in my heart." The list could go on and on.

Medical science had assumed that the heart is a mechanical device, a pump to move blood through the body, adequately replaced by a transplant or even a plastic facsimile. Doctors presumed that it was controlled by the autonomic nervous system like all the other organs and physiological activities.

Science is now realizing that the heart has its own special form of intelligence. This intelligence becomes available when mind and emotions come into balance and coherence. Recent scientific research is demonstrating clinically what the yogis and poets have been saying for millennia. Its language is a little different, but science is finally validating esoteric traditions. The heart is the perfect meeting place for science, mysticism and poetry.

The Waveform of Ecstasy.

The human heart has seven distinct muscle groups, each producing a different vibration pattern which can be individually monitored by an EKG. The combined pattern of the seven vibrations is usually a chaotic jumble, like noise, representing scattered mental activity. When the person being monitored is experiencing feelings of love, caring, non-judgement or acceptance, all seven waves take on the same rhythm. They reinforce each other, becoming clear and

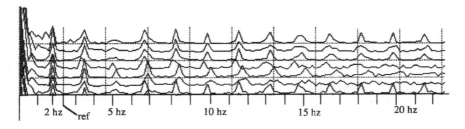

coherent, like music. This song of the heart produces a calm sense of well being.

One way of picturing vibrations is to analyze/compare the activity of harmonics at different frequencies to see what frequencies get activated. This diagram shows the similarity of the seven heart vibrations in a moment of love.

In harmonic analysis of a coherent love wave, the frequencies of activity peaks turn out to be in a phi ratio (the Golden Mean). The heart then provides access to higher dimensional cascade of communication and understanding, this most efficient path of energy from heaven to earth. This slow love frequency is the basis for nesting the higher informational vibrations.

The regular vibration of the body comes from a standing wave in the aorta, the major artery. When the heart ejects blood the aorta balloons out. A pressure pulse is created in the artery. The pulse travels down the vessel to the point where the vessel divides and part of the impulse is reflected back. If the outgoing and reflected pulses are synchronized, a standing wave is established at a frequency of about 7 Hz. This coherent mechanical wave creates several resonant systems including electrical vibrations which entrain the brain (see Chapter 8).

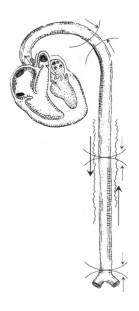

When vibrations come into coherence there is maximum energy efficiency in the system. No energy is wasted by one part fighting against another. More energy is available for clarity of mind and vitality of body. Stress, when not handled consciously, creates heart wave incoherence. Incoherence creates additional stress. This is a vicious debilitating circle in which many people are caught.

Effect of Heart Coherence on the Body.

When the heart waves' harmonics are coherent, emotions are resonant and harmonious "Negative" thoughts or emotions set up erratic vibrations in heart rhythms and imbalance in the nervous system. The autonomic nervous system has two parts – the sympathetic which stimulates the body to activity and the parasympathetic which slows things down and produces serenity. When the signals are confused both systems send messages and the body gets muddled. It's rather like driving a car with one foot on the gas pedal and the other foot on the brake. Continually responding to many situations as if they were life-threatening increases incoherence of the inner vibrations, placing higher levels of stress on the whole system.

Loving thoughts and feelings create balance in the nervous system, reducing activity signals in the sympathetic system and increasing the calming effects of the parasympathetic system. The two sides work cooperatively and harmoniously. The coherent love vibration also creates in the mind clearer perceptions and intuitions, greater creativity and focus. The brain is better able to process information, solve problems and make decisions.

Messages from a loving heart intervene in the emotion process, toning down the body's stress response. You have begun this process by Witnessing your upsets, consciously recognizing emotional reactions to upsetting situations.

With some practice, these situations lose their power and you no longer see them as threatening. You can even learn to stand quietly in the center of your being, in your Heart, while the world whirls chaotically around you. You don't have to get caught up in it. This information, this sense of calm within the storm, is sent from heart to brain. Your response to a "threat" is now mellow, no longer an automatic reflex action.

Coherent vibration/heart resonance is the physical component of the Bliss state, a necessary requirement for vitality of the cells and of the body. A cascade of neural and biochemical events result from the heart's transmission, which affects every system in the body:

- Chronic stress and its many side-effects are relieved.

- With less stress, production of the stress hormone, cortisol, is greatly reduced. This frees up materials, allowing production of more DHEA, an important regenerative and anti-aging hormone. Both cortisol and DHEA are made from a limited supply of the same precursor.

- In messages sent to the cells, coherence means self-replicate while incoherence means self-destruct.

- The immune response is enhanced. The love-based, low frequency vibration from the heart strengthens the immune system via the thymus gland which is the physical correlate to the heart chakra. It sits right above the heart, vibrating in resonance with it, translating the heart's life-affirming information into hormones that protect body cells. This makes the body super-resistant to all infections and degenerative diseases, a process essential for longevity.

In most children the thymus gland is quite large and is the body's main producer of chemistry for the immune system. In most adults the thymus is non-functional and atrophied. In an effort to protect your tender heart feelings you have also compromised your life expectancy. That can be reversed by "reopening" the heart, reactivating the thymus.

A loving heart is the best protection against AIDS and cancer. Simply bringing the coherent heart vibration into play is the solution to most of the health problems of this time.

Heart as a Balance Point.

The heart is a beautiful place to learn discrimination. From its position above the lower three chakras you can watch Ego play out its strategies, and from below the higher three chakras you begin to sense the workings of Soul. You can determine which voice is guiding you, can hold Ego in alignment and allow Soul to manifest its divine destiny.

The heart serves as a point of balance and integration for your physical, emotional and mental natures, as well as the connection to your spiritual nature. A distinctive wave, as measured by an EKG, is produced in the heart during the experience of love. The ratio between the power peaks is the Golden Mean ratio. This ratio allows energy to change scales or harmonic octaves without losing any of its power or information. Thus a loving heart is the intermediary, the communication center, between the various aspects of your being.

The DNA in every cell of the body is built on the Golden Mean ratio (comparing the width of the DNA coil and the length of one segment). Coherent heart sounds, with their harmonics also appearing at that ratio, weave a nest which fits the braid angle of DNA. Genetic material is efficiently transmitted because there is so little negative interference. The loving heart then supports DNA in maintaining optimal health in the body.

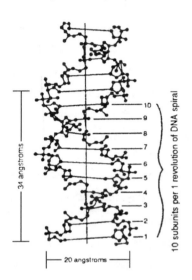

Entraining the Brain.

Vibration patterns generated in the heart are detectable in the brain, measurable by EEG (electro-encephalogram). Since the heart produces the strongest rhythm in the body and the strongest field, it can entrain the other parts, including the brain. When heart and brain are working in harmony, singing their song together, body and mind are able to perform optimally. allowing coded intelligence for higher brain functions

If you sustain that love space you sustain the entrainment. Continued focus on the heart increases synchronization with the brain. When you experience harmony and connection with something external, like a beautiful sunset or piece of music, you are actually experiencing being in sync with yourself. This produces a feeling of at-one-ment and a profound sense of well-being.

Accessing the Heart Wisdom.

First you learn to quiet the mind, using any of the techniques already presented (watching the breath, breath mantra, khechari mudra.) When the mind is still, you can access your inner wisdom. It feels like Shiva energy around the head. The Inner Smile allows it to enter your physical system.

Then focus on the heart. (Simply paying attention to any body part brings an increased energy to that part.) A few minutes of such focus allows the heart and brain to connect. You might think of that as the Shiva consciousness streaming into the heart space. It brings clarity, serenity and wisdom.

Finally, to come fully into a loving space, bring in Shakti passion. Move energy from the genitals up into the heart to join Shiva so that the full power of love can be expressed.

Begin Safely with Neutrality.

The physical heart and physiological phenomena described so far are always working in concert with the subtle energies of the heart chakra (Anahata). That energy center is tightly closed and guarded for most people. Proceed slowly in opening the heart chakra to the flow of love. To open it prematurely creates the risk of leaving a wounded Inner Child unprotected.

Love can be frightening at first. You've gone to great lengths to avoid it. But you needn't miss out on the values to health that come from a loving heart. You can be protected and still get the benefits by taking a neutral position.

Most people live in a negative way, which produces chaos and stress in the heart. Begin by changing some life-long habits. Begin moving toward neutrality:

• Change from complaining about situations into **acceptance** of them.

• Release blame and resentments for past indignities with **forgiveness**.

• Replace criticism of others and yourself with **non-judgemental observation**.

This takes away the paralyzing effects of negativity. If you are taking responsibility for the authorship of your life, there is no place for these negations. This can all happen without making the heart feel too vulnerable and it's enough to make an enormous difference in your body and emotions.

> Judgements are a device that the mind
> uses to maintain the illusion of separation
> from others. There must be two entities for
> one to be standing in judgement of the other.
> Similarly the mind engages in self-judgement in
> order to maintain a separation from the Soul.
> The Soul simply cannot be present where
> there is judgement (i.e., Coherent vibration
> is neutralized by judgement vibration). Guilt
> and shame are the surest way to keep the heart
> vibration incoherent and chaotic, which locks
> out the Inner Beloved from your heart.

Opening the Heart through Devotion.

The god of your heart, who or whatever you feel that to be, represents the highest expression of life. Whether a personal god exists or just an abstraction really doesn't matter. By recreating the relationship of a child to a father or mother through prayer and worship, many people bring themselves into a simple loving space.

Your sense of devotion might be clouded by old resentments. Many people blame God when their life doesn't go according to plan. That is a hold-over from a time when the only wisdom offered by the church in the face of trauma was "It's God's will." When you assume responsibility for creating your life, blaming God is no longer an option.

Some people find it useful to honor spiritual masters, advanced beings. They are seen as role models who have attained a high level of development. Just be careful whom you chose for adulation. Occasionally "masters" turn out to have human weaknesses, so idolizing them can be disappointing.

You can honor the Divine in your beloved partner, in every being, in every aspect of creation, realizing that they are human and will occasionally do things that "push your buttons." To keep recognizing divinity as an abstraction allows you to come safely from the heart without being too vulnerable.

Why You Protect the Heart.

You probably learned early in life that pure love was not part of your earth reality. Reaching out for love in your primal innocence, you came up against parents who had no experience of love without conditions. In order to survive in an unloving world you were forced to protect your tender heart, to shut down the natural flow of heart energy. It was simply too painful to know about love in a world where unconditional love was not available.

Later in life when you want to open yourself to a deep relationship, you feel a high risk factor. The more you care about someone the greater the potential for pain – the chance of loving someone who doesn't love you back or finding that great love and losing it. This is among life's most frightening possibilities. Most people choose the safety of never opening fully, of staying separate.

Before the heart can re-open safely, the Witness needs to be securely in place and major emotional issues must be identified and defused. The heart is potentially a receiver of the most transformative energy you can know, but transformation only happens when there is no judgement, especially self-judgement. It only comes in a space of loving acceptance.

When you begin to open the heart chakra there is usually a lot of pain and sadness. Your Limited Self remembers all the times you have longed for love and it wasn't available. Based on past experience, love is very frightening.

An existential sadness comes from feeling cut off from your Divine Source. You long to be reconnected, to return home. This barrier of sadness and fear stops most people from going forward in opening the heart.

As the heart chakra develops, you truly become an "awakened one," intent on living in the Bliss state. That opening, when emotions are flowing freely, brings you to a place of joy, of exquisite pleasure, of true Bliss. It is huge, overwhelming – so much bigger than the fears and strategies you have used to keep it contained.

A dear friend recently said,"I am truly beginning to be less frightened of relationship because I know I will always have my own personal connection to Divine Source, sexually as well as in the heart. It releases my fear of dependency on another individual for this sweetness. It helps me to just enjoy love wherever I find it."

When Soul manifests in the body it is experienced in the heart. With a little practice any anxiety can be dismissed by taking a single deep breath which pulls the Soul back into its place (pulls vibrations back into coherence and your life-line back in place) and reminds you that all is in Divine Order.

Heart is Reclosable.

The lower three chakras are "closed" when they are hiding subconscious memories that you have not yet looked at. These chakras become "open" when those banished issues have all been recognized, experienced consciously and accepted. After that there will be recurrences but no more big surprises.

The heart chakra however can open and close. This is protection that allows you to open up when you are in a safe place and want to share that precious energy with a Beloved or a trusted group, with Nature or Existence. But when you go back into the marketplace or are in the company of less conscious beings, you can put your protection back up. In earlier times tantric work was practiced in the safety of a monastery or an ashram. Now you are required to do it in the world. Take care to protect the heart in the early stages.

Stages of Opening.

A safe sequence for opening chakras is as follows:

1) The mind – with added clarity of heart intelligence (Shiva Consciousness) assisted by Cobra Breath Level 1.
2) The lower body, the ego chakras, the Inner Child, with benevolent Witness present, assisted by Cobra Breath Level 2.
3) The heart and finally the throat, with the help of Cobra Breath Level 3.
4) The connection to the Divine Love of all creation that is in all things, through Cobra Breath Level 4.

Love and Sex.

This society is preoccupied with the hidden power of sexual energy. It uses the lure of sex to merchandise every imaginable product. Over a million websites are sex-oriented. You harbor a mix of fear and fascination with this unattainable mystery and an embarrassed excitement in its unrealized potential – unrealized because you look for it in the wrong place. The media promotes the idea that sex is the same as love. Many think they are in love when they are only in lust. In truth, casual sex is only a small aspect of love. Sex, when substituted for love, leaves you empty and unfulfilled. Its satisfactions are fleeting. Some men give the promise of love in order to get sex from a woman; and some women give sex, hoping to get love. This bartering process has broken many hearts, left a residue of bitterness.

With the consciousness and techniques of tantra, you expand lust into love. Lust is taking – objectifying and using someone for your own pleasure. Love is giving, honoring and sharing for mutual enjoyment. Passion doesn't disappear. That special chemistry continues to be the driving force but it transforms into something greater and more satisfying (see Chapter 11).

What is Pretending to be Love?

If you perform loving service or spiritual practices because you expect a reward, you are not acting out of love. You are bartering with Existence. How many times must you be disappointed before you outgrow this temptation?

Music, entertainment, fashion, everything in your environment feeds into your hunger for love. Songs and movies are often about love, usually neurotic and distorted love based on need. "I want you. I need you. I love you." ... "I want to gain complete control of you, to handle even the heart and soul of you." ... "People who need people are the luckiest people in the world." ... "Once you have found her, never let her go."

"Love" has many meanings at different levels of consciousness. "Loving" at the level of 1st chakra awareness means looking for security by demanding fidelity, being possessive, jealous and suspicious. Loving at 2nd chakra perspective means looking for comfort and pleasure from nurturing, stroking, being cared for. People are often attracted to someone because they see there a high potential for pleasure. The singles scene is an ongoing rating game, based on the premise that the more beautiful the form, the greater the pleasure and the greater the conquest. Love at the 3rd chakra means wanting to dominate or be dominated (needed), wanting approval or a partner who would upgrade your social status. Again the rating game enters. Ram Dass observed that those "on the make" see only three kinds of people: 1) the prey, 2) the competition, 3) the irrelevant. What a limited view of humanity!

Initially, "love" appears to be dependent on someone or something outside you. It springs from the responses and actions of the other. When you experience the magnificent expansion which love brings only with respect to a certain person, you might assume that s/he is the source of your experience. S/he is just a catalyst. Real love flows as a natural state of your essential being, part of the great mystery. Tantric loving is an overflow from the abundance of love that is your essence.

> Once you awaken to the source of love within,
> you will no longer need to search for it outside.

This note was written by an Ipsalu teacher (among her many other accomplishments) to a tantrika who, separated from his beloved, felt his heart was breaking.

Dear M,

It was great to see you again with your heart unzipped. Whenever my heart aches or breaks I find it ultimately opens and heals. A huge shift came for me when I decided to stop yearning for love and started Being Love, living on the path of Love, no matter what. I started loving every-thing and everyone in my day. I asked, "What can I do for the people around me today to really serve them and be kind to them?" I found myself making love to the air and sky, to plants and water. I brought food from my (catering) events to parking lot attendants and valets. I helped people carry heavy objects and did things for them that I knew they didn't like doing. Recently I worked in hospitals with kids and elderly people and let God teach me love through them. I really practiced Namaste, seeing others as divine beings and they all became radiantly beautiful souls. I do this in the bank, the grocery store, on the road, whenever I remind myself to be a channel for Love and my life is transforming completely as a result. I almost always feel full, joyous and radiant. I took the love I had for the unavailable beloved one and gave it out to the world. And so my heart healed in ways I never expected. The love became suprapersonal instead of personal but more rewarding in new ways. I am still a ways away from being in service and in love with all life all the time, but this is my Bodhisattva goal and my feet are on that path.

All Love,
L.

Love Expressed as Service.

When the heart is opening, many people report a shift in their values and priorities, especially in their professional activities. If their livelihood is not making a difference in the lives of others, they become dissatisfied. Some have an urge to go back to school and study therapy or body work. Others want to use their training and skills in assisting worthy causes.

At least one well-known guru simply gives hugs to her devotees. They gladly wait in line for hours for the privilege of hugging her. She holds this balanced, coherent Bliss vibration. By being close to her, people can entrain themselves to that vibration and instantly feel the ecstasy. The devotees probably won't be able to hold that vibration or recreate it initially but at least they have had the experience and will never be satisfied with less. Hopefully they will be motivated to do the work necessary to achieve that state as their own permanent reality.

Great artists, teachers and healers work by the same principle. Their vibrations are characterized by a slow, coherent waveform.

12-Pointed Star.

The traditional symbol for the heart is a 6-pointed star. A triangle pointing down represents masculine (Shiva) energy, and a triangle pointing up represents feminine (Shakti energy.

Two such stars superimposed with a twist make the 12-pointed star which is also useful when you are ready to open the heart chakra. Contemplating and visualizing the balanced, 12-pointed figure suggests to the organism a balanced wave pattern in the physical heart. It is a pattern that mathematically represents ecstasy.

Each spinal chakra (body oriented) is associated with a chakra in the brain (spiritually oriented). Esoteric traditions teach that the 12-pointed star shows a balancing of the six spinal chakras with the six brain chakras, a state of harmony between heaven and earth. A traditional heart yantra has twelve petals, representing a fully opened heart blossom.

The 12-faced figure, a dodecahedron, is the only shape whose angles create sides in the ratio of the Golden Mean. It can be seen as twelve spiral vortex cones, a basic shape in the weaving of energy into matter.

In a two-dimensional image it appears to have ten sides. Many biological forms are based on this shape. The DNA strands which hold the blueprints for life forms, appear in this form when viewed from above.

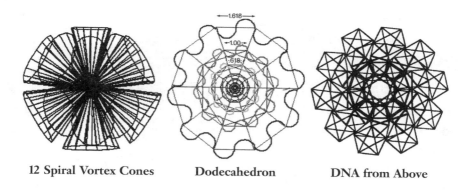

12 Spiral Vortex Cones   **Dodecahedron**   **DNA from Above**

The low-frequency coherent heart vibration is the perfect carrier wave for high frequency information being stepped down from higher octaves. As old body cells are replaced by new cells, the DNA information must be correctly copied. When the heart is producing coherent waves, i.e. when it is experiencing love, the cells receive accurate instructions to make healthy DNA. When anger or sadness is the operative mood, the information cannot be correctly communicated and the cell is not accurately replicated. This accounts for aging and degeneration.

Humans now have two strands of DNA holding their genetic endowment. There are indications of potentially twelve strands and that the missing information is stored in each cell, but it is scattered, not yet braided into workable strands. When the heart is coherent in the Bliss frequency the DNA is instructed to perform this braiding process.

When coherent or orderly enough to phase lock or nest, emotion's **long wave**[A] programs DNA (the **short wave**[B]) by braiding the genetic material, aligning the active sites. This braiding is the structural switching which decides the codon groups to be turned on or off.

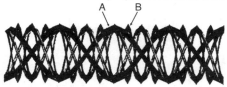

Bringing the DNA into a new configuration virtually produces a new life form, the new human, with a new body and new consciousness. Great seers (Edgar Cayce, Nostradamus and others) have spoken of changes in the earth's energy that will transform it into a planet of light, a system of higher vibration. Those living here will have bodies suited for that refined environment. Earth changes are happening. You are encouraged to be prepared for the new world that is rapidly emerging.

Coming into Resonance.

The Earth is surrounded by its atmosphere, and outside that is another layer called the ionosphere. The space between Earth and the ionosphere serves as a resonance chamber. Electro-

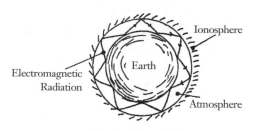

The earth's atmosphere shown as a resonant cavity.

magnetic radiation creates a vibration by going out from the earth, bouncing off of the ionosphere, and returning back to earth. This natural resonant frequency of the planet is between 7-8 Hz (called the Schumann resonance in honor of its discoverer).

The energy of the earth has been referred to here as Shakti Kundalini (i.e., creative energy or sexual energy).

• When two vibrational systems operate near each other, the stronger one tends to entrain the weaker one. Experiments have shown that introducing the earth frequency into a room creates a state of euphoria in the people present.

• Whenever the mind is quiet, as in deep meditation or yoga nidra, it produces radiation at a frequency around 7-8 Hz.

• When the heart is experiencing love (i.e., vibrating with coherent resonance) it creates a vibration at about 7 Hz.

• When the mind, heart (Soul) and genitals are all vibrating in the same frequency you experience an exquisite wholeness (holiness) and the mystical inner union, being at one with physical reality and the Consciousness that supports it.

The diagram below shows those three vibrations in harmony.

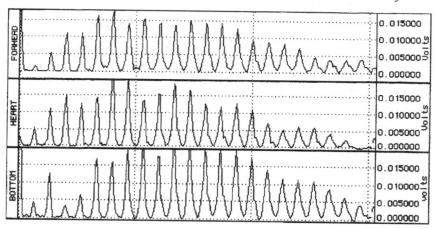

The mantra AUM quickly creates this wonderful attunement. A (ah) stimulates the heart, U (oo) stimulates the sexual energy, M (mm) quiets the ego mind and connects all the energies.

Imagine two lovers, each in that holy vibrational resonance as they exchange energy. They disappear into each other because they are operating at the same vibration. There are no artificial barriers, no distinctions, only love and harmony manifesting at all levels. This is the ultimate gift from the human experience. It is understandable, learnable and easily within your grasp.

Healing Society, the Planet and Beyond.

Social change can be brought about by a critical number of people holding a coherent vibration. A Transcendental Meditation group meditating in Boston produced a significant drop in the crime rate. Guidance suggests that even 10,000 people in this country holding the Bliss vibration could transform this society.

Many people have discovered the value of being in nature and living close to the land, for their healing or for vision quests. You can allow yourself to be entrained to the planet's vibration. To add to the excitement it has been demonstrated that the planet can be entrained to the Bliss vibration. Groups gathered in loving meditations have actually altered the vibrations of the planet where it had been damaged by human thoughtlessness. With a critical mass of people holding the coherent heart vibration, it is possible to bring Mother Earth into ecstasy as she comes into sympathetic resonance with the love of her children.

Coherent emotion feeds the earth. The long emotional waves, as in whale songs and the ring of human hearts, braid the fabric of the planet's grid system. (Another topic too big to handle here but too important not to mention.)

The range of effectiveness even reaches into the solar system. During Earth Day meditations a few years back solar flare activity was favorably influenced. The power of love knows no limits or bounds.

Heart Space and Mystical Experience.

Research featured on the cover of a recent Newsweek demonstrated that the mystical experience, that feeling of being at one with God and all Existence, is produced by shutting down certain control centers and circuits in the brain. Your orientation in space and time, your sense of self awareness, your sense of boundaries, hence of separateness, are created by a continual stream of sensory information being processed by these brain circuits.

After years of meditation, or long focused prayers, or by being in love, one shuts down that delimiting device. Scientists were happy to learn that mystical states were all in your mind. Suppose rather that the mystical state of unity is the reality and the mind has to work continually to create the illusion of separateness.

The experience of timelessness is related to the heart space. Time is the fourth dimension, and the heart, the 4th chakra, governs your experience of time. (Type A personalities are compulsive about schedules and are at the highest risk for heart failure.) When you are in the present moment, when love is in your heart, you are oblivious to the passage of time. This is how hours of tantric lovemaking seem to be timeless.

Maintaining Bliss.

You can maintain a continuously open heart and enjoy uninterrupted feelings of well-being. The secret is to stay in gratitude.

This culture spends little time in thanksgiving. The one day so designated is usually an excuse for excessive food and football. Blessing food at meals (saying grace, gracias, thanks) used to be much more common. Three times a day people reminded themselves to be thankful. Many now take plenitude for granted and miss this opportunity. You might occasionally thank God when something you really want happens, or when you expected something terrible that doesn't happen. You are likely to take for granted all the things that support your peace and comfort, and focus attention on those things you feel are lacking. You see the cup as half empty, not half full. Complaint and criticism are your constant companions.

There is a Sufi story about a saint who thanked God for everything that happened. If it rained on him, he thanked God for the rain. If he had no place to sleep, he gave thanks for the sky and stars above him. The story means that every problem and inconvenience includes an opportunity to learn. It wouldn't have showed up unless there was something within that needed to be examined. Therefore everything can be seen as a blessing.

There is also a deeper meaning. Realize that gratitude and the loving space it produces are so valuable on every level they don't have to be justified. The continual state of gratitude is not a response to changing circumstances. It is a choice you make moment to moment. It is the way to stay healthy, blissful and wise, a way to keep the Soul within the body as Divine Presence.

At least once you have had a mystical moment when the spirit soared and the heart opened. You weren't taught how to recreate this. You knew God was involved because you recognized, you were thrilled by, the Divine essence, but you considered it "an act of grace," beyond your control. In fact you can choose to create this blessed moment. An ongoing state of grace comes from continually saying "thank you."

> Gratitude is the
> secret to living in Bliss.

Qualities of Enlightened Beings.

Certain qualities characterize highly evolved beings. As you work your way toward that state, be conscious of expressing these qualities in your life.

You live in the moment, and are not concerned about past or future.

Clearly everything is in Divine Order.

Discrimination is still important, but there is no judgement or blame.

The Witness is constantly present.

You are unconditionally loving.

Each moment is as if it were your first, free of opinions or positions.

Feeling grateful in all circumstances keeps the heart open and holds Ego and Soul in the proper balance.

The Limited Mind is quiet when nothing is required of it.

Emotions are responses to the moment not patterns from the past.

Chakras are open and clear (i.e., Endocrine glands are balanced and healthy).

Nadis are clear (and physical correlates, vascular and lymph systems, are open and unobstructed).

Male/female dualities are balanced (Ida/Pingala).

Sympathetic and parasympathetic systems are balanced.

Two brain hemispheres operate simultaneously.

Psychic perceptions are clear. Other dimensions are easily perceived.

Kundalini is activated and fully flowing.

There is an ongoing feeling of oneness with creation.

Sexual energy is abundant but free of fantasy and not requiring release.

The body requires careful maintenance and is sensitive to toxins/impurities.

Doors are open to the Collective Unconscious/Akashic Records.

Godliness is evident in everyone you meet and in everything around you.

Life is joyous, not taken too seriously.

A first person pronoun ("I – me – mine – myself") is seldom spoken.

It feels like things are moving but that no one is making them move.

Ego is consistently in loving service to the Bliss Body.

Going Deeper

You are ready now to bring the greatest mystery into your body, the merging of polarized energies, to feel yourself finally becoming whole.

1. Inner Smile. (Chapter 4) Keep bringing clarity and peace down to the heart.

2. FireBreath. (Appendix C) Bring energy up from the earth to the heart.

3. AUM mantra. Inhale deeply and on the exhale intone the mantric sounds "ah oo mm," giving 1/3 of the breath to each sound. For extra effect focus on the resonance in the chest cavity during the "ah" sound, gently contract and relax the genitals during the "oo" sound and feel the buzz in your sinus cavity during the "mm." Continue for several minutes. Feel what happens.

4. Give Thanks. Throughout each day feel gratitude. As you prepare to sleep, review your day and give thanks for every experience, whether sweet or challenging. This will allow you to wake up the next day in a wonderful state of mind, eager for another Blissful day.

Resources

The Heartmath Solution, Doc Childre, Institute of Heartmath, P.O. Box 1463, Boulder Creek CA 95006. website: *heartmath.org*.

The Alphabet of the Heart, Dan Winter. (out of print) *DanWinter@aol.com*.

Stalking the Wild Pendulum, I. Bentov.

Chapter Seven

MALE/FEMALE POLARITY

Balancing the Inner Man and Woman

Suppose that souls incarnate in both female bodies and male bodies in order to explore both ends of the polarity. Within each individual is a male and female aspect with the potential of developing and coming into balance. Only in that balancing do you discover your full magnificence.

This chapter shows you why and how to accomplish this balance.

There have been long periods in earth's history when matriarchal societies were dominant, and periods when equality and partnership existed between male and female beings. Archeological studies bear this out. We are coming out of a long patriarchal period, now moving toward a time of balance in polarities. Because everything unfolds in Divine Order, this is the way it needed to play out. Each aspect needed its gestation time.

Reflecting the cultures from which they arose, most current spiritual paths have been dominated for centuries by male energy, while female energy has been maligned and repressed.

Men are usually stronger physically and mentally, and women have proven to be physiologically and emotionally stronger, according to many sources. Women are also more capable of turning sexual energy into transcendent experience. The female body is designed to access the energy of creation through sexuality, to perform the miracle of birth, of mani-festing new life.

Tantric paths openly revere and tap into feminine power. Buddha told his disciples "Enlightenment resides in the sexual parts of women." (Buddhatvam Yosityonisamasritam) That teaching doesn't appear in many translations available today.

Repression of the Female Essence.

The thoughts that follow are not meant to scold the male reader. That would be preaching to the choir. Any man reading this material has probably come to appreciate feminine energy and is learning to reconnect with it in his own being. This is not an easy task in the climate of these times. For a man to undertake this balancing process he must have a real hero spirit, one that follows his heart regardless of social pressures.

Just step back now and review what has been happening in the world for the last 3,000 years.

Many traditions pay great homage to Divine Mother in her various forms but only as a spiritualized woman. Tantrikas honor the gutsy, lusty, primeval female energy as well, as part of the highest materialization of the divine.

In daily life the Hindu woman is given little authority or respect. When a couple walks down the street, the woman walks several paces behind the man. Women are considered lesser beings who can't become enlightened except through their husbands or by being reborn as a man. Until recently in India a widow was expected to jump onto the funeral pyre with the burning body of her dead husband. Widowers, however, were not required to display such devotion.

In the Western world, Catholics adored the Madonna but burned thousands of women at the stake for using herbal healing methods or exercising their intuition. Healing or psychic powers were considered to come from the "dark side," from dealings with the devil. The Christian churches are very afraid of female power and have controlled its expression for the last 2,000 years.

The Church established itself as the sole intermediary between man and God. If people discovered they could reach God directly and didn't need the Church anymore, then the Church would lose its power over its members. If anyone displayed spiritual understanding independent of the Church, they were excommunicated or executed. As a result, many women today are reluctant to recognize and display their spiritual power. 2,000 years of conditioning doesn't go away quickly.

Cultures with a heavy Catholic/Christian influence still maintain the saint/slut dichotomy. They reward women who repress their sexuality and view women who enjoy their sexuality as whores. It is said that if you don't enjoy sex it isn't a sin, and its obvious converse.

There is strong evidence that Mary Magdalene was not a prostitute at all, but rather was a tantric adept, and that she instructed Jesus in the tantric arts. This information certainly was long since expunged from most histories. (See Resources.)

In the last century repression has continued. Women in eastern Europe, recently released from Communist domination, have lost contact with their femininity because it was severely dishonored. An attitude impressed on a society for two generations works its way into the culture and doesn't have to be taught to the third generation.

Middle Eastern and Asian cultures are, or have been, the most abusive to women, treating them like property and giving them no voice. Certain Islamic sects perform clitoridectomies on young girls in the name of purification. Thereby they ensure a woman's feeling of powerlessness and prevent her from experiencing sexual pleasure.

Tantric schools of India, China and Tibet are all based on the principle of balancing, blending and reuniting the male and female energies. The resulting fusion theoretically provides a dynamic expansion into a higher plane of Existence. In practice, many cultural traditions fall short of this ideal.

For centuries Taoism was based on a process of single cultivation. It encouraged the man to balance his energies by using women as objects in his own pursuit of immortality. This view was an extension of the prevailing culture in which Taoism arose. At that time in China women were thought to exist solely for men's use. Taoist men were trained to absorb the LifeForce from their female partners. Consistent with the no-victim principle, you can assume the women had agreed to such a system.

Taoist masters renowned for attaining incredibly long lives have done so at the expense of many women. Master Li Ching Yuen, founder of the Wu Chi Tao rejuvenation system, was reported to have lived over 250 years, and during that time buried twenty-three wives. His longevity resulted, in part, from his diet and exercises but primarily because he could absorb the essence of each wife for his own benefit.

Even though most of the practitioners of this type of Taoism were male, there were women in this tradition who became equally skilled in extracting the male essence to maintain their youth. The priestesses in temples of Tibet and Egypt were also said to have relieved the young monks of their excess energy.

Lovers frequently draw from their partners unknowingly. After sexual union one partner might be consistently energized and refreshed while the other feels exhausted. This subtle drain is the cause of many marital tensions, usually going unrecognized, with the irritations manifesting in other ways.

Dual cultivation, where energy is equally shared and exchanged between male and female partners, came into practice in China during the Ming Dynasty, a Chinese spiritual renaissance beginning in 1368. Consciousness of the people started elevating at that point, and men could see women as divine entities.

The practice of binding women's feet was not originally done for aesthetic reasons alone. All of the yin energy points are in the feet. When normal growth and development of the feet is prevented, not only is there great pain and difficulty in walking, but the yin points in the feet atrophy, causing the energy to go into the groin, producing more Yin essence for the men to drain.

This practice seems barbaric, but even today it is fashionable for women to wear high heeled shoes which puts constant pressure on the Bubbling Spring, the point in the sole of the foot where earth energy enters the body. That energy is drawn up into the sex center causing the hips to sway more seductively, an erotic visual treat for men. Styles have taken advantage of the design of the female body for men's pleasure and arousal. Women go along to get attention, and also to enjoy the extra rush of feminine energy.

In this culture, as liberated as it pretends to be, the incidence of physical violation of women is appalling. Domestic violence is at frightening levels. Rape is rampant, especially date rape. Until recently it was mostly unreported because of the insensitive way it is handled by the legal system. It was assumed that the woman provoked the attack and got what she deserved. A woman was publicly humiliated when trying to prosecute. That has improved a bit.

The incidence of incest is staggering. Violated girls usually assume the blame and spend their lives in hidden shame and mistrust. Until recently it was the unspeakable taboo. Now that taboos are lifting and people can talk, they are discovering that an astounding number of children, even little boys, have been molested by family members and teachers. Keep reminding yourself that there are no victims. Transcending this trauma can produce enormous spiritual growth and compassion and is an experience many souls have chosen.

Men and women alike have dishonored female energy for thousands of years, but this is changing. Now is the time for goddess energies to reemerge on the planet to balance with the male. Women are reclaiming their divine heritage as the goddess who brings forth life. Men are reclaiming their sensitivity and their appreciation of things feminine.

Traditional Worship of the Divine Feminine.

Many cultures have identified various feminine qualities and created for each quality a deity who can be worshipped as an abstraction of the quality. The Tibetan practice includes focusing on an image, such as the divine mother Tara, and pulling that image/energy into your body, thereby incorporating the attributes that deity represents.

The Hindu tradition reveres many female deities including Saraswati, goddess of arts and science, Lakshmi, goddess of grace and abundance, Durga, the warrior spirit, Kali, who destroys egos, and many many more. The ancient temple in Hirapur, India celebrates sixty-four yoginis as female nature spirits. Through chanting and ceremonial offerings to the appropriate deity, the supplicant would hope to receive her particular benefits.

The ten Mahavidyas offer a form of goddess energy you can explore. Each represents one step in the cycle of creation and destruction. If your personal efforts at creation get interrupted in some predictable way, focus on the deity representing that difficult phase of the cycle could help you remove the obstruction and return to the flow. A complete description of this cycle and ten gorgeous yantras that support the energies are available from Tantrika International.

Polarity in Relationships.

Yogic techniques teach you to balance and blend polarized energies. The energies that you embody reflect your attitudes about male and female characteristics. Practicing Ipsalu techniques helps you develop a new awareness of, and appreciation for, your own inner male and female aspects.

Most of you live out your lives in a highly polarized condition. Your culture has defined masculine and feminine roles. Men are trained to be unemotional, at least emotionally uncommunicative, resistant to intuitive promptings, uncomfortable at nurturing. These female qualities are seldom expressed by men because they aren't approved by family and society.

Traditionally women have accepted a subordinate role as caretakers for their men and children, in part because the display of male characteristics by a woman has been discouraged until recent years. Women who are assertive and competitive, or who seek professions in science, construction, law, medicine or military, areas long claimed as male domain, have had a real battle against the prevailing current. A woman in a managerial role is considered a manipulator for doing exactly what a man in the same position would do to be considered a shrewd businessman.

Now women are more fortunate. Many are encouraged from an early age to develop their minds, competitiveness and their physical potential, qualities formerly associated with masculinity. The women's lib movement struggled to regain women's power, but they went about it in a way that didn't bring real satisfaction. They tried to outdo men at being masculine rather than tapping into the incredible power of their latent femininity. Role definitions have certainly blurred in the last few decades, often leaving people confused. Men seem particularly set adrift by these changes.

Many women find that psychic abilities come to them quite easily. Their intuitive nature is inborn. Men usually have to cultivate these abilities. The tantric sciences develop in men qualities that come naturally to women. Men can become more intuitive, more soft, more in tune with nature, allowing psychic impressions to come through. For a man to truly honor the female essence, he must recognize feminine energy within himself, his Inner Woman, and trust his "dark side." It is unfamiliar and initially frightening, but it soon grows on you.

One male student recently wrote, "Going into the (Ipsalu) Level 2 puja, I expected we men would recognize and adore the divine feminine in our sisters. We did. I expected my heart to swell with gratitude for the gifts of grace, strength, beauty and loving-kindness they brought us. It did. I loved softening and opening in their arms – becoming a brother, a teenage lover, a young husband, a baby, a daddy – each sweet lotus polishing an aspect of this jewel. Now the scent of lotus is everywhere. I rest in the lotus always. More and more I experience the world as feminine. I find it easier to surrender each day. As my own goddess self develops, I'm able to move in ways that were never possible before."

Polarity as an Expression of Hormones.

Sex hormones determine the expression of polarity in the body. Every body produces both estrogen and testosterone in varying degrees at different times of their lives, a process controlled by the pituitary gland (6th chakra) and the gonads (testes or ovaries – 2nd chakra).

Around age eighteen, men and women are most highly polarized. Men have the highest level of testosterone they will ever have, women have the least. Testosterone is responsible for both sexual and violent behavior. Denied a sexual outlet, and not having learned how to transmute sexual energy into higher expression, a man might turn toward violence. This is seen in cultures that limit men's sexual activity – like the Irish-Catholic in a pub brawl or the Moslem terrorist. Some people use violence to get sexually aroused and/or satisfied.

Military training takes advantage of this hormonal abundance. Not long ago young recruits were directed to march in formation, carrying a rifle on one shoulder and holding their scrotum with the other hand to stimulate more hormones. They would sing a marching song: "This is my rifle and this is my gun. This is for fighting and this is for fun." By forbidding any sexual release, including masturbation, the knowing drill sergeant was able to quickly transform a gentle young man into a killer.

As a man matures, he gradually produces more estrogen and less testosterone. He becomes softer, more sensitive. In East Indian society a man uses his first twenty-five years for education, his second twenty-five years to raise a family and earn a living. At age fifty, the male change of life, he can look forward to retiring from family and business life and devoting his full energies to meditation and spiritual development.

In the Western culture men at that age are more likely grieving the loss of their male drive, chasing after younger women trying to recapture it, while downing millions of tablets of Viagra.

As the man is becoming more feminine, the woman is becoming more masculine. Women's estrogen production drops off sharply at about age fifty. The change of life can be very smooth. Hot flashes and emotional swings can be controlled by practicing tantric techniques such as Sahajoli Mudra and Alternate Nostril Breathing, so the decline of estrogen is gentle and balanced. The increasing male energy allows her to become the sorceress, to take on wisdom and power previously unavailable to her. Again, this is a time for celebration, a rite of passage, not for mourning lost youth.

The fully realized masters, whether male or female, reach a place of perfect balance between their masculine and feminine aspects. They don't come to a neutral place, but rather expand to include the entire spectrum. People looking at Babaji's picture for the first time sometimes see the image as female, but looking more deeply into the picture they see a complete masculine aspect as well.

Myth of the Soul Mate.

Some mythologies hold that each individual was originally androg-ynous and at some point was split into male and female parts. Each then wanders through life in search of their other half so they can return to that original wholeness. This belief forces you to look outside yourself for completion rather than turning within to own and integrate the inner male and female parts of your Being.

One woman recently shared "I've always been a strong 'Shakti' and consequently felt a strong need for a 'Shiva' in my life. Since I started practicing the Alternate Nostril Breathing Technique I have experienced a sense of balancing my own feminine energy with my own masculine energy. My reality has been altered because I finally 'got it' that I was already complete within myself. How freeing! No longer needy of a man, I have found my Beloved (life partner). I am experiencing fulfillment in a way I never knew was possible."

A Theory on War Between the Sexes.

Because the earth energy is feminine, a male child in this culture feels out of place here. Also when a male child realizes that he is separate from his mother, he feels cut off from his Source. He must rely on his wit or brute strength to survive. The prospect is frightening and a man's psyche is built on a foundation of fear. Society has set up severe penalties for a man who admits to feeling fear. This simply isn't tolerated. Children humiliate the "chicken" who won't go along.

Cowards on the battlefield are shot. The sensitive, gentle, frightened boychild is forced to create an uncaring facade to take refuge.

On the other hand, the female child does not suffer from this cutting off because she resonates naturally with the earth. She carries within her body the same creative powers as her mother. In a society based on male domination, men realize that women have a huge advantage. Men go to great lengths to keep women from discovering their true power. Repression of women has resulted from men's fear. A woman's response to the repression is a deep boiling anger and frustration because she is not allowed to express herself. Her psyche is based on this anger. Again, society has set it up that a woman is not allowed to express her anger overtly. And so she finds devious and covert ways to express it and to get back at men: manipulative schemes, punishing remarks, sexual teasing, emasculating behaviors. Each gender seems to find pleasure in abusing the other.

A man can find that Shakti force within himself, can rediscover his latent "feminine" aspects and can reunite with his Source. A male student reported, "There is no doubt that tantric practices, particularly the (Ipsalu) Level 2 course, have helped me access what are generally considered feminine energies: warmth, compassion, receptivity, and above all, surrender. Like many men, desiring continuous strength, I recoiled from the idea of surrender and equated it with weakness. The depth of my emotional pain, created by needing to control outcomes and my perpetual resistance to the now, motivated me to practice surrender. This surrendering process was encouraged and facilitated by all my contacts with tantra and has resulted in an ongoing state of peace, freedom and joy that I had scarcely dreamed possible."

The Second Level Cobra Breath is Ipsalu's best technique to support this shift in consciousness, this balancing of energies.

Seeing the Divine in the Opposite Sex.

Currently in somewhat tantric circles, women are often referred to as goddesses. Sometimes it feels like a new form of flattery, a refinement on an old predatory game. The term is also being used to market leg razors, clothing, etc. In the Level 2 Ipsalu course, Bliss in Relationship, a tantric ritual (puja) is performed where a man learns to truly honor the feminine goddess force. This practice allows for a major transformation of consciousness.

In puja the men create a circle where each has his personal space, his temple. The women, dressed in divine costume, rotate through the temples, sharing a sweet (non-sexual) energy exchange for a few minutes with each man in turn. The focus is on recognizing and honoring the highest aspect of each Being. Women, finally receiving the recognition denied them their entire lives, step easily into their magnificence, and are then able to truly express their full capacity for boundless love.

Man's relationship to woman shifts from a game with offense and defense strategies to a genuine love. One student reported his experience: "Going into the puja of the goddess, the feeling of love and acceptance flowed so strongly between us, I felt this feeling was possible with all women. Every one of the goddesses were so different. Each experience was as different as the goddesses. And yet every one of them was so beautiful and magical, all held a piece of the whole. So different, yet you could love all women through any one of them."

UNITY FROM DUALITY

This is a brief digression into a more theoretical, intellectual approach, in the interests of maintaining a balance.

Polarity in Vibration.

The physical universe is based on the principle of duality. Every tradition expresses this in some way, including ancient Tantric scripture. Before the Universe came into being, pure consciousness existed in a static state of perfect equilibrium. The Universal Mind is light at rest, a mind not functioning, where there is no movement. But together with the desire for inertia was the conflicting desire for creative expression. The inherent potential for creation existed in the Universal Womb/Mind, like an unlimited seed (represented by Bindu). From this point of light (consciousness) all creation unfolded.

The vibrations that make up the life force spectrum consist of points of contraction (negative) and areas of expansion (positive) within a waveform. Each wave creates an action and reaction. We perceive the action, but the reaction is not perceptible to your limited senses. This creates the illusion of movement, of physical reality.

Just as a movie is a projection of film images, creating the illusion of movement, still the picture never leaves the film, and we don't perceive the gaps. So the Universe is a projection of mind ideas which never leave the mind.

A whole course could be devoted to this complex subject. (In fact there is an excellent but very technical home-study course available. See Resources.)

Within Bindu were two poles of energy, positive and negative, extending out from the fulcrum, the still point of pure consciousness. In the body the optic thalamus serves as a fulcrum for the pineal and pituitary glands, the male and female centers. The positive pole is represented by Shiva, the negative pole is represented by Shakti. When they come into perfect balance, etheric vision is possible. The male and female must always remain in balance with each other to maintain the illusion, but they can be out of balance with the fulcrum, like a see-saw.

Shiva is the static principle, pure consciousness, beyond qualities. Shakti is the dynamic aspect of reality, the world face, cosmic energy in motion. These are the forces which created and maintain the physical universe. Taoism calls them yang and yin. The Old Testament gives us Noah (which means stillness) who had three offspring: Ham (light), Shem (form) and Japeth (beauty).

In practical terms, masculine people tend to day dream about their ideas until a feminine person comes along to urge the idea into realization. It's been said "Behind every successful man there is an exhausted woman," that is, Shakti energy propels an idea from static consciousness to dynamic manifestation. Some people have learned to access both their masculine and feminine aspects and can do the whole job themselves.

As long as Shiva and Shakti were joined, they were dormant, but once a split occurred, the spark of creation began as they played and interacted with each other, trying to rejoin. A great explosion took place which formed the nebulae of creation. These nebulae vibrate at an incredible speed, setting up ultrasonic waves, the first manifestation of cosmic prana.

Scientists agree that, wherever there is life, there are electrical properties. Science confirms the existence of electro-magnetic flows, which are influenced by positive and negative ions and by the earth's electro-magnetic field.

The earth appears to be a huge magnet with the North Pole being positive and the South Pole negative. Each pole attracts opposite particles and repels similar, setting up energy circuits around the planet. These currents affect your minds and bodies in ways you may not realize.

The ElectroMagnetic Body.

The body, like the earth, can also be considered a magnet, with the top of the spine a positive pole and the base of the spine negative. This creates a continual flow of energy between the two poles. Electric current creates magnetic fields that spread infinitely at the speed of light.

Science is beginning to see the brain and central nervous system as transmitters and receptors of electromagnetic waves, transmitting and receiving information. Every thought and body function produces a vibration which is transmitted to every form in creation. As you practice, you learn not only to maintain harmony within your bodies, but to project harmony into the atmosphere around you.

Electro-magnetic fields are composed of ions – tiny particles with positive and negative charges which penetrate all matter. Every organ and process of your bodies and minds are very much influenced by the ions in and around us. In crowded city environments, positive ions predominate and people can become irritable, depressed and lethargic. On a beach or in the mountains, negative ions are abundant and the body and mind become refreshed. The absorption of ions is an essential function of respiration. You are well advised to seek an environment that is pure and simple.

It has been shown that the negative pole of a magnet has a dramatic effect on the body's ability to oxygenate the cells and that sleeping with your head pointed north or even with the negative pole of a magnet at your head has powerful effects on the body's self-healing capacity.

The Trinity – Ida, Pingala and Sushumna.

There are three main nadis near the spine for distribution of energy and consciousness in the human body: The most important is Sushumna, the neutral central canal, beginning at the root chakra, traveling back to the spinal column and up the center channel of the spine. The current flowing down the right side of the spine is called Pingala. This is the positive, electrical, male current. Flowing up the left side is Ida, the negative, magnetic female prana. Sometimes these are pictured as running in front and back of the spinal canal.

Sushumna connects with Ida and Pingala at the base center and again at Ajna where Ida and Pingala terminate. Sushumna continues on, terminating at the crown chakra above the head. Often they are pictured crossing at each chakra.

Actually, the channels form a three-dimensional helix around the spine, a form much like the DNA coil. That would be challenging for most people to visualize.

The images serve, by mental projection, as a way to draw in cosmic energy. After some practice you can feel the helix form.

Shiva is always depicted carrying a three-pointed staff, the trident, representing Ida, Pingala and Sushumna. These three energy flows make up your internal trinity – body, mind and Soul (Prana, Chitta and Atman). Your every action in life can be categorized as either physical, mental or spiritual and is dependent on these three energies. Each of these three currents has its own distinctive qualities and properties and produces its own effects.

Tantra equates Shakti and Shiva with body and mind (prana and chitta), manifesting in the human form through Ida and Pingala. It is through Sushumna that Kundalini, that high-powered spiritual force, has to move. This passage opens up only when the male and female channels are equally open. Then the mental and physical energies become even and rhythmic. The mind is quiet and the body relaxed.

Consciousness and Mind.

Pingala is responsible for external awareness and motivating the body. It controls the sympathetic nervous system. Ida withdraws the mind and activates internal awareness through the parasympathetic nervous system. Sushumna is the passage of transcendental consciousness. These correspond to the three states of consciousness which you regularly experience: the waking state, the dream-sleep state, and the dreamless state of deep sleep.

In the waking state the mundane world is perceived through the gross body. Here pleasure comes from sense gratification as your connections with the world come through the sense organs, all functions of Pingala. For most people, life is experienced only in the lower level of the mind, the "mental pool" of the 3rd chakra, the Limited Mind. There is a higher strata of mind called the Cosmic Mind or Unlimited Mind, accessed through the 6th chakra, of which the unawakened person is completely ignorant. It is a subtle strata, although all vital energies are active in that cosmic area of the mind.

At a deeper level, you encounter the subconscious realm of the dream state. There you experience as an etheric or pranic body, your stored memories and perceptions (2nd chakra). There is no input from the senses, so the experience is totally subjective, the domain of Ida.

When you sink into the deep sleep state, you enter the unconscious layer of mind and experience your astral body (4th chakra). Here the lower mind and body are inert and you are unaware of your existence. This unconscious realm is associated with the Sushumna channel before it is awakened.

We continually pass through these three levels of consciousness, usually with no awareness of the experience. The yogis found that through concentration and meditation on the breath and prana, they could pass from one state to the next without losing awareness. They could learn to experience all three levels simultaneously. They could even pass beyond the barriers of the finite mind into the infinite, ascending to the Cosmic Level of your minds.

Yoga Nidra, yogic sleep as described in Appendix B, is your most powerful tool for accessing and healing these other strata.

Dual Brain.

The human brain is really two distinct organs, each with different functions. Medical research has demonstrated that when the bridge between the two hemispheres (corpus callosum) was cut, the two body sides initially acted very differently. The left hemisphere is an efficient computer, fine for mathematics, linear logical processes, verbal language and rational detail work. It also is colorless, predictable and utterly out of touch with the emotional or spiritual aspect of a being. Most meditation practices focus on the stillness of Shiva energy, ignoring the Shakti. The meditator becomes very mental, the body becomes old and wasted.

The right hemisphere works through intuition and is non-linear, musical, emotional and creative. It controls the interior body functions, the visceral activities. Conscious use of this part is not developed, not encouraged and not even recognized as a valid mode of operation. It works unconsciously. When it does demand occasional expression, the results are often irrational, bewildering outbursts from a fragmented emotional body. In its immature state, full of repressed material, it is a child out of control. Potentially, it is the organ of higher faculties, the font of mystical experience.

Most people haven't learned to use both aspects of their natures. There is an intercerebral competition, a dominance or inhibition blocking the cooperative use of these hemispheres. You have only to watch any movie made in the forties to see how your heroes and role models were totally polarized. The men were portrayed as cold and unfeeling, the women given to hysteria and incapable of reason. Anyone locked into either mode is severely limited. Society has made considerable progress from that highly polarized time.

The most successful people have naturally integrated right and left brain functions. They've learned how to use the right brain to get the intuitive "Aha," the gut feeling about a problem, and then turn to the left brain to work out the details to implement that solution.

Research has shown how greater brain hemisphere cooperation can be learned through biofeedback. After a stroke, one hemisphere can learn to take on the functions of its damaged opposite. Jnana Yoga is devoted to shutting down the thought process, bringing the two brains together to receive illumination. Tantra uses the breath and sexual energy to achieve that union.

Alternate Nostril Breath.

As you closely observe the breath, you usually discover that the nostrils are not equally involved. One nostril is doing most of the breathing at any given moment. The dominant nostril changes at regular intervals, about every forty-five minutes.

Extensive research has been done in correlating the alternation of cerebral hemispheric dominance with nasal dominance, concluding that the more open nostril indicates the control by the opposite brain hemisphere. Researchers could have turned to the yogic tradition which has developed highly efficient methods for balancing the two hemispheres and studied this rhythmic alternation. An entire science, Swara Yoga, has grown up around this subject.

When the right nostril is open, mental energy is dominant – the male principle flowing through Pingala channel. It controls the sensory nerves in the eyes, nose, tongue, ears and skin. If you try to meditate while this nostril is predominant, your mind will wander. You will be inclined to review something in the past, plan something in the future, or solve a problem.

When the left nostril is open, lifeforce energy is dominant – the female principle. It flows through the Ida channel, controlling the organs of action: speech, hands, feet, reproductive, and excretory organs. If you attempt meditation, the body will be restless, wanting to wiggle, to walk, talk, or eat.

During the moments when dominance is switching and a point of balance is achieved (both nostrils equally open), spiritual energy is in control. The energy travels through the Sushumna channel in the center of the spine. At this moment you can easily experience deep meditation, perceive the colors or sounds of subtle energies or contemplate the higher truths. Your spiritual potential can be activated. This is the goal of all yogic practice.

By adjusting the breath patterns, you can prepare yourself appropriately for the demands of the moment. If you need quick vitality or to be aggressive, close the left nostril, breathe through the right. If you wish to be more nurturing, close the right nostril, breathe through the left. Before you go into meditation, create a balance in the openness of the nostrils.

Union in Yantras.

Contemplating the sacred geometry of certain shapes, yantras, stimulates specific energies in the body.

The Shri Yantra, the greatest yantra, graphically represents the integration of male and female energies, reflecting the male and female components of the chakras, coming to the central point of Bindu. The triangles pointing down represent the vulva, the yoni opening up into cosmic space. The triangles pointing up represent the lingam entering the yoni, to create life at the point of Bindu, giving birth to your expanded consciousness, your ability to transcend duality to enter the state of Absolute reality. The smallest triangle in the center represents the Cosmic Womb, holding the Bindu dot of cosmic fire. The points of the triangles form an egg shape, representative of the Cosmic Egg.

OM is the seed mantra, the sound of creation. The Shri Yantra is the graphic representation of OM, depicting the forces of creation. Iron filings scattered on a surface, surrounded with the OM sound, arrange themselves into the Shri Yantra form. Meditating on this yantra stimulates the Third Eye (pineal gland) and opens etheric vision. Focusing on Bindu (associated with the optic thalamus) pulls you back to that still point of pure consciousness.

On the cover of early editions of *Jewel* is the image of a serpent swallowing its tail. This ancient symbol represents the completion of duality. The male (head) reconnects with the female (tail), the coming together of polarities to form a circle, which represents completion or wholeness. This can be seen as coherent vibrations where the male (fast) frequencies are nested in the slow (female) carrier waves.

Polarity in Tantric Practices.

Mastering this duality in your yogic/tantric practices and in your relationships prepares you to master your physical embodiment and transcend its limitations.

Sexual arousal, when done tantrically, activates the Kundalini and creates the potential for a sublime spiritual experience. This can happen for an individual by balancing the Ida and Pingala channels and allowing Kundalini to well up within Sushumna. For a couple, the female body serves as the Ida channel, easily pulling up the earth's negative magnetic energy through her vagina, while the male body serves as the Pingala channel, with ready access to the heavenly electric energy through his crown.

When you share Cobra Breath with your mate, your coupled energies take you both into transcendent states. In the passion of Tantric practice, each man becomes Shiva and each woman becomes Shakti, but then the polarities switch and Shiva becomes Shakti, Shakti becomes Shiva.

If the energies between partners are well balanced and shared, their etheric bodies join into a single body at the moment of orgasm. Each neutralizes the other's polarity, each completes the other, and both experience the Kundalini ascending.

A woman in this culture can reach Bliss through orgasm more easily than a man because she is able to pull her own negative energy up her spine to meet her own positive energy in the brain. She doesn't require a partner to do this because she is fairly comfortable with both poles of her energy spectrum.

A man usually has to tap into a woman's dynamic to move his lower body (negative) energy since men are often resistant to the emotional experiences that are invoked. Therefore bringing Shiva down to meet Shakti is not a well-known process. The special power of Ipsalu Tantric Kriya Yoga comes from its ability to help you access, fully experience and embrace the entire range of your divine humanness, the entire male-female spectrum.

Going Deeper

1. Read "Cosmic Unity of Opposites," Lesson 4 in *Jewel*.

2. Make a list of qualities you associate with the members of the opposite sex, especially qualities that put you off. If you have such generalized judgements, begin to explore where they came from and bring those memories up for healing. Remember the mirror principle. Attitudes about external personalities reflect attitudes about your internal male/female qualities. If a man has decided he can't trust women, he won't trust his own intuitive promptings. If a woman believes powerful men are dangerous, she might suppress her own outgoing power.

3. Continue with daily practice, adding the Alternate Nostril Breath. Your routine could now take this form:

ACTIVATE THE BODY

- Complete Breath (Chapter 2)
- Rishi Isometrics (Chapter 2)

STILL THE MIND

- Alternate Nostril Breath (below)
- Hong Saw Breath Mantra (Chapter 2)

AROUSE SEXUAL ENERGY

- Vajroli Mudra for men or Sahajoli Mudra for women (below)

TRANSMUTE

- Solar/Lunar Breath (below)

ENJOY

- Quiet meditation for 5 to 15 minutes. Do nothing. Just be.

Alternate Nostril Breath

By the process of alternate nostril breathing you can balance the pranic flow through the three main currents of prana in the body –

169

Ida, Pingala, Sushumna. A slightly different version of this breath is presented in *Jewel in the Lotus*. This special way of alternate nostril breathing produces different results:

- To renew the human pranic battery and electrify all the body's nerve currents, clearing away negative energy.
- To stimulate organic functions to high activity and bring well-being and harmony to your mind/body complex.
- To purify the body and assist in expelling wastes.
- To put Sushumna into operation for Kundalini awakening.

1) Sit in easy pose or a chair.

2) Begin by thoroughly exhaling the air in your lungs, using both nostrils.

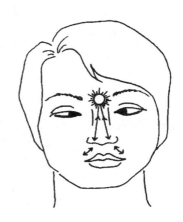

3) Using the right hand, close the right nostril with the thumb, position forefinger at Ajna Chakra, resting second finger alongside left nostril (Shiva Mudra). Inhale through left nostril for 6 counts. See a laser beam of light entering the nostril, striking the Third Eye.

4) Retain breath for 3 counts.

5) Press left nostril closed, release right nostril, and exhale through right nostril for the count of 6, seeing a beam of light flowing from the Third Eye out the nostril.

6) Hold the air out for 3 counts.

7) Keep left nostril closed and inhale through right nostril for 6 counts.

8) Hold breath for 3 counts. Then release left nostril, closing off right nostril and exhale through left nostril for 6 counts. Hold air out for 3 counts. This constitutes one round.

9) Perform seven rounds. Then rest.

Vajroli Mudra (for Men)

1) Sit on a thin cushion or folded blanket in cross-legged position.

2) Relax with eyes closed. Focus on a point at the top center of the pubic bone.

3) Using the muscles that would stop urination, lift the lingam upward. Maintain relaxation in the perineum and anus.

4) Hold the contraction for 10 seconds, then relax for 10 seconds.

5) Continue to contract and relax for a few minutes.

Sahajoli Mudra (for Women)

1) Make sure your foot is clean.

2) Sit on a thin cushion or folded blanket in cross-legged position. Place your heel inside the vagina entrance. If that's uncomfortable, sit on a rolled sock.

3) Relax with eyes closed. Focus on a point at the top center of the pubic bone.

4) Contract and relax the vaginal muscles, becoming more intense.

5) Contract and hold for 10 seconds, then relax for 10 seconds.

6) Continue for a few minutes.

Solar/Lunar Breath (Polarizing Pranayama)

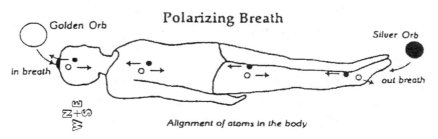

Polarizing Breath

Golden Orb

Silver Orb

in breath

out breath

Alignment of atoms in the body

Lie flat on your back in the corpse pose with your head pointing north. This helps to align the prana currents in your body with the earth currents.

The Solar/Lunar Breath rejuvenates the entire body. It refreshes the complete nervous system and the 72,000 nadis It is healing to every other part of the body by allowing prana to flow throughout. This helps to bring balance between you and the environment. Maintaining balance saves you many years and lifetimes by eliminating the accidents and karma created by an unbalanced mind and body.

1) Imagine a golden orb just above your head. Inhale, and bring the warm, solar energy into your head through the crown chakra, clear down into your feet. At the base of the feet imagine a silver orb. As you exhale, feel the energy of the silver orb enter through the soles of your feet. Continue pulling the cool, silver energy up through your body to the crown.

2) Repeat twice more.

3) As you inhale, apply root lock and feel the silver orb enter through your feet. Pull the cool, silver energy up through your body just to the heart (Anahata Chakra.) Hold the breath there a moment, feeling the lunar energy.

4) Exhale, releasing root lock, and stay aware of silver energy at Anahata.

5) Inhale, apply root lock and bring the warm, golden solar energy down into Anahata Chakra; this time allowing it to mingle with the cool lunar energy.

6) Exhale, releasing root lock and sending solar energy up towards the head, lunar down towards feet.

7) Repeat steps 3 to 6 twice more.

8) Inhale, apply root lock, and this time send both lunar and solar energies to the heart. Hold the breath, mixing the energies at the heart. It appears as white light. Feel the warm expansion of your heart center.

9) Take a sniff of air, then slowly exhale, releasing the root lock and sending lunar energy out of the feet, solar out of the head. Relax in corpse pose for at least 10 minutes.

The gold color represents the sun, the father. The silver represents the moon, or mother. Balanced polarity (Shiva/Shakti, yang/yin, male/female) restores the primordial unity of life.

Set aside a certain time each day to do these exercises and each day try to extend the time a little longer. With practice you will find that you are more relaxed, have increased vital energy, look and feel younger and more healthy. Give yourself enough time to see results, and never force or over-tire yourself. Breathing, like meditation, is a lifelong practice, and the better the breathing, the longer the life.

Resources

The Chalice and the Blade, Riane Eisler, for information about pre-biblical civilizations based on partnership and honoring.

Gnostic Gospels, Elaine Pagels, for information on Mary Magdalene. References from Egyptian scrolls buried in 300 AD how Jesus favored Mary, kissed her on the mouth frequently and openly, referred to her as the woman who knew the all.

Mahavidya documented by Kirby Jacobson. Ten colored yantras and brochure available from Tantrika International.

Kundalini Tantra by Satyananda Saraswati for Vajroli practice. A wealth of Kriya techniques. Available from Tantrika International.

Russell's Home Study Course in Universal Law, Natural Science and Living Philosophy, University of Science and Philosophy. Swannanoa, P.O. Box 520, Waynesboro VA 22980, phone: (800) 882-LOVE, website: *philosophy.org*.

Chapter Eight

AWAKENING KUNDALINI

The Next Plateau in Human Development

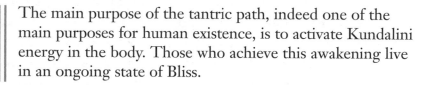

The main purpose of the tantric path, indeed one of the main purposes for human existence, is to activate Kundalini energy in the body. Those who achieve this awakening live in an ongoing state of Bliss.

*K*undalini can be defined as Consciousness, the substratum of Existence, the most refined form of energy on the material plane, the most subtle manifestation of the One from which it is inseparable. Coming into full expression of that universal consciousness marks a quantum leap from the limited human condition into cosmic capabilities. Every spiritual path is designed to accomplish this awakening, the yogic path being the most explicit.

The Key to Humanity's Future.

Kundalini awakening is the next step in human development. Science may suppose that the human brain has attained its highest stage of evolution. Yogis have always known that the brain continues to evolve. It molds itself slowly, imperceptibly. in the direction of a definite target which represents the next plateau in human development. It is within the scope of your imagination and not very far away. What in the world can be more important than this?

Currently the average person uses only 10% of the brain and science is unaware of a purpose for the other 90%. Working with a superior type of consciousness would bring into play much more of the brain's unused capacities. This awakening involves a reconfiguration of the central nervous system, allowing expanded perceptive sensitivities, superior cognitive abilities, intuitive knowingness, inter-dimensional awareness and ability to perform what are now considered miracles.

With this awakened consciousness you will access the secret Source from which all philosophy and science was born, the fountain

175

of all literature, music and art. You will be in touch with the Source of all creativity, nobility, and psychic powers in humankind.

Your most revered teachers have lived in the light of awakened Kundalini where Consciousness becomes aware of its immortal Self in all of its celestial grandeur, sublimity and mystery. In the West this state has been called Christ Consciousness, Cosmic Consciousness, Mystical Consciousness and the Beatific Vision. In the East it's referred to as Self Realization, Enlightenment, Buddha Consciousness, Samadhi, or Satori.

Saints and sages throughout the world have agreed that the essence of this state of being is indescribable. Gopi Krishna, one of the best known Kundalini experts, described four qualities displayed by a person with activated Kundalini:

1) Living in continual Bliss,
2) Having impeccable integrity,
3) Opening to latent genius, and
4) Accessing cosmic wisdom – knowing just what is required to make the most of each unique moment.

Once it is widely understood that life has this innate purpose, and that this possibility is equally accessible to all individuals, perhaps that understanding will mitigate the ideological and religious differences that are now tearing the world apart.

Techniques for working with Kundalini are found in every advanced culture. Similarities between the Tantric Schools of India, China, and Tibet make it apparent that all emerged from a common source. That source is the Immortal Mahavatar Babaji, creator of Kriya Yoga who has worked tirelessly for many centuries from his home at Siddhasharam in Northern Tibet. Babaji is dedicated to advancing the consciousness of the human race.

Kundalini Energy.

The place in the body where dormant energy lies, from which all potential might be accessed, involves a gland tucked under the sacral bone at the lower end of the spine. In Sanskrit it is called the Kunda. Medical science is aware of the organ and refers to it as the coccygeal body, but doesn't understand its function. "Kunda" literally means "reservoir." This reservoir lies dormant as a pool without a single ripple. The energy is sleeping so deeply that one could go through an entire lifetime unaware of it.

"Kundalini" is a little pool of energy that has been activated. Kundalini is not the whole of the Kunda but only a little wave that has been aroused and brought into consciousness. It is a hint of what is possible when the infinite reservoir of primal power is accessed. When that awakening happens, when that energy moves upward to nourish the brain, you are startled to find the dimensions that open and the knowledge and capabilities that are suddenly available. They have always been present but are not in your awareness until Kundalini is activated.

A tiny trickle of Kundalini is already awakened. It animates your body, providing just enough consciousness to get through the day but not enough to access the higher realms. This minimal flow of Kundalini energizes all the senses. As the flow increases, you can access the invisible spiritual dimensions beyond the limits of the senses. As Kundalini awakens you begin to perceive matters of the Soul.

Traditional Model.

Kundalini has traditionally been depicted as a serpent, coiled and sleeping at the base of the spine. When disturbed, it opens its coils as it climbs up to the crown. The undulating Kundalini movement is much like the movement of a serpent and so, for thousands of years, the serpent has been used in many cultures to symbolize rising consciousness. It  is interesting to note that a recent poll showed the snake to be the animal most feared in this country. (Bad press or fear of change?)

 Ancient pictures portray the snake, particularly the cobra, twirled around the hemispheres of the brain. In the center a serpent's head arises representing the awakened crown chakra. In ancient Egypt, Pharaoh wore a headband ("Uraeus") with a serpent image at his forehead.

Kundalini is activated by the energy of Shakti, worshipped in India as the primal energy that created the cosmos. It's the sexual energy that generates love and desire, the driving force of your development, the libido, the "other face of God." In Hindu mythology Shakti, the female divine principle, is required to make the arduous climb to reach Shiva, the male divine principle. Shiva sits above the crown in deep meditation until Shakti arrives to activate him. Once united they realize transcendent Bliss. The techniques of most yogic paths serve to bring Shakti up the spine to meet Shiva and from there they go out of body into transcendental space.

Not many yogis working in this model have achieved the goal, and many who do go mad in the process. Kundalini activation is considered a rare phenomenon in India. Ipsalu suggests that Kundalini awakening requires that Shiva come back down to meet with Shakti at the root chakra. (Kriya yoga is the only school that includes this step.) Once balanced and blended, this mixed energy then ascends the spine through Sushumna.

One who has just been through this ecstatic awakening might attribute that event to your guru or favorite deity, but the awakening always comes from within, from the Inner Beloved.. No one can activate another person's Kundalini.

How it Works.

Physiologically the Kunda interacts with the reservoir of cerebro-spinal fluid at the base of the spine. The fluid continuously flows up to the brain bringing nutrients and bathing every cell. Then the fluid moves back down the spinal circuit carrying away metabolic residue.

The movement of the LifeForce (Shakti) energy magnetizes the spinal fluid. When this magnetized fluid reaches the brain many neurons, formerly dormant, become activated.

There are two main types of pranic energy. The energy accessed at the base of the spine is lunar prana, "Shakti," magnetic feminine energy related to physical manifestation and the lower chakras. The energy accessed in the brain is solar prana, "Shiva," electrical masculine energy coming from the heavens. These two energies are constantly intermixing through your body. If it were not so, life could not continue.

The four ventricles (cavities) in the brain all serve as reservoirs for the cerebro-spinal fluid. When the fluid is magnetized by Shakti energy, the brain reservoirs become a magnetic field which attracts Shiva (electrical energy). Thus the ancient myth is played out in your own physiology.

The energy at the base of the spine and in the genitals is more dense and therefore easier to perceive. It comes from the root chakra. You can feel the rising energy when you do Cobra Breath. If you put your hand slightly above the crown chakra you will feel a cool breeze. That's the LifeForce coming up. It is called serpent fire, but it really is a cool, female energy vibrating up the spine. The solar energy, Shiva, goes down the spine. You cannot feel Kundalini in the brain until you have refined your sensitivity. Tantra teaches you how to upgrade the raw, sexual lustful energy. As you practice the techniques for moving energy up the spine this energy becomes more refined so that it is perceptible in the brain.

Practicing the Cobra Breath pulls more and more magnetic Shakti into the cerebro-spinal fluid to bathe the brain. As a result more electrical Shiva energy, attracted by the opposite polarity, is drawn into the body. Maintaining a balance between these energies is the essence of tantric practice. If the masculine energy predominates, as it does for most people in this culture, the feminine energies are not permitted to move. Only when balance is attained do you experience the ascent of the Kundalini.

Awakening Kundalini.

The full awakening of Kundalini in the body is the most intense spiritual experience available at your stage of development. It might happen suddenly, or gradually over a period of several years. For many people a natural Kundalini boost occurs around age forty. Some get a dramatic preview, a temporary opening, perhaps to inspire them to do what is necessary for a permanent awakening.

The process can be stimulated by a variety of methods:
• Many years of meditation,
• Mechanical vibrations,
• Electro-magnetic currents,
• Sound vibrations,
• Using breath to increase and balance prana, or
• Using sexual energy.

In Ipsalu, Kundalini activation is more systematic. The potential energy lies very close to the 1st chakra and can be activated by stimulating that chakra. Several powerful exercises are suggested later in this chapter.

The Shakti reservoir at the base of the spine is also activated by stimulation of the medulla, that indentation at the base of the skull.

This is the feminine portal of the 6th chakra and it is linked directly to the Kundalini reservoir. The medulla is stimulated by the sounds of the Cobra Breath.

Breath as an Activator.

You can tune in to the movement of this spinal fluid, a process which normally goes on outside of your conscious awareness as does the breath. It is simple to turn conscious attention to the breath, so the breath is used to pull this energy into the spinal fluid. Becoming aware of the movement of spinal fluid takes a little more practice.

Breath is a physical phenomenon which allows you to access the etheric dimension where Kundalini is based. You can also stimulate the sacral reservoir with a rapid intense breath. Increased breath brings in more oxygen to enliven the physical dimension and more prana to stimulate the etheric body. Kundalini is closely related to the amount of oxygen in your body. If you are breathing intensely you are increasing the ratio of oxygen (life energy) to carbon dioxide (death energy). The more oxygen in the system, the more the Kundalini is activated.

Various spiritual paths offer a variety of Kundalini Yoga methods to stimulate the students' energy level and facilitate a rapid awakening of the serpent. The distinctive feature of Kundalini techniques is that they utilize energy (prana/Shakti) as a means to awaken consciousness (Shiva) in the body.

The Tantric Approach.

The tantric path sees sexual energy as one expression of Kundalini. Hence, awakening Kundalini is accomplished simply by bringing consciousness to sexual arousal and orgasm.

Quoting again from Gopi Krishna, "The Lingam-Yoni, the masculine and feminine (genital) symbols, which have been in India from the remote past, denote the reversed action of the cerebro-spinal system, utilizing every spare ounce of the bio-energy normally used for amatory purposes, for the remodeling of the body and brain under high pressure, in which all organs of the body become inextricably involved. With the flow of the Nectar, distilled by the nerves from all parts of the body into the brain, the area of rapture is transferred from the genitals to the cerebrum. The phenomenon is ancient and so widespread it is amazing that modern science has no inkling of it even now."

Conscious, extended lovemaking produces a surplus of hormones, which bring about healing and rejuvenation of the body. Sex hormones, estrogen and testosterone, bring about major changes in the brain during critical development periods – the final trimester of pregnancy, the first four years of life, puberty, change of life (male and female). These hormones enter the nuclei of cells and turn genes on and off, creating permanent changes. They play a part in the Kundalini quantum leap.

The female body has a natural advantage. Intercourse provides some Kundalini stimulation as the G-spot on the vaginal wall is touched. This is one reason why women experience Bliss (Samadhi) during and after sex more often than men. To further enhance her experience, a woman might appreciate manual stimulation of G-spot massage.

The unaware male functions sexually without disturbing Shakti Kundalini. The male body is programmed so that visual stimulation from seeing an attractive female is often enough to activate the 2nd chakra, to produce an erection and ejaculation. The energy can bypass both the heart and the Kunda (1st chakra).

If a man wants to include more Kundalini in his arousal, special techniques may be used to stimulate the prostate (which automatically stimulates the root chakra) including: 1) massage of the perineum, 2) anal stimulation and internal prostate massage, and 3) aswini mudra (tensing and relaxing the anal sphincter).

Directing Kundalini movement is a matter of manipulating sexual energy. In an unaware person orgasmic energy flows down and returns to Mother Earth. The tantric goal is to reverse this flow by sending Kundalini up the spine through the chakras, reaching for the heavens. At the moment of orgasm, if your mind is filled with lustful thoughts and desire for gratification, the energy evoked will be sexual and move downward. If your mind is filled with love and longing for God the orgasmic energy will become Kundalini and move upward to connect you with the Universe. It will circulate with your partner's energy as your bodies merge in many dimensions.

Most people put great value in the bit of pleasure they receive from sexual activity. That arousal is simply the activation of LifeForce energy. Even the limited way people use that energy has produced some of their most important life experiences. Try to comprehend what experiences are possible if they were using this sexual/ Kundalini energy to its full capacity.

When you are in the presence of someone whose Kundalini is awakened and moving, you may experience sexual arousal. A spiritual arousal would be occurring as your energy vibrates faster to match this advanced being, but you have only known this sensation with respect to sexual activity, so that is how you might interpret the sensation.

Both sexual energy and Kundalini are activated by the breath. The breath is the meeting point, the bridge between body and Soul. In Ipsalu, breath is used to access the reservoir of potential energy in the body. The several levels of Cobra Breath are extremely powerful tools to awaken these energies.

Normal sexual arousal is accompanied by rapid shallow breathing. Deep breathing, as in the FireBreath (Appendix C), can produce arousal as the breath stimulates that potential energy. It is unusual to experience the sex act with a quiet breath. When you are able to do so, you will have completed the compulsive phase of your sexual history.

Kundalini Hazards.

This topic is timely. Because of new energies available on this planet, the Kundalini in many people is spontaneously awakening, often without preparation.

There are many documented cases of people who slipped into "Kundalini psychosis," often after periods of intense spiritual practice and/or interaction with a powerful spiritual master. It can actually produce physical illness, hallucinations of demons and divinities and the symptoms of psychotic break. In that startling moment when Kundalini awakens, people suddenly attain an alternate reality where the background energies behind the physical world come into perception. They realize their divine nature and commune with other beings at that level. They experience boundless energy and know with certainty of their immortality.

To illustrate the difference between ordinary consciousness and superconsciousness, remember the story of Helen Keller as depicted in a wonderful movie *The Miracle Worker*. There was a rapturous moment when she suddenly realized the relationship between signing and objects. She realized that things have names and people can communicate through words. Imagine that her vision and hearing suddenly returned in that same moment. Imagine her being flooded by impressions, emotions and information. It would be overwhelming. A sudden awakening of Kundalini produces that sort of bewilderment.

The Kundalini psychosis can be compared to an LSD experience. Suddenly there appears another dimension of reality. Those who have "bad trips" often are unable to accept the truth and clarity that comes to them. Their reaction and resistance to unfamiliar perceptions make the experience highly distressing. The Ego has constructed a sense of reality where it feels safe and competent. When that is ripped away, Ego becomes frightened.

Concerned loved ones usually insist on getting "professional" help in these cases. The accepted medical response to such expanded perceptions is to sedate and dull the mind until it can be controlled. There are countless cases of people who have been hospitalized for spontaneous Kundalini risings. The people have no idea what is happening, nor do those who are caring for them. They only know that it is out of the ordinary and frightening.

The DSM (catalog of all recognized mental disorders) now includes a condition called "Religious Experience." Therapists now have a diagnostic category for Kundalini crises. This is encouraging.

Psychosis occurs when the energy moves too quickly or prematurely before a person is prepared to handle the new energies. The unpreparedness may be at the emotional level. A person who has not brought full awareness to the emotional body and is unwilling to deal with that aspect, could "flip out" rather than face their rejected parts. The unreadiness may stem from attachment to old beliefs and attitudes that one is unwilling to examine.

When this fire of consciousness is burning within, any emotional state will be greatly amplified. Old resentments might turn into rage. A person who lives in loving harmony will find that expanded and increased. This is why it is essential to clear the emotional body before the Kundalini rises.

The Ipsalu methods systematically prepare mind and body to receive this new consciousness by stimulating/activating the channels and chakras in a certain sequence. The issues that lie buried in body tissue and sub-conscious mind are addressed and resolved gradually so they don't come up too quickly.

Your body is a perfect three dimensional manifestation of your beliefs, attitudes and coping mechanisms. As self-limiting attitudes and judgements are dropped, the body reorients itself to the new situation. When Kundalini is activated the body undergoes total transformation. The DNA is being reorganized and upgraded every time you come into the Bliss state.

Kundalini has been referred to as Cosmic Fire. It is a high voltage electromagnetic force that burns differently from normal metabolism. When this energy awakens, programming that no longer serves the higher purpose will be burned away. Internal guidance will suggest lifestyle changes regarding diet and self-maintenance.

Gentle Kundalini Rising.

There is nothing to fear. The Kundalini experience can happen gently in a way that allows you to continue to function in the world as an enlightened being instead of retreating to a hermitage, or being locked away, dysfunctional and unable to care for yourself. In order for Kundalini to rise gently, the Ego must be willing to gradually let go of its attachments. The only thing you have to lose is your idea of who you are as a limited being and what you thought life is about. Since that was all an illusion anyhow, it is a small loss. Something will die in the process: namely limited ego consciousness, that system of beliefs, memories, attachments and attitudes by which you define yourself.

This process requires an enormous leap of faith. You must be willing to admit that your prior life was based on erroneous assumptions. None of your strategies work any more. It requires you to go through a period of time not knowing who you are or what life is about. It requires an emptying out before you can be filled with a new level of understanding.

The unknown is a great challenge. Spiritual seekers are willing to spend endless hours in meditations and rituals and practices, but hesitate to dive into the void. Trust Existence enough to give over control of your life. Surrender to your own higher power.

Notice how willing you are to accept and complete all the unexperienced emotional fragments that are stored at each level of the psyche. These will come to surface in cathartic meditation, in therapy, while making love, or just in the process of life. To deal most effectively with these emotional moments, simply experience them fully and remain present as the non-judgemental Witness.

Creating Your Moment.

The process of awakening is going on all the time for all beings. By doing the Ipsalu Tantra practice you can greatly accelerate that natural process. If you continue to practice regularly, the moment will come when you feel the Kundalini energy rise within you like a gentle electric shock beginning at the sex center rising into the brain. It is a flame yet cold, penetrating as a thorn yet delicate as a flower. Prana is like visible light flowing everywhere but Kundalini shoots up the spine in a thin shaft similar to the coherent light beam of a laser.

When this begins to happen, trust it and ride it as a river raft following the current. Surely everything on this rafting trip is new and frightening. You are entering a new reality and will undergo the same insecurities you felt as an infant suddenly launched in a world you didn't understand. When Kundalini fully awakens, you go through a birthing of the higher Self, a true rebirth, you being both the parent and the child.

Kundalini Moving through Chakras.

Chakras are way-stations along the upward path of the Kundalini. The serpent passes through each chakra and rests a moment, opening the chakra's potential, just as watering a plant brings forth its blossoms. You may have heard of Jacob's Ladder or the Seven Steps to Heaven. These are symbolic references to energy moving up through the seven chakras. (Chakras are discussed individually both in *Jewel* and in the Practicum.)

Tantric practice is designed to stimulate Kundalini energy through the root and sex glands, pulling that sexual energy, via the spine, to the spiritual centers in the brain. It's only a short journey – two or three feet at most – but an arduous one. You must penetrate every level of the psyche along the way. It may be that you have already taken countless lifetimes trying to complete this journey. The time is coming soon for this long-cultivated seed to sprout and come into full blossom. Most people continue to live in the first level of consciousness, the material plane, only two to three feet from their Godliness. Mired in their opinions, they have lost sight of their spiritual heritage.

As you begin to awaken Kundalini and it rises from one chakra to the next, new energies begin to flow through your being. You might occasionally experience involuntary movements (kriyas) indicating resistance to its passage. As the flow becomes steady, goals and desires which you once thought to be important lose their fascination. Consciousness becomes more refined, vibrating at higher frequencies. At each level of consciousness, new dimensions of your Being begin to open up. Eventually you transcend the sensory plane and enter more subtle bodies (etheric, mental, astral.) With new extra-sensory perceptions you access knowledge of the extension of the body into the bodiless, the Soul. Thus Kundalini is the preparation for experiencing your Divine Essence.

When the energy centers are fully activated and Kundalini flows freely, you will for the first time feel like a whole person. In the Ipsalu system this has been designated as the fourth level of spiritual development. (Levels are described in *Jewel,* page 99.)

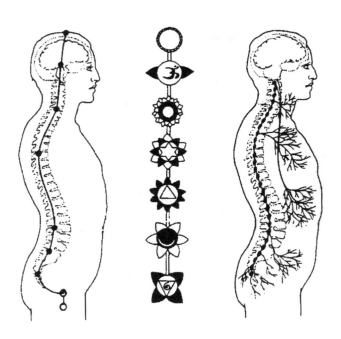

The Granthis.

The spine contains three psychic knots (granthis) which obstruct the flow of Kundalini. These Wisdom Knots are nature's way of preventing a premature Kundalini rising. Each knot represents a barrier in your development which must be transcended. As each knot dissolves it indicates that the body is ready to receive energy at a higher level.

The first knot (Brahma granthi) is at the base chakra. The obstacle is your attachment to outer security, material possessions and selfishness. You can also be stuck at this point through negativity, lethargy and ignorance. Open it with the Root Lock (Moola Bandha).

The second knot (Vishnu granthi) is the doorway to the heart chakra. It deals with the neediness in your attachments to people and to your opinions. You become entangled in strategies for control, ambition and assertiveness and cannot find your way to compassion. Use the Diaphragm Lock (Uddiyana Bandha) to assist in this opening.

The third knot (Rudra granthi) works behind the throat at the seventh cervical vertebrae. This is the first spiritual chakra and the hardest one to open. Here you can become enthralled with your emerging psychic powers and phenomena. You still want to see yourself as a special and separate individual. When Ego-based individuality is relinquished you open the space for further spiritual development. Here the Chin Lock (Jalandhara Bandha) is helpful.

The Triple Lock on page 129 of *Jewel in the Lotus* is one technique to deal with all of these barriers. The locks create a hydraulic pressure. When they release, the energy shoots up. The technique must be accompanied by a willingness to let go of the attitudes and attachments that go with the barriers.

Current Research.

Satyananda Saraswati, source of the Kriya Yoga teachings, declared that the whole universe is contained within the cranium. The space in the center of your brain, the third ventricle, is called the Cave of Brahma (the Creator). There you can experience the Milky Way, which he said (and science concurs) was the point of origin for this galaxy. Once your Kundalini energy is awakened by Tantric practice, an orgasmic consciousness is going on all the time. It's not a visualization. You actually see this happening within you. (See diagram A.) This phenomenon can now be explained in physiological terms.

It was proposed in Chapter 4 that all mystical experiences can be explained in terms of the body. In "Stalking the Wild Orgasm," Itzhak Bentov describes research into the effects of deep meditation on the heart and brain. A recording of a meditator's heart frequencies takes on a rhythmic sine wave pattern caused by a standing wave in the aorta. (More detail in Chapter 6.) This vibration sets up a chain reaction, producing four other vibration patterns in the brain, resulting in polarized currents flowing through the brain and around each brain hemisphere. (See diagram B.)

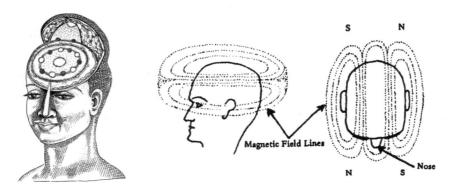

A. Diagram drawn by Satyananda of his vision in deep meditation.

B. Diagram by Bentov of fields entrained by coherent heart vibration.

These polarized currents flow along the sensory cortex in each hemisphere crossing an area that contains a pleasure center. Stimulation of this center creates for the meditator an experience of ecstasy.

In the brain, polarized currents create a magnetic field which becomes an antenna able to tap into information encoded in waves in the environment, information including all knowledge and all wisdom. Tuned to a certain range of frequencies, the brain is both transmitting and receiving information. It is directly in contact with the Cosmic Intelligence.

The tone produced in the heart (EEG) during deep loving state vibrates at about 7 Hz, (the upper theta range) accessible in the brain (EKG) by practicing yoga nidra. Overtones, higher frequencies contained in these heart sounds, set up resonance in the ventricles of the brain – the reservoirs of spinal fluid. This stimulus is conducted up the left side of the neck (Ida channel!) into the skull. This resonant vibration is the "inner sound" reported by many seasoned meditators.

The lateral ventricles project into each hemisphere. Their vibrating fluid sets up resonant vibrations in the corpus callosum, the nerves connecting the two hemispheres. Thus the hemispheres, your male and female aspects, come into a synchronized and balanced state in meditation.

The exact relationship of Kundalini with the fields under investigation has not been determined but bit by bit science is validating this ancient spiritual tradition. The research has just begun. As credibility increases perhaps more people will appreciate, and be open to exploring, the Kundalini phenomenon.

Going Deeper

1. Read *Jewel*, Lesson 7, for more about Kundalini.

2. Read *Moola Bandha, the Master Key* from Bihar School of Yoga to appreciate the many benefits and the power of this vital practice, capable by itself of activating Kundalini. Learn in detail how it effects body, mind and energy. Several advanced forms of the practice are presented for the serious student. Available through Tantrika International.

3. Continue with daily practice, adding the Moola Bandha and Sushumna Activation.

Your routine could now take this form:

ACTIVATE THE BODY

- Complete Breath (Chapter 2)
- Rishi Isometrics (Chapter 2)

STILL THE MIND

- Alternate Nostril Breath
- Hong Saw Breath Mantra (Chapter 2)

AROUSE SEXUAL ENERGY

- Vajroli Mudra for men or Sahajoli Mudra for women
- Moola Bandha (below)

TRANSMUTE

- Sushumna Activation (below) or Cobra Breath, Transmutation Breath, Solar/Lunar Breath

ENJOY

- Quiet meditation for 5 to 15 minutes. Come out into spontaneous movement, BodyFlow.

Moola Bandha (Root Lock)

This technique is presented in *Jewel*, instructing you to contract the anal sphincter. That is a beginning, since that contraction initially includes a perineal contraction. Here you are asked to isolate the perineal muscles for better results.

1) Sit comfortably, pressing the left heel against the perineum or vaginal opening if possible. If that's not comfortable, sit on a knotted sock or small pillow to apply pressure against the perineum. Breathe naturally and relax. Men focus on the perineum (between genitals and anus.) and women on the cervix.

2) Slowly contract the muscles that lift that area up into the body, then relax.

3) Localize your focus so eventually the front urethral muscles (vajroli/sahajoli) and anal muscles (aswini) can remain relaxed during the perineal contraction.

4) Continue for a few minutes.

5) Coordinate the contractions with the breath for more powerful effects. Inhale deeply, lift the perineal area, tuck the chin and hold as long as is comfortable.

6) Relax the chin and the contraction as you exhale. More details and discussion can be found in *Jewel*, page 173.

For clarity compare the three genital contraction points:

For women:
1. Sahajoli mudra (clitoris, lower vaginal muscles and urethra)
2. Moola bandha (upper vagina, near cervix)
3. Aswini mudra (anal muscles/sphincters).

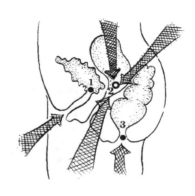

For men:

1. Vajroli mudra (penis)
2. Moola bandha (between anus and scrotum; perineal body)
3. Aswini mudra (anal muscles/sphincters).

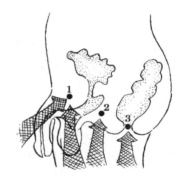

Sushumna Activation

This is another way of balancing male and female currents. Normally energy runs up Ida and down Pingala. By alternating that sequence with its opposite (up Pingala, down Ida) you neutralize the polarity. An energy vortex forms around the spine as a result of this oscillation.

This process charges the dormant Kundalini with prana, causing the "serpent power" to stir and eventually ascend the channel of Sushumna.

Hold the spinal column free by sitting erect. During the practice of pranayama there is a lot going on within the body. Nerve currents are displaced and given new channels. New vibrations begin. The whole body constitution is remodeled. The main part of this action lies along the spinal column, so take care to sit tall and relaxed while performing these mystical practices. If you sit slouched or twisted you risk injury.

1) Close the right nostril and in 4 counts slowly inhale through the left nostril. Focus the mind and visualize the prana going down the left side of the spinal column and striking the base center, the seat of Kundalini.

2) Hold the current of pranic energy there for 16 counts.

3) With a sniff of air, visualize slowly drawing the current through the triangular-shaped sacrum to the other side of the spinal cord.

4) Release the right nostril and close off the left nostril. Slowly, for 8 counts, exhale the breath through the right nostril as you visualize the current passing up the right side of the spinal column.

5) Hold 4 counts.

6) Similarly, inhale the prana down the right side, exhale it up the left. That is one round.

7) Repeat for a total of 7 rounds.

Resources

George Tompkins for decades of pioneering efforts to publicize the Kundalini potential. BioEnergy Research Foundation, P.O. Box 1957, Columbia CA 95310, email: *rebirth83@hotmail.com* or contact Tantrika International.

Stalking the Wild Orgasm, Itzhak Bentov, for breakthrough research on the mechanics of consciousness. 1977 Inner Traditions International.

The Serpent Power, Dr. Raymond Bernard for the Sushumna Activation breath ratio.

Moola Bandha, the Master Key from Bihar School of Yoga, available through Tantrika International.

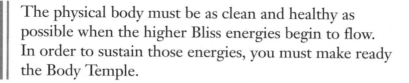

Chapter Nine

PREPARING THE BODY TEMPLE
Lifestyle Changes to Nurture the Body

The physical body must be as clean and healthy as possible when the higher Bliss energies begin to flow. In order to sustain those energies, you must make ready the Body Temple.

*Y*our physicality is as holy as any other aspect of your being. Honor your body as an extension of your Soul. Enjoy its beauty, its imperfections, its capacity for pleasure, its vigor and vitality. As you admire its strength and capabilities, remember it is a temporary abode and you are much more than a physical body.

Pleasurable activity and nourishing food are naturally attractive to a vital, healthy, integrated body, but many people who are working on their bodies are motivated by unconscious pressures, issues associated with the first three chakras:

1. Survival. Some people who jog, go to the gym, watch their diet, etc. do so with an undercurrent of fear of their mortality. They wish to postpone that inevitable unknowable transition. In the Taoist tradition people work to extend their lifespan so they will have more time to develop spiritually. They want to proceed slowly to minimize their emotional experience.

2. Pleasure. Some realize that they will have more opportunities for sexual play if their bodies are attractive. If they are convinced that sexual gratification alone will bring them happiness, this can become a real addiction. Sex brings a rush of endorphins, a hormonal "high" which feels good for a brief period, but if sexual energy is not transmuted it soon dissipates leaving a craving for another "fix." For those who rely on their body image for satisfaction, advancing years and loss of attractiveness present a serious challenge.

3. Vanity/Approval/Power. Some want to look good so they will be admired. Athletes train to compete and win. Some want to do their "personal best," but that is still based on a need for achievement to boost self-esteem. Some want to attract desirable partners so they will be respected and envied. Some, particularly women, become aware of the power they have over people, both men and women, when they are visually attractive and desirable.

If these ego-based motives drive your physical conditioning program, if you work on your body in order to find love or safety, you are probably trying to compensate for a deep emptiness and a sense of unworthiness. No matter how good your body looks, it will never be good enough to fill that emptiness.

Good Intentions Short-Lived.

So many people have started diets and exercise programs that are soon abandoned. The ego includes self-sabotaging elements. You may have attitudes and judgements that disconnect you from parts of your body. There are usually good reasons for your body being in its current less-than-optimal state and you may be heavily invested in maintaining that state.

What if you get to looking good and still don't experience the love you want? What if your partner feels threatened when you look more attractive and get attention from others? What if you start to get attention and don't feel deserving of it? Maybe being sickly gets you extra attention. Maybe being physically limited relieves you of unwanted responsibilities or allows you to avoid frightening challenges. Maybe your physical state supports you in staying numb and protected from life's uncertainties. There are many strategies to preserve safety.

Eventually you realize that the only thing that really matters is returning to your true nature, with your body in the flow of exalted energy. The barriers to that reunion gradually come into conscious-ness – Mental barriers: limiting attitudes and beliefs; Emotional barriers: attachments and incompletions; Physical barriers: toxicity, malnourishment, dehydration and resulting low energy. These are the factors that prevent the Beloved from fully functioning in the physical temple. Once you allow these hidden agendas to come into consciousness, and disempower them, then the way is clear. The body's wisdom will prompt you to do what is necessary to prepare the temple, to host that Presence. Only in this mystical union of body, mind and Soul will you find true fulfillment.

Obstructed Flow.

Vibrant health results from a free flow of body energies, nourishment, fluids, chemical signals and electrical impulses. When that flow is compromised, fatigue, illness and aging result. Today's typical lifestyle seriously challenges that flow.

The LifeForce has been processed out of most foods. Most people are not well nourished. A "normal" body ingests an ongoing barrage of unfriendly substances from: air and water pollution; foods pumped up with preservatives, insecticides, hormones, antibiotics, mysterious chemicals; mercury fillings; prescription and recreational drugs; hybrid or genetically engineered plant forms unrecognizable to the body; irradiation, etc. Countless micro-organisms continually enter the body. This is all common knowledge.

Life forms and materials not useful to the body must be processed, detoxified and eliminated. This uses up energy and materials that would have been better spent maintaining healthy cells. Toxins waiting to be removed are stored, a little in each cell and in the inter-cellular spaces. Much energy is expended in holding that poison in isolation in order to protect the body. Prana is not allowed to flow through those body parts, because it would release the stored toxins. Material is plastered onto the walls of tubes, impairing circulation. For many people bowel function is sluggish and elimination compromised. If you ingest poisons faster than the body can eliminate them, you are continually increasing your toxic deposits until the body is overwhelmed and dies.

If you live in your mind, out of touch with your body, you will have lost your sense of what the body wants and needs in terms of food and drink, breath and movement. You are oblivious to what the body sees as toxic and traumatic.

The human body is like a magnificent steed that carries the mind wherever it wants to go. It is a perfect servant, an outpicturing of your attitudes and feelings. If you saw someone deliberately abusing such a fine animal, feeding it poison, denying it water, contaminating its air supply, confining its movement or ignoring its need for affection, you would be outraged! Notice how you treat your body.

This situation continues because of your unconsciousness, because you do not honor yourself enough to take care of yourself, or because of a hidden agenda, even a death wish. You could choose toxicity as a way to hold your consciousness at a low level. Lethargy, toxicity and the resulting poor health are effective distractions and deterrents to spiritual awakening.

Certainly you could control many harmful factors with filters for air and water, healthy food choices, regular exercise, avoiding drugs, etc. More importantly, you can live in a polluted environment, even survive an epidemic, by maintaining body consciousness and holding a high vibration. Improved lifestyle enhances consciousness which inspires further improvement, creating an upward spiral.

Returning to Flow.

When your energy level increases rapidly through spontaneous Kundalini opening or extended period of love-making, or increases gradually through regular spiritual practice, your body immediately directs that extra energy toward a cleansing and healing process. A body that has been congested might feel uncomfortable for a while, dealing with the toxins that are being released. Similarly a profound meditation may leave you disoriented. You can't sustain that peak energy level until the body is clear and flowing. Only then can you fully receive and embody the Divine Presence.

(When writing/transmitting Jewel in the Lotus, *I had just completed an intense three-week cleanse on wheat-grass juice. The book came through quickly and intensely as I worked compulsively sixteen hours a day for about a month. It would not have been possible to do that work without the cleansing. It is an interesting synchronicity that the opportunity and impulse to do a cleanse showed up when it was time for the book to come forth.)*

Design a program for yourself to begin purification. Many books, systems and products are available. For more detail you can order a brochure "Preparing the Temple" from Tantrika International. The subject is too big to include here.

To sustain the body flow, adopt a lifestyle of diet, elimination, exercise, meditation, breath and sleep that allows a gradual and thorough cleansing to take place. Find a style that is comfortable and can become a consistent part of your life. Sometimes you will go off the track, or even backtrack. Find something that always steadies you and brings your physical being back on track.

DIETARY CONSIDERATIONS

Bringing Consciousness to the Table.

• Make your eating time a meditation. Bring total consciousness to the process.

• Do not eat while driving or reading or watching TV. Be present.

• Make eating a celebration. Take a few extra moments to create a pleasurable ambiance, a sensory feast. Arrange the food attractively. Place fresh flowers on your table and have soothing music playing.

• Prepare and receive the food with gratitude and an open heart. In that sacred space all body systems work better. The vibration of the food actually changes.

• Bless the food to work with your body so that which supports the body can be easily assimilated, and that which offends the body can be easily eliminated.

- Take your time. Don't eat when tense or rushed.

- Take pleasure in the aroma, texture and taste of the food.

- Chew food thoroughly. This produces enough saliva, which contains essential enzymes, to mix with the food so digestion is quick and complete. When properly chewed, food reaches the stomach in a liquefied state, easy to digest. If the pieces are too large and digestion too slow, the food, especially meat, putrefies and produces toxins which the body absorbs.

- Refrain from drinking liquids with your meals. This encourages "washing your food down" before it is properly chewed, also diluting digestive fluids, further compromising digestion. This health rule applies even more strongly to iced drinks which dampen the digestive fire and stop the digestive process entirely.

- Consume only moderate quantities. Stop eating just short of feeling full. Freeing your body energies from the burden of digestion makes more energy available for healing and enjoyment. Longevity research has demonstrated that low calorie intake is definitely a vital factor in life extension.

- Finish dinner at least three hours before bedtime. Late night meals don't have time to digest before the system shuts down. Food sitting in the gut overnight, putrefying, makes you feel sluggish the next morning. If possible have your major meal midday.

Basic Dietary Principles.

- LifeForce comes into the body through food.

- Food is most alive when it is as fresh as possible, not processed in any way.

- The body's pH balance (acid/alkaline) is essential to good health and is dependent on food choices. (This can reflect Shiva/Shakti balance in the body.)

- Choose organically grown produce, free of pesticides, waxes, dyes, etc.

• Choose organic dairy and meats, free range, free of hormones and antibiotics. Many people do better without dairy and/or meat. Check your body reactions.

• Cook minimally. Microwaves destroy food's LifeForce and nutrients.

Finding Your Optimal Diet. Bodies differ in their metabolism, bio-rhythms and sensitivity to various foods. Changing seasons call for different choices. No ready-made diet system is going to be just right for you. Create a personalized plan to suit your individual constitution, honoring your body's preferences.

There will be times when you deviate from the optimal. Enjoy those moments fully, free of guilt. Guilt closes the door to consciousness. If you remain conscious and blissful, the body is forgiving of occasional indiscretions.

Medical research has established beyond question the existence of a brain in the digestive canal called the enteric nervous system. It contains as many nerve cells as the central nervous system. It gathers and evaluates information about interactions between foods and emotions and governs digestion accordingly. "A gut feeling" and "body wisdom" are not just figures of speech. There really is an intelligence, a belly brain, ready to advise you in your choices.

Since there are countless miracle foods, supplements, herbs, homeopathics and essences available, you might need help in making good choices and in establishing a new relationship to regular food. Rather than being constrained by rules and restrictions, learn to hear what your body wants at any given moment using these tools:

• **Kinesiology**, a form of muscle testing, gives good feedback. Hold different substances in one hand while a friend tries to push down your other arm extended. Have the friend push initially without food present to establish a norm, a basis of comparison. Holding foods your body can't digest weakens your arm muscles. Touching foods your body needs and wants strengthens your muscles.

• **Pendulum Reading** is a simple way to dialogue with your body, a way to tap its innate wisdom about what it needs and what it can't handle. You can use a fancy piece of jewelry on a chain or a simple washer on a string. It doesn't matter. Hold the string lightly with your left hand, with the pendulum point hanging over the circle center in the chart below. Simply take yourself into a focused meditative space, hold the food or supplement in question close to your belly, and ask the body to send its evaluation through the pendulum.

Using the scale of -10 to +10, consider -10 to be poison and +10 to be optimal nutrition. "0" is neutral, doesn't hurt, doesn't help. Set up your own experiment. keeping a record for a few days. You may observe that choosing the bulk of your diet from foods rated +5 or more leaves you feeling more alive. See if it is true that the higher your standard, the better you feel. Occasionally foods with a rating of -2 or -3 might be allowed if it is something you really enjoy. Some observations have showed that the Soul had difficulty staying present after the body had ingested foods rated less than -2. Find out what your body says.

The ego can interfere with this process. If you have strong beliefs or feelings about a certain food, that can influence the outcome. Remain attuned to your body wisdom and to your Higher Self and allow that to influence your food choices..

The way food is prepared has a dramatic effect on its quality. Try this experiment. Cut an acorn squash in half. Gently steam one half, microwave the other half. Don't be surprised if your body rates the steamed squash a +8 and the "nuked" squash a -8.

Related foods might score differently. White rice and brown rice might have very different ratings, as might grapes with and without seeds.

Ask what quantities are appropriate, what dosage for supplements. Ask about food combinations. Your cereal and milk might check out OK together, but adding a banana might get a rejection.

Test yourself every few weeks to see if the ratings change. Sometimes after a cleanse you are better able to tolerate certain foods. Once you have begun a cleansing program, stay with it at least forty days. That's how long it takes to replace every blood cell in the body, to know the fluids are clean.

Pendulum Scale

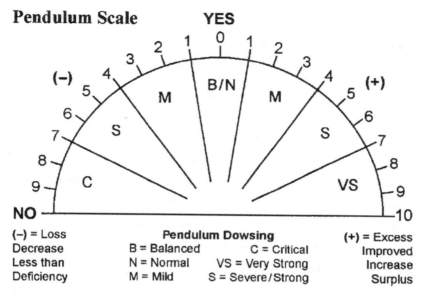

(−) = Loss
Decrease
Less than
Deficiency

Pendulum Dowsing
B = Balanced   C = Critical
N = Normal   VS = Very Strong
M = Mild   S = Severe/Strong

(+) = Excess
Improved
Increase
Surplus

Addictions – Allergies.

There is a correlation between allergies and addictions. If you eat certain foods every day and feel anxious when they are missing, you might well be addicted to those foods. Often people are allergic to the addictive foods. The body, lacking the necessary enzymes, is not able to fully digest the food. Undigested toxic residue is trapped in the body and stored. When you don't get your daily dose of the addictive substance, the body begins cleansing by dumping the toxin into the system for disposal, which could feel like withdrawal. If you eat or drink more of the food, the cleansing stops.

Once you are caught in this allergy/addiction cycle, unable to stop yourself from self-destructive behaviors ("I can't believe I ate the whole thing."), you might feel guilty, and that's the glue that holds compulsive behavior in place.

> Guilt is the price you are willing to
> pay for the pleasure of not living up to
> your own impossibly high standards.

Yoga Nidra is one of Ipsalu Tantra's best tools against addiction. An appropriate affirmation planted into the sub-conscious relaxes the body's craving for the compelling substance and lets the cleansing process proceed.

Another potent tool is bringing consciousness and permission into the cycle. A chocolate addict, who was compelled to eat chocolate several times every day, tried an experiment. She gathered together all her favorite forms of chocolate and arranged them beautifully on a silver tray. She prepared an altar with candles, incense, etc, and performed a series of techniques to reach deep meditation. In that highly conscious state, maintaining the non-judgmental Witness, she gave herself total permission to eat as much of the chocolate feast as she wanted. The first day she ate until she was uncomfortable. The next day, repeating the process, she found she wanted much less. After seven days she found the food unappetizing. Chocolate had lost its power over her for years thereafter.

This technique has been used successfully to stop smoking. Allow yourself to smoke but only in a highly conscious meditative space. Release judgement or guilt and focus on the pleasure of the smoke. Be the Witness. See what happens.

The same principles apply here that were recommended for bringing to light emotional/subconscious material (i.e., feelings are felt deeply with non-judgemental awareness until they lose their emotional charge.) The principles work just as well on the physical behaviors which grow out of those repressed subconscious attitudes and belief systems.

Distinguish Physical Hunger from Emotional Hunger.

Many people turn to food when they are happy and want to celebrate. Some turn to food when they are unhappy and want comfort. Eating produces endorphins, the body's pleasure chemical. As dieters attest, depriving yourself of that pleasure often sets up a backlash as the Ego rebels and protests.

Eating for sensual gratification can be a part of your sadhana (daily practice.) When you bring total consciousness to each moment of eating, tiny portions are just as satisfying as binge-size portions stuffed down unconsciously. An ascetic approach to food is not consistent with the celebratory spirit of Tantra. Neither is unconscious over-indulgence.

Attachment to Food.

Many people live to eat, rather than eating to live. They choose primarily foods that are familiar and associated with fond childhood memories of love and safety. Some foodophiles get defensive when their favorite treats are said to be unhealthy. Every form of psychological protection is employed: denial, invalidation of the critic, getting hostile, finding justification, etc. How would you react to the inner conflict of loving something that hurts you, or to the threat of losing a major source of comfort or pleasure?

Sugar provides an experience similar to the ecstatic connection, the flow of cosmic energy. For those unaware of an authentic sense of union with the divine, or for those unwilling to go through the process of awakening consciousness, sugar provides a momentary respite from the pain of spiritual separation.

Water.

Almost everyone in the world suffers from chronic dehydration. 75% of Americans fall in that category. Virtually every disease that ravages this generation can be linked to dehydration. The body requires at least half a gallon (two liters) of pure water every day, even more in hot dry climates, more yet for large people. When thirst prompts you, instead of water you often turn to coffee, tea, fruit juice, or soft drinks. The caffeine in coffee, tea and most soft drinks is a diuretic. Rather than supplying moisture, it prompts the body to release water. The sugar which is contained in most soft drinks and juices is so toxic that the body must retain a great deal of water to store the sugar in solution. That pulls water out of the system so there is even less available for proper cell function. For every ounce of these beverages you consume, increase your pure water intake by one ounce.

When water metabolism is askew, calcium ions cannot stay in solution and are deposited in the joints, causing some forms of arthritis. Other important ions are eliminated because there isn't enough water to hold them. That causes an oxygen shortage in some cells, making them vulnerable to cancer-causing viruses which thrive in anaerobic environments. Even five glasses of water daily decreases risk of colon cancer by 45%, bladder cancer by 50% and breast cancer by 79%!

Lack of water is the Number One trigger for daytime fatigue. Adequate water eases pain in the back and joints for 80% of sufferers. Just a 2% drop in body water brings on fuzzy short-term memory, trouble with basic math and difficulty focusing on printed matter or a computer screen. Even mild dehydration slows metabolism.

The DNA molecule is in the form of a helix, held together by a water matrix. When there is inadequate water in the cell, the helix collapses and the cell is unable to replicate itself accurately. Therefore, dehydration is a major cause of the cell damage recognized as aging.

It is interesting that a culture so fascinated and compulsive about 2nd chakra issues (sex and unintegrated emotion) is in such short supply of water, the element governed by the 2nd chakra. The failure of people to come to terms with their sexual energy and their karmic responsibilities (2nd chakra archives) is literally killing them.

Rewards for Conscious Self-Nurturing.

The body has other basic needs that have been discussed in previous chapters. Self-nurturing includes providing yourself liberal amounts of sharing love, giving service, being stroked and hugged. It includes making time for fun activities, sunshine, and conscious breathing. It is based on a deep trust in the goodness of life. In addition, if you provide the quantity and quality of food and drink that rates high for your body, and if you stay present to its feelings moment by moment, your body will express its appreciation in many ways. You will have boundless energy, need less sleep, and have beautiful skin and shining hair. You will easily attain and maintain normal weight. Aches and pains will disappear, and disease will pass you by. Your meditations will be deeper and more satisfying. Your mind will be clear and creative. Your sexual energy will be more intense and sexual experiences profoundly satisfying. You will be naturally drawn to tasks and activities that further support your health.

Every seven years the body is completely regenerated – every cell having been replaced. If you are consistently conscious of your body's needs, you can literally have a healthy new body in seven years.

SEXUAL HEALTH CONSIDERATIONS

Your sexual organs and glands play a key role in generating energy for the tantric practices and the resulting expansion of consciousness. The health of those parts and their functions deserves special attention.

America is the world leader in infertility, PMS, hormone imbalance, menopause related illness, pelvic inflammatory disease, frigidity, prostate disease, low sperm counts, premature ejaculation and impotence. A recent study produced startling figures – 57% of the women in this country are sexually dysfunctional (either non-orgasmic or simply not interested.); 46% of the men are impotent or ejaculate prematurely.

The sexual health crisis can be attributed to:

• Toxicity and poor nutrition as discussed before. (See Resources at end of the chapter for specific herbal support.)

• Drug use (prescription and recreational) and alcohol,

• Sedentary lifestyles, and

- Shallow breathing (inadequate prana).

- The prevailing schizophrenic approach to sexuality, celebrating and repressing it at the same time. This confusion, and associated guilt or shame, shuts down the flow of prana (LifeForce) into the sexual organs.

- Widespread ignorance and lack of sensitivity in making love.

- At the deepest level there is indeed the lack of love.

- Remember, a steady flow of pranic energy and occasional experiences of ecstasy, the Bliss State, are required for survival and health of the cells, of the organs, of the body as a whole.

WOMEN

Breast Cancer.

The breast is designed to pour out loving energy to a mate, the children and the home. When the flow of energy is blocked or not received, the risk of disease is much higher. The breast cries out to be caressed and honored as a fountain of love. Notice which women are stricken by breast cancer. You will see that they, and their partners, often have issues around giving and receiving nurturing. Women who freely express love have a far better chance of being cancer-free, especially in the breast.

PMS.

Almost every fertile woman in this country suffers some form of menstrual disorder. For many the effects can be debilitating – physically and emotionally. PMS is caused by a sudden drop in hormones (estrogen and progesterone) in the three to four days preceding menses. This can be mitigated by adopting a healthier lifestyle and better attitude about the feminine role. The hormone fluctuation is softened by regular practice of tantric exercises – like Sahajoli Mudra, MoolaBandha, and breath techniques (especially Cobra Breath 2 and FireBreath). Be the Witness as you bring to consciousness whatever comes up during those days. It's the body's monthly emotional release session. Use it to full advantage.

Menopause.

Women who do tantric techniques can greatly reduce, or eliminate entirely, the discomfort, mood swings and hot flashes associated with the change of life. Like PMS, these symptoms result from a drop in hormones, not just for three to four days, but permanently. The same tantra methods recommended for PMS apply here. Even after the ovaries have shut down, other glands (adrenals) and tissue (fat cells) can produce estrogen.

Menopausal distress is uncommon in China and India. Women don't need to suffer through this transition. If viewed as a loss, it is even more distressing. How much better to celebrate it with a rite of passage, a crowning, honoring the strength and wisdom a woman comes into at this point in her lifecycle.

Breath is the key because it is your carrier wave of energy, strengthening the immune system and balancing the endocrine system. You will feel vital and youthful as you continue in your tantric practice.

The common hormone replacement therapy offers estrogen taken from the urine of horses. This treatment produces high risk of cancer and liver problems. Herbal alternatives are effective for many women, with far less risk.

Pelvic Inflammatory Disease.

At least one out every seven women suffer some infection in the reproductive organs. Half of them don't realize when it is happening, since there are no symptoms. Much of this is caused by introducing spermicidal cremes, bleached tampons, even panty hose and antibiotics. The healthy bacteria get killed and unhealthy micro-organisms flourish. There are herbal products to assist. (See Resources.) The effectiveness of your immune system is greatly enhanced when your heart is open and loving.

Hysterectomy.

Half a million women each year agree to have their uterus and ovaries cut out. Many of these surgeries aren't necessary, and many more wouldn't be required if the women were doing tantric practices. After the fact, women sometimes ask whether tantric exercises will be of value to them, since they have no ovaries to stimulate. The chemical dimension is certainly compromised, but the energy body cannot be surgically altered. It continues intact, perhaps calling for additional practices. With some experimenting you can discover what practices are effective for you.

WOMEN AND MEN

Infertility.

Over ten million American women are infertile. Nine million of them used medical infertility services just last year, services costing over $2 billion, but with an appalling 87% failure rate. Many of those women could have had children if their bodies were healthier. There is a built-in protection. When the female body knows there is insufficient strength and LifeForce to support another life without compromising its own survival, it won't allow pregnancy to occur.

The American male's sperm count has dropped to half of what it was only seventy years ago. This is a reflection of unhealthy lifestyle and confusion about the male role. Being a macho man is not encouraged any more in many circles, but women still are drawn to male power, and the sensitive guy often finishes last. These double messages could be enough to confuse the male body.

Safe Sex.

In the early phase of tantric practice, it is certainly advisable to use a condom. It doesn't stop the flow of energy and, by desensitizing the lingam, may even assist the man toward longer staying power. A committed relationship for tantric practice is the best preventative for sexually transmitted diseases. If you choose to have multiple partners, select partners with healthy diets, lifestyles and attitudes. Meditate deeply and ask for guidance before each new encounter.

Once your heart chakra opens, the thymus gland becomes increasingly active, thereby strengthening the immune system. An increasing number of people carry the HIV virus. Those with a strong immune systems (i.e., heart chakra open) will have a much better chance of surviving.

MEN

Impotence (Erectile Dysfunction).

Ten percent of American men can't ever achieve an erection. Almost every man has occasional difficulty. Most of this problem can be attributed to bad circulation, hormone imbalance, prescription and street drug use. Compounding this is men's confusion about their masculine roles and women's unconscious anger which finds ways to emasculate men. Viagra's sales top one billion dollars a year, despite the drug's dangerous side effects and even associated deaths. Men are desperate enough to risk losing it all. Vajroli Mudra and certain herbal formulae will greatly help the physical problems. The psychological issues need some serious attention. Apply the dialogues and processes described in Chapters 3 through 5.

Premature Ejaculation.

In former days, when intercourse was typically a five-minute process, "premature" simply meant ejaculating before fully penetrating. In tantric terms, when lovemaking is stretched out for several hours, there is a new standard for "premature." Vajroli Mudra is the classic training device to increase staying power. Applying the teachings for transmuting energy, men can expand orgasm while delaying ejaculation indefinitely. (See Chapter 11.)

Prostatitis/Prostate Cancer.

Half of the American men have prostate enlargement. By age fifty, 35% have cancer growing in their prostate. This is an epidemic! The surgical solution is a multi-billion dollar industry. The Root chakra is related to the prostate. By regular practice of Aswini Mudra and Moola Bandha (Root Lock), a man can keep his energy pumping and stimulate the prostate gland. Anal contractions, plus healthy lifestyle including specific herbal formulas, will be a great help in protecting against prostate problems.

Going Deeper

1. <u>Be Aware of your Eating Habits</u>. Record everything you eat for a week, including the times and quantity. Be honest about your habits and take responsibility for your food choices. Rate the foods. Notice how you feel an hour after eating. Has that particular food increased your energy and sense of well-being or has it made you dull and scattered?

2. <u>Bowel Cleanse</u>. Most people carry old fecal material lodged in the intestines for years. This accounts for much of the body's disease and distress. Removing it has cured a wide variety of ailments. There are many products and programs to help deal with these deposits and return you to a natural flow. See the reference in Resources below for an excellent herbal program. You can also look in your area for a colonic therapist for high enemas.

3. <u>System Cleanse</u>. Consider doing a five-day cleanse to cleanse and strengthen your kidneys (if you tend to be fearful) or your liver (if you are holding anger). An excellent herbal combination to cleanse the blood and lymph will serve you well. (See Resources for a recommendation.)

4. <u>Yoga Nidra</u>. Let your practice of the Yoga Nidra technique focus on improving your food choices. Use a resolve like "I prefer foods that my body digests easily." Or "I give my body what it needs to create optimal health."

5. <u>Stomach Rubs</u>. Massage your abdomen with circular strokes, going up on the right, down on the left. Starting with small circles move to larger ones, and back to smaller. Traditional Taoist practice would suggest 36 clockwise and 24 counter-clockwise circles but just do as much as your body wants. This stimulates the digestive organs.

6. <u>Diaphragm Lock</u>. See Appendix A for Uddiyana Bandha, an exercise that is wonderful for digestive organs and also helps open a Granthi Knot, a barrier to Kundalini movement.

7. <u>Nauli</u> is another great aid to digestion, and a potent practice to open Manipura, to activate the body's fire. It also produces energy to assist in the activation of Kundalini. Hold the root lock, exhaling while rolling the belly in and up, inhaling while rolling out and down, in a pronounced circle. Continue for about a minute. Now exhale completely and roll the stomach for another minute. Breathe deeply, and push the fire down into the genitals. Make a sound like a grunt. Repeat three times. Notice if there are any new sensations in the lower body.

8. <u>Vajroli or Sahajoli Mudra</u> is the best way to ensure sexual health (Chapter 7), along with <u>Aswini Mudra</u> (Chapter 3), <u>Moola Bandha</u> (Chapter 8) and <u>FireBreath</u> (Appendix C.)

9. Get pH test strips at your drugstore. How close to neutral is your body's acid/alkaline balance?

Couple Exploration

<u>Prepare a Sensual Feast</u>: A temple atmosphere, provocative music, incense, flowers, candles, and a variety of bite-size delicacies of various colors and textures, arranged beautifully on a platter. Dress festively. Feed each other as sensually, as creatively, as possible. Try "lip service" for sure, and use any other part of the body to offer the morsels. Be playful, even outrageous!

Resources

Body's Many Cries for Water, by Fereydoon Batmanghelidj, MD. The clinical journals from his research on dehydration are available for those who understand body chemistry. See website at: *www.watercure.com* .

For herbal formulas and Bulletins on Colon Health, Kidney Cleanse or Liver Cleanse and Sexual Health by Dr. Richard Schultze, contact American Botanical Pharmacy, 44143 Glencoe Ave., Marina Del Rey CA 90295, phone: 800-HERB-DOC (437-2362).

A Second Brain, by Dr. Gershon on Enteric Nervous System (Belly Brain) research. *www.hosppract.com/issues/1999/07/gershon.htm* . See also *www.ananova.com/news/story/sm_105441.html* .

Chapter Ten

BLISS IN RELATIONSHIP

The Ultimate Challenge

> If handled consciously, emotional clearing can take
> place much faster and more deeply in relationship than
> in isolation. Someone is always there reminding you of
> your unfinished issues. Polarity balancing also goes faster
> and deeper for a couple than for an individual. A tantric
> relationship is a great boost toward Bliss.

In an ideal tantric relationship, two beings recognize each other as embodiments of the Infinite. They have each found their own strength independently, but they find together more joy, more clarity and depth than they could sustain alone. They delight in each other's company. They find ecstasy in sexual union. Their souls commune as two hearts merge into each other.

That's the vision. Here's the reality. This culture is engulfed in an epidemic of failed relationships. Emerging from an era of great freedom for sexual and romantic exploration, many have come away wounded and despondent. Millions of men and women, the survivors of countless romantic disasters, now distrust and resent the opposite sex. Many have given up hope. Celibacy has become very popular. What has gone wrong?

Love in relationships is conditional. There is the feeling that it must be earned: "If you fulfill my needs, I will love you. If you don't, I will leave." This unspoken basis creates an undercurrent of subtle resentment and stress. It is difficult to relax and be authentic when you feel your performance is being constantly evaluated. Conditional love is all you have ever experienced, but it is a poor substitute for the real thing. Many people settle for being needed instead of being loved.

All relationships are governed by the Ego living life through a past or future orientation. Ego is incapable of being in the moment. Love, on the other hand, only happens in the moment, the eternal now. But when you come into the moment, you discover all the frozen emotions stored in the perpetual present. Everything you wanted to avoid comes up to greet you. It comes up to be healed.

Relationship as a Primal Therapy.

The lower three chakras are closed as long as issues, usually from childhood, remain subconscious, unresolved. The issues involve what you wanted from your parents and didn't get (attention, approval, love) or what you got from your parents and didn't want (abuse, abandonment, unattainable expectations.) There is enormous pressure within the psyche to heal these wounds, to complete these experiences. The Ego recreates the experiences over and over, in dreams and in reality, hoping each time to get satisfaction.

Everyone chooses sexual partners who replicate the situation with a parent, usually the opposite sex parent. If the parent was controlling, you would be drawn irresistibly to a controlling partner. If the parent was critical, you would be attracted to a critical partner. A hundred other potential partners might come along, non-controlling or non-critical, and you would find them boring. It is not that you love being controlled or criticized. What fascinates you about this new love is not who s/he is, but what s/he will be after you fix her/him. You secretly plan to get her/him to love and respect you, and to be what you wanted Dad/Mom to be, thereby healing you and healing the parent vicariously.

One lady in England, upon hearing this idea, replied indignantly that it certainly didn't apply to her. Her marriage of twenty-two years was perfect and there was no such process going on. Curiously both she and her mate asked for private sessions. Each of them was desperately afraid of losing the other, based on feelings of inadequacy that were residual from their child-parent experiences. This fear of abandonment severely limited their sexual expression. Each was a perfect parent clone for the other.

Coming into relationship usually means that both partners have found in the other a surrogate parent, another opportunity to get what they wanted as a child. Their scripts match well. Each can play the role required by the other. For example, say he needed a controlling partner and she had that potential. She wanted a critical partner. He could be that. In a different context she might not be controlling at all, and he might not be critical, but they each present those qualities to hold the other's interest.

The blush of "new love," while intensely exciting, is nothing more than a rush of hormones triggered by the anticipation of completing primal issues. Both lovers project onto their partner "stuff" from the past – expectations, needs, resentments, fears, etc. The honeymoon effect doesn't last very long because the harsh reality of fulfilling these expectations comes into play. If you try to be what the other wants, you are never able to be authentic or spontaneous. You can never reveal who you really are because that's not what your partner wants.

Relationship consists of two people trying to get what they need from each other. They become frustrated and judgemental when their needs aren't met. Both blame the other for their unhappiness. Each is oblivious to what's going on, mechanically acting out old patterns, never really seeing the partner for who they are. Each only values in the other the part that fits the script, the reenactment.

If you decide to give up on a relationship before you have cleared the primal issues, you will most certainly be drawn into another relationship where exactly the same issues come up. It may appear you have had ten relationships, but in fact you had one relationship ten times. Women who escape from one abusive husband will probably soon find themselves another abusive husband, etc. Existence (Higher Self) doesn't let you (the personality) off the hook until you have completed the task, learned the lessons that these relationships were designed to teach.

> The one constant factor in all
> my failed relationships is me.

Tantric Relationships.

It is possible for two people to work out their issues together by expanding the principles already presented in this course: being the Witness to your partner's process; not getting caught up in the drama; not taking the "stuff" personally; not judging or criticizing, but just holding space for your partner to process it through. The trick here is to not both go into process at once, each reacting to the other. That's how it usually has gone, and you know that doesn't work. One must be the designated adult.

If you do both get caught up in the drama, it might be helpful to pull back for a cooling off period and then try again to work it through.

It's possible that two people could have, together or independently, worked out their issues, learned their lessons and attained a state of completeness. Then they are not looking to another to make them happy or fulfilled. Then there is a chance for a more fulfilling tantric relationship where they are together because they enjoy each other unconditionally.

The Maharishi (of Transcendental Meditation) used to tell his students "I love you, but don't take it personally." When your Ego hears those three magic words, it invests heavily in the person offering love, thinking its lifelong hunger for love can only be satisfied by that one person. In a flowing relationship, when two people are "in love with each other," each party would be "in love," having realized independently a state of loving. Then they are free to choose to be "with each other."

What Your Lover Really Wants.

Specific sexual techniques are presented in the next chapter. The work you are doing with your self awareness and daily practice (as suggested at the end of each chapter) will turn you into a far more sensitive and passionate lover. This happens as a side-effect even without specific techniques. You are becoming increasingly skilled in matters which are far more important to sexual satisfaction. You are working to become a more developed human being rather than human "doing." You are looking for humor and lightheartedness, for compassion and understanding, for patience and spontaneity. What you want most, and fear most, is true intimacy. That includes the following:

• **Emotional honesty.** Recognizing your feeling states and allowing them to come into your conscious reality does wonders for communication within a relationship. When you realize, for example, that the anger you hold toward your mother or father is being projected onto every subsequent relationship, that realization gives you the ability to release the past and come into the present.

Repressed anger is the most lethal poison for sexual passion. Anger you have projected onto your mate and been unable to resolve and release will extinguish the sexual fire or turn it into violence.

Both partners need the space to have and express their feelings without being misinterpreted, without the other personalizing something that isn't really about him/her.

• **Emotional maturity.** This means taking responsibility for your own feelings and upsets instead of blaming your partner. When your buttons get pushed, be grateful to your partner for showing you where there is still need for awareness. Acknowledge that you chose this partner because s/he could push your buttons better than anyone else! Once you release the unconscious energy on that button a most amazing transformation happens, not only in you but in your partner and your relationship as well.

• **Vulnerability.** If you have guarded yourself, never trusting enough to expose your tender essence, you have never really made love. You may have had sex but that is totally different. When you come into a relationship with an open heart and with no agenda, only then can your partner truly relate to you as a totality. Let yourself be vulnerable. It takes great courage to allow another to really see you. You concluded as a child that who you really are doesn't inspire love. You learned to play the role your parents required in order to get from them some semblance of love, highly conditional, on their terms. Most people keep their charade going and aren't available for an authentic connection.

• **To accept and be accepted.** You both want to be recognized and appreciated as you are, not as a project, something needing to be fixed. There is no room for one-upsmanship, no sense that one is superior to the other.

• **Being present for an extended time.** Have you had a sexual partner whose lights were on but nobody was home? More often than not that is the case. A lover whose Soul is actually present in the moment, delighting in whatever happens, is a treasure. You can make your lovemaking a meditation, with one Soul touching another. This is sublime beyond description, even without intercourse.

Marriage counselors sometimes advise their clients to fantasize in order to improve their sexual "performance." If the relationship is not working it's usually because one or both are not present in the moments when real intimacy could happen. They are off in their imaginations with a former lover or a favorite superstar, someone who is not really involved. That is the problem. To do more of that is certainly not the solution. If a couple choose to explore alternate realities together, that is quite another matter. Both are present to the experience.

• **Trust.** If you feel secure enough in yourself it won't be threatening to you when your partner enjoys another person. In your earlier programming the only reason someone (male or female) appeared to be interested in another, or paid attention to them, was because they had ulterior motives – sexual conquest. That would understandably set off a huge reaction from the other partner. A possessive tantrum was your only way to defend your "territory."

Relationship tries to set up boundaries and limitations. Love must have room to expand. It can't be limited to just one person. You and your partner will discover that there is much to be learned and enjoyed in sharing love with many people. That heartful sharing can be juicy and enlivened by sexual energy without any sexual/genital agenda. When you hold on too tight and don't allow your partner any space to interact with others, you strangle something. Trust your partner. Have an understanding that each will always behave as if the other were present and will never knowingly behave in a way that would dishonor your agreements, whether or not the partner is present.

Meeting Your Partner at Every Level.

People often report that they feel a lot of energy in the sex organs, and a lot of energy in the head, but very little in between. These people are, of course, only able to make connections sexually and intellectually, with little or no love involved. They have no trouble finding partners with the same energy pattern. They are legion.

How many times have you found yourself with someone where there was amazing chemistry and sex was fantastic, but you had little to say afterward and felt strangely separate? Or have you had friends you could hang out with and feel totally understood and connected and nurtured but there wasn't a trace of interest in sex. Or someone whose conversation excited you and exchanging ideas could go on all day but you still felt a separation and no passion.

People usually connect at one level. If you manage a two level connection you feel like you have won the lottery. Attaining tantric Bliss in relationship requires sharing energy at all three body centers simultaneously:

<u>Mind</u> – clarity of vision, a shared sense of what life is about. Mind-chatter stopped long enough to allow clear perception. Heavenly energy pulled down to grace the body.

<u>Body</u> – the sexual energies, fully activated and transmuted to a higher level. Earth energy pulled up into the heart.

<u>Heart</u> – clarity that reveals the Divine Presence in the physical temple. Boundaries, the sense of separateness, dissolved.

The Incest Factor.

As Freud pointed out, there is a powerful sexual energy operating within children and every child-parent relationship is a romance. This sexual aspect is suppressed to the sub-conscious because of social taboos but it continues to spill out into people's lives, adversely affecting all subsequent relationships. There are many variations to this theme but almost everyone needs to bring this stifled energy back into the flow to free themselves from its influence.

The Oedipal Complex.

Many men report that they had felt passion at the beginning of a relationship but as the love bond became deeper the sexual energy grew faint. They could still get turned on but only by women for whom they have no real love. This is a pattern left over from childhood.

Every little boy is in love with his mommy. She is the source of his life, his nurturing, the love that is essential for his survival. She is his goddess. He wants her total attention and doesn't want to share her. The father and siblings are his competition. Freud noticed the power of the Oedipal Complex, as had the Greek dramatists long before him. The sub-conscious urge to make the father go away, even to kill him, seems to be basic part of the male psyche.

Normal Male Development. At about age four to five this energy comes to a peak. Normally at this time the boy realizes that his mother will never be available to him exclusively or sexually. He then begins to model himself after the father in hopes of someday attracting someone just like his mother. This is one way family conditioning is transmitted from one generation to the next.

A young boy associates the loving, nurturing heart energy with his mother but realizes that the mother is not available sexually. So he creates a barrier between the energies of heart and sex. The diaphragm is the physical wall that separates the chest and abdomen cavities. It becomes chronically tense, an armor to stop the energies of love and sex from connecting.

Men find it difficult to make a commitment to any one woman. As long as that split exists in them, they know deep down that there must be at least two women, one for love and one for sex. Many cultures, especially European, have resolved this problem by allowing men to take a mistress. He has a wife to bear his children and receive his undying love and a mistress to inspire his passion.

For millennia societies have played out the theme of the sainted wife/mother and the desirable but despicable whore/mistress. Women were categorized into one of these two types, often depending on whether or not they enjoyed sex. That was how a man related to them. Women have compromised themselves in this way partly because that is what it took to maintain a relationship. In fact it has been a collusion of all parties concerned, an attempt to deal with the force of sexual energy or the resistance to it.

Women of this time don't have to participate in this limited definition. They are by nature prepared to be both loving/nurturing and sensual/sexual. For them to have to make a choice and only be half of who they are is no longer acceptable. Granted many women have closed down one or the other of these aspects, or even both. For someone to fully activate both the sexual and loving natures and heal this split through tantric work is one of the most heroic accomplishments possible. It is the greatest enhancement to a relationship and the noblest gift to the beloved. Uddiyana Bandha, the diaphragm lock, is a good exercise to relax that rigid wall. (See Appendix A.)

After a puja experience a male student recently shared "I didn't anticipate that my surrender to this adoration and gratitude would be such a turn-on. The river from the heart to the sex flows both ways; or maybe it's an alternating current. Love-making has become wider, deeper and richer."

Interrupted Male Development. During this critical time in a boy's life, (age four to five) if the father abandons or divorces the mother, or dies, the boy effectively wins the Oedipal conflict, wins the mother. He still can't have her sexually but now he becomes so emotionally attached to her that it is almost impossible for him to be deeply involved with another woman. No matter which way the Oedipal drama plays out – normal or interrupted – a great challenge is presented to the male.

The Electra Complex.

Similarly every little girl has a strong sexual connection to her father. She might be outrageously seductive and flirtatious, often in competition with her mother for his attention. Her sexual behavior is cute when she is very young, but by age five it could become a problem for the father. He could be feeling subtle arousals that aren't appropriate.

Normal Female Development. Often the only way the father knows to control his conflicted energy is to withdraw. They may have shared a bath before but can't any more. She isn't allowed to come snuggle in his bed any more. He creates a barrier and is no longer available to her in a sensual way. Sometimes the father withdraws emotionally as well.

The little girl feels abandoned, rejected, no longer lovable. She will doubt her self-worth and be drawn to emotionally unavailable men. Fortunately, due to the male programming, there are plenty of those around.

Interrupted Female Development. If the father is unable to restrain his urges, and involves his daughter sexually to fill his neediness, it could take several forms. If he is tender and loving in his sexual advances, she may enjoy it at the time, treasuring that special connection, until she learns that fathers aren't supposed to behave that way. Then she will feel betrayed and find it hard to trust men. Alternately if the father is insensitive and forces himself on an unwilling child, she suffers feelings of worthlessness, helplessness and shame. As the topic of incest becomes more openly discussed it is revealed that incestuous behavior is far more common than previously imagined. Once again, whether the Electra energy plays out normally or aberrantly, the female faces a challenge.

Fortunately there are many parents who are conscious enough to stay present with sexual energies and not close off or take advantage. They trust themselves to handle the energies in a healthy way.

Deeply exploring incest issues and bringing them into loving consciousness is an important feature of the Ipsalu second level course, Bliss in Relationship.

Circumcision and its Aftermath.

The penis foreskin contains reflex points that are connected to the heart. Removal of that skin is an additional way to exclude a heart connection from the sexual experience. This makes men into warriors. The foreskin also has abundant nerve endings so the uncircumcised penis is more sensitive to touch. The rubbing created by the foreskin moving over the penile shaft adds even more stimulation. Circumcision lessens sensitivity.

It also drives a deep subconscious wedge between men and their mothers. Most circumcised men carry deep resentment from the violation and the pain. They carry a deep sadness and loss for what was taken from them by this cruel procedure. They resent and distrust their mother (and by extension, all women) for allowing it and for not protecting them. Being held down and powerless created a terrible rage, and releasing this rage is an essential process for a man.

Relationship Cycles.

Relationships seem to run in seven-year cycles. The seven-year itch is a well-known phenomenon. Most divorces occur seven, fourteen, or twenty-one years into a relationship. You start a relationship expecting your partner to change, hoping your dissatisfaction with him/her will be resolved. Seven years seems to be the life expectancy for hope. At that point, if nothing has changed, you admit that it's not going to change. You either resign yourself to the situation or decide to move on.

If changes have occurred and issues have been resolved, a couple usually takes on a new set of challenges at the beginning of a cycle.

They might start a family or business, buy property, etc. Be aware of cycles so they can be managed more consciously.

Alternative Relationship Styles.

Considerable interest has been expressed recently in exploring types of sexual relationships other than monogamy. There are newsletters and organizations building up around this theme. Several couples have written books describing their experiences with open marriage, two-couple marriage, group marriage. In almost every case, after a period of time the original couple was no longer a couple.

People give up on monogamy because it hasn't worked. They figure that changing the form will solve the problem. Without the emotional healing and spiritual unfolding described in this book, the other forms of relationship will not produce fulfillment. The variety of partners provides a distraction and the repeated excitement of new relationship provides titillation, but they won't heal the inner child and won't lead to Bliss.

Some of these movements are, ostensibly, based on a spiritual foundation. But on closer examination, there is usually a powerful figure holding it together, a parent clone for all to work with. Lacking consciousness of this transference to a parent surrogate, the people can get hopelessly muddled in their attachment and loyalty to the group and its leader.

Even in Tantric practice, casual sex will not take you into an illumined state and will not produce Bliss. It is dangerous to your health to play around with different partners in this age of AIDS and other sexually transmitted diseases. On a subtle level, each partner with whom you share genital/sexual energy leaves a residual connection, like a leak in your energy system. If they wish to, and you subconsciously allow it, they can draw from your energy at a later date.

You have to know your partner. Love and mutual respect have to be there. Tantric sex does not work without love.

Honor the Divine in Your Mate.

Often it's easier to see things externally than internally. Certainly you can see the other person's faults more easily than you can see your own. By the same token, it's easier to see the exalted nature of your partner than to see your own. When your partner really sees your grace, it is easier for you to find it.

The roles of men and women and the ways their egos interact were once clearly defined by society, but now the role definitions are crumbling. In this confusion it can be useful to refer to ancient male and female archetypes, the quintessential divine energy: Shiva is sitting high above the tumult of life, with clear vision and wonderful ideas, deep in blissful meditation. Shakti is sensual, intuitive, creative, manifesting and nurturing. See this potential in each other and honor it.

Many men, even men with spiritual inclinations who have not had tantric training, function sexually more from instinct. They haven't learned to integrate their sexual behavior into their spiritual life. (Things are changing and now many men are showing up, with no formal practice but with a very tantric style.)

Traditionally, in the tantric temples, the women teach the men about tantra and about love. Women experience arousal and orgasm more intensely than men. Women are the initiators. Men do very well when they let her take the lead.

How You Keep Yourself Single.

There are periods in life when the work you need to do can best be accomplished alone. You oscillate between introverted periods and extroverted. Sometime you simply need your own space. The mind may not accept that fact, and come up with a drama around wanting a partner, but it may not be a true reflection of your Soul's current plan.

You may be avoiding relationship. If prior relationships were painful (more to the point, brought up primal issues which were not handled consciously) you may be ducking that pain and holding yourself apart with certain reasonable attitudes, saying, for instance, "I want a relationship, but there aren't any men (or women) out there who have the qualities I require." Existence continually adjusts itself to conform to your expectations. With such a protective barrier, you will not see, will not recognize, will not attract a suitable partner. Take responsibility for having created the barrier and all that could change. When you admit you are avoiding relationship, and are not the victim of circumstances beyond your control, then that truth will set you free from your distress. You will either choose to remain single and enjoy it, or you will open up to the possibility of relationship.

Attracting a Partner.

When you practice the Cobra Breath, you create a magnetism around you. You exude a charisma that could draw that special person to you. People who are interested only in sexual encounter tend to avoid someone who is radiating heart energy. They find it frightening. When you are in your heart energy, no one operating at a lower consciousness will come close to you because you always attract someone who is vibrating on your own frequency.

Going Deeper

Relationship issues are dealt with in the very powerful Ipsalu course, Bliss in Relationship. Dealing with them on your own only works if both partners are able to Hold Witness when the issues come up.

<u>FireBreath with Partner</u>

1) The FireBreath (Appendix C) has been recommended earlier as a solo practice. If you have some skill with that, you can share the experience with your partner.

2) If the movement of energy activates an emotional release for one of you, let the other hold space for that releasing.

3) Several couple practices are included in Appendix C.

Chapter Eleven

BEING ORGASMIC
Tantric Sexual Attitudes and Practices

Enlightenment has been defined as perpetual orgasm, the ultimate Bliss. Harnessing sexual energy provides the fuel for the tantric journey. This chapter shows you how to attain that mastery.

Most people are at the effect of their unconscious sexual drives. This relentless pressure shapes their actions and decisions. Many feel guilty about this powerful drive, especially if they use masturbation or superficial sexual encounters to keep the energy manageable and if they have a negative judgement about doing this.

The traditional way for the spiritual seeker to deal with sexual pressure was to repress the energy, often taking vows of celibacy. This doesn't solve the problem. Many convents have secret burial places for embarrassing newborns. Note the recent flurry of reported child molestation among the clergy. There are countless stories of "gurus" or "advanced yogis" having covert sexual involvement with their students. Celibacy is not a decision you make. It's a state that you attain by fully expanding and transmuting the sexual energies. Self-judgement is the quickest way to cut off your connection to the Divine. Only when guilt and repression have been released can you come into the Bliss vibration – the integrated energy of the human and the divine.

A popular CD by Enigma features a sultry female voice, over a background of Gregorian chant. She murmurs seductively, "The principles of lust are easy to understand. Do what you want, and do it to the end!" This is reminiscent of Osho's advice. The point is not to avoid desires, sexual or otherwise, but rather to express and fulfill the desire consciously, <u>appropriately</u>, being the Witness, without guilt or judgement. The urge will be satisfied only when you discover that a lustful predatory encounter is not what you really wanted.

One step toward attaining spiritual maturity is learning to use this wild, raw sexual power in new ways. After practicing transmutation for a while, you find the energy ascending on its own, without your direction. That force is there when you want it, tingling throughout your body, but it no longer lingers in your genitals, distracting you. The energy can then be used as a powerful fuel for your spiritual journey.

Many people suffer from having too little sexual energy. A recent survey revealed that 24% of women are not orgasmic and 33% are simply not interested in sex. An astounding number of men don't have much sex in their lives. Their energy has been shut down by sub-conscious beliefs and attitudes acquired in their early years, traumatic experiences and disappointment with insensitive lovers, and physical limitations from an unhealthy lifestyle. Low energy leaves that nagging feeling of inadequacy.

Sexuality Essential to Spirituality.

One of the most precious experiences you can have is an encounter with another Soul, meeting as closely as is possible on the physical plane. Sexuality without love dishonors both partners. Sexuality in the context of love is sacred, to be revered as a holy sacrament.

Sexual energy is the energy of creation. As you gain skill in sensing and moving this force, you open up the possibility of awakening and manifesting your latent divinity by awakening the power of Kundalini. Sexual energy is one expression of that essential LifeForce that allows you to meditate deeply while staying grounded. When doing the Kriya practice, you rotate sexual energy through subtle pathways in the body, often an orgasmic experience in itself, a practice which has produced many enlightened beings.

Connecting sexual energy to spiritual energy is the essence of alchemy. The key that makes this possible is the Cosmic Cobra Breath. When this breath is practiced in a sacred space with a partner, male and female energies merge and you propel each other into transcendental states. This powerful technique deserves your deep respect.

The practices described in this chapter assume you have Cobra Breath. If you don't, you can substitute the Transmutation Breath in Appendix A.

The most powerful energy available to you is your sexual energy. Every time you have an orgasm you reach Samadhi (deep Bliss) at least momentarily. In that blissful state, the mind stops, the breath slows, you are suspended beyond time and space. It is the moment when God gets to play in the human drama. Sometimes that orgasmic moment can be stretched to five or ten minutes or more and it seems like eternity. Women often feel this orgasmic Bliss more intensely than men because most women are naturally more open to the internal flow of energy. Anyone can learn this openness with some practice.

A woman who recently completed all the Ipsalu courses shared the effect on her sexual experience:

> "I have been experiencing sexual fulfillment in a way that I never knew was possible. Penetration sex has a longer lasting impact on me because I am transmuting 2nd chakra energy up to my heart chakra. The difference I feel inside from making this connection has redefined sex for me. I experience the ordinary act of intercourse as something extraordinary.
>
> I can experience internal orgasms from energetic sex without the need of intercourse. My partner and I can finish lovemaking and after he has withdrawn from me, I will continue to experience orgasms from the feeling of the energy which remains in my yoni. Even after his lingam is out of me, the sense of the energy remains very present. This I know is an extension of energetic sex. I feel so fulfilled, there isn't the urgency to repeat the act so soon. The memory and awareness of the energy remains with me for days.
>
> My partner and I find ourselves laying close to one another and our breath will synchronize on its own. Our bodies will transcend into an expanded state of consciousness for hours. The inner tranquillity which we both experience is like nothing we have ever known before. People are asking me what I am doing because they see me as looking years younger. The practice is reversing the aging process of my cells.
>
> I am eternally grateful for the many ways Ipsalu Tantra has impacted my life."

Overcoming Conditioning.

Those raised in this Christian culture have been taught that there was something inherently degrading about sex and that you all came into this life through the sexual sin of your parents. This insidious idea has been around for so long it has worked its way into your DNA. What an incredible relief it can be to discover that this is a fallacy and that all parts of you are sacred. There is nothing to reject or suppress. It is a major leap in consciousness to accept the idea that sexuality and spirituality are manifestations of the same energy. Experiencing them together completes both. The sexual union called maithuna is the essence of your connection to Existence.

Sexual Politics.

Sex is at the root of most of society's problems. This primal energy has been perverted and poisoned for thousands of years by those who want power. Politicians and priests have used sexual restrictions to control the masses. When you control someone's sexual energy, you make him/her a slave. Consider the spirited bull and the docile ox, his castrated counterpart. The bull is filled with unremitting fire. The ox plods along, useful, uncomplaining, spiritless.

When a religion declares sexual energy to be evil, with severe penalties for its unauthorized expression, it creates an inner split, cutting off the believers from their own creative power. At an early age children are brainwashed to believe that their very nature is bad. Guilt and shame, the most powerful crippling attitudes, are deeply instilled, destroying authenticity. A false self is created as they disown their true nature.

Spirit simply cannot abide where guilt and shame prevail. Thus the believer can no longer access God directly, and must be dependent upon the church, the sacraments and the priesthood to satisfy his/her spiritual longings.

If people expressed their sexual energy, they could not be controlled – not by the government, by the church, or by society. Imposing antisexual religious doctrines, sexual taboos and social mores helps the ruling powers to curtail people's creative force. Rulers feel they then can channel that energy to suit their own agenda.

The subjugation is intensified further by limiting the experience of love. A taboo must contain some truth in order to be effective. And so society teaches everyone how wonderful love is They talk of the glories of "higher" love but at the same time denigrate the "lower" love.

In truth, lower love is a vital component of higher love. The physical must be embraced, transformed and integrated to attain spiritual awakening. The controlling system doesn't want people to have this experience.

An infant, when deprived of love expressed with touching and stroking, although fed and kept clean, grows weak, and doesn't develop properly. Sometimes it even dies. Many people have reached adulthood, but something inside has not flourished. Starved for the physical expression of love, people are suffering from that lack of nurturing.

See clearly how this entire scenario is a collusion.

> The rules of conduct and limitations society has imposed reflect your own barriers, and protect you from being vulnerable and being hurt.

It has been taught that only husbands and wives can share in the expressions of sexual energy. In the attempt to control that energy, you might end up turning it off altogether, so there is no energy for even the approved recipient. Denied the expression of love, you become miserable and bitter. Those energies might be expressed as violence, either overtly or in a passive aggressive way. Tantric practices allow the sexual energy to flow freely, but channel it upward to be expressed through the heart without genital involvement (when that's not appropriate.)

Those who choose to be with many partners are usually disappointed in the quality of the casual genital/sexual experience. They keep coming back to try again because they are driven, but the satisfaction is minimal and short-lived. They continue to bring along their fears, defenses and limitations into each new sexual opportunity, and the results are the same.

When people are in love and feeling in union with the beloved and the world, they are at their most creative, most sensitive, most beautiful. They aren't afraid to take risks or to explore new possibilities. When love is absent, they remain disenchanted, lacking inspiration.

Did you find yourself feeling victimized by a repressive system while reading this just now? That's a trap to be mindful of. As long as you look outside for the solution to your problems, as long as something external has to change before you can experience your own expansion, as long you see yourself as the victim of circumstances beyond your control, you are hopelessly stuck.

I once visited an intentional community near Berlin. It was dedicated to reforming social and religious restrictions that limited people's sexual freedom. I tried to share my perspective with some of the leaders. They simply couldn't grasp that the real barriers to freedom and Bliss are internal and that the repressive system is only mirroring their own programmed repression.

The experience of Bliss is hidden in the here and now, with things exactly the way they are. Nothing has to change. Struggling against external barriers can be valuable if done consciously, helping you to discover your own internal limitations.

Multiple Partners and Cobra Breath.

Practicing Cobra Breath sexually with more than one person in the same time period can create distress, as can practicing outside a committed relationship. Sharing the Breath produces a powerful energy connection. If one partner is eager to share the Bliss and becomes open and vulnerable, and the other partner is still guarded, just going through the motions, this bonding can be painful. It's similar to unrequited love, but on a much larger scale. As you move into the higher levels of Cobra Breath this connection becomes even more profound. The open sensitive one can often feel the emotions, even the thoughts, of the other and can lose their boundaries. This can be confusing and disturbing. There are many practices you can share with a friend, but honor the power of the Cobra Breath and save sharing it sexually for someone you really know and trust.

Tantric Lovemaking.

Among the profusion of "tantric" books now available are many which focus almost entirely on super-sexuality. There are videos out on sacred spot massage, methods to stimulate the prostate and G-spot. The methods are presented as a way to get aroused and to enhance orgasm but obviously they are also going to stimulate the Kundalini. The instructions don't tell you what to do if that happens.

There are several books and videos out, very detailed and explicit, about sensual massage and arousal methods. You can turn to the *Kama Sutra* or *Taoist Sexology* books for innumerable sexual positions and techniques. *Sexual Secrets* has a wealth of information and things to try. There are many more.

Some couple practices can be found in Appendix A and a Lovemaking Guide is included at the end of this chapter. This is basic information including a few sexual techniques that will enhance your lovemaking experience. Just remember that the sex act is not the heart of Tantra. Tantra is about feeling energy and moving it through the bodies. That doesn't require a vast repertoire of sexual techniques. Once you have mastered a technique, you can release it and be available for whatever the energy wants to do. Then you are free and that's when the tantric magic happens. Ipsalu doesn't focus directly on sex technique. Transcendent experiences come as a side-effect of your practice as you become more balanced, more able/willing to stay present.

Vama Marg.

Vama Marg is the left hand path of Tantra, which for centuries has been feared and condemned. Since the left hand (right brain hemisphere) controls creativity and intuition, the left hand path allows you to access and express these qualities.

In the Vama Marg you practice with a partner, each aware of the other's divinity. Using yogic techniques you circulate energy. You clearly feel your own maleness and femaleness simultaneously, and finally fuse those polarized parts in the moment of orgasm.

"Vama" in Sanskrit means to spit out or vomit. "Marg" simply means path. Vama Marg practice helps you release all illusions of separation, of who you are and how you fit in. When you are free of the illusions, you are ready to enter a new dimension of making love and being love.

Create the Time.

Allow at least an hour and a half of uninterrupted time for your tantric adventures: approximately half an hour for warm up, half an hour for intercourse with transmutation, half an hour to cool down. Quickies can drain your energy, especially if you are rushed and tense in pursuit of an orgasm. If you find that happening, just notice how you feel afterwards. If you choose to spend more time, you'll soon become accustomed to a much more satisfying experience and won't want to settle for less. Use that shorter time to be close and relax together, to share energy, to play and to communicate.

You may be more comfortable making love in the dark, with the sheets over your bodies or partially dressed, because you carry feelings of embarrassment or guilt. You hurry to get it over with, instead of celebrating and embracing that divine connection.

Many couples, before they have sex, insist that everything is just right: no headaches, work all done, children in bed, dishes washed, pets fed, not too tired. Very seldom does all this happen at any one time, so they have "quickies" as they pass in the night. Tantra teaches not to wait for things to be right. Create the moment by being available to your partner and by generating the energy to get started. You can use Vajroli or Aswini Mudras, or the FireBreath.

Making love twice a day can be considered morning and evening prayers. It's not necessary to penetrate and reach orgasm. Just a few minutes of touching, sharing, caressing, holding is very nourishing and very healthy. Energy is exchanged on a subtle level. The spoon position is especially nice for this. The couple lies each on the right side, the man behind the woman. His left arm enfolds her, perhaps the left hand on her heart, receiving her loving energy. His heart is just behind hers so she feels his love coming into her heart. Just breathing together in this position is very sweet.

Waking up to love in the morning sets the mood for the day. You can't be gloomy if you are feeling erotic energy rushing through the body. It puts a smile on your face. Carry that energy without feeling pressure to release it. If you become too aroused then transmute the arousal with the Cobra Breath or Transmutation Breath.

Early morning intimacy is often avoided because people wake up feeling, tasting and smelling like a trash can, the result of eating/drinking unwisely the day before. If you have refined your diet and refrained from eating during the three hours before bedtime, your body won't be obliged to do a major cleanse every night and early morning becomes much more appealing. Consider making some adjustments which truly honor your body temple so that it can be enjoyed to the fullest.

Extended tantric lovemaking, pulling energy into every cell of the body, is recommended once, maybe twice, a week. More frequently could overload your system in the beginning. Eventually you might choose to include lovemaking in your daily spiritual practice.

Prepare Your Tantra Temple.

Make your bedroom into a tantric environment. Remove the TV. Meditate there so that a sacred energy builds. Set up an altar, complete with incense, candles, fresh flowers, objects and images significant to you. Make this room a place of higher consciousness, not just a place to dump clothes and crash out. Then even your sleep time becomes useful, your dreams become healing and instructive.

Illumination is important to create a sensuous atmosphere. Light candles – sensitively selected and arranged. Use colored lights: red or amber to work with mother earth energy, ultraviolet light or cobalt blue to take you into abstract spiritual realms as you make love.

Music also assists in creating the right vibration. Remember that the frequency of earth energy (Schumann Resonance), the brain frequency of meditation (upper Theta) and the frequency of a heart in a loving space are all the same frequency range – 7 to 8 Hz. Classical Indian music, such as the ragas, are based on overtones of that frequency range. Indian music is an ideal choice. Much of the "New Age" music is either spacey or primitive. It's important to pull those two extremes together. Look for something grounded, yet expansive.

Tantra for Singles.

The Dakshini Marg path, the right hand path, uses many of the same techniques as the left-hand path but it is done without a partner. You can arouse your own subtle energies by self-pleasuring, bringing yourself to a point of intense excitement. At the moment of orgasm transmute the energy. This completes the circuit, keeping your energies inside while relieving the pressure in the genitals. On the exhale, as you relax, the energy diffuses through the whole body.

Self pleasure is the first step in being able to give pleasure to somebody else. Many women haven't yet experienced orgasm with a partner. Once you can feel dynamic energy within your genitals and learn to move this energy into higher centers in the body, then you will become sensitive to that happening in a partner.

To complete the tantric experience, you eventually will attract a partner with whom to share energy, to bring that positive and negative force into union that awakens you to Bliss.

Sexual-Spiritual Enhancement.

You can be orgasmic at any time. When your partner wants to make love but you feel tired or not turned on, five minutes of FireBreathing will leave you totally aroused. (See Appendix C.) The same technique can also be used when you want an experience by yourself.

In the FireBreath, orgasm becomes a distribution of energy throughout the whole body, the whole being, rather than just a localized genital experience. Women naturally experience a full-body orgasm, due to the nature of their nervous system. Most men, however, have never known anything other than an isolated genital release.

You can do this practice: 1) solo, with just the breath and movement, 2) including self-pleasuring, or 3) with a partner. The FireBreath orgasm can be ecstatic as the vibration takes over the whole body. You may immediately get to the peak, or might choose to stretch out the experience for a long time, reaching higher states of orgasmic energy, over and over and over again. This is a beautiful way for men or women to have multiple orgasms. Include FireBreath in your lovemaking and you might experience an orgasm that climbs from one chakra to the next until the entire body is in full orgasm.

Once you get to a highly aroused state, if you are with a partner, come right into the yab yum position (woman sitting on the man's lap) and continue pulling energy up into the heart. When you feel orgasm getting ready to climax, lift the energy with a Cobra Breath (or Transmutation Breath), touch foreheads in the tantric kiss, then lean back and exhale down. Try it and see what illuminating experiences occur for you. Feel the presence of your souls. See them merging in space in the Cosmic Orgasm.

Tibetan Tantric Rebirthing.

A very advanced rebirthing process from Tibet is offered in the Ipsalu Tantra third level course, Bliss of Cosmic Union. Special breathing patterns and mantra, together with profound sensory/sexual stimulation, produce for many a mystical peak, a tantric marriage and the beginning of a new level of awareness.

TANTRIC LOVEMAKING GUIDE

Greater awareness, a bit of basic knowledge and a few techniques can transform your sexual experience into ecstatic communion. There are references here to the Cobra Breath. If you have not received it, use the Transmutation Breath in Appendix A.

Foreplay

Notice that the term isn't "forework." Let yourself be playful and creative, never letting lovemaking become predictable or mechanical.

No Expectations.

Enter into loveplay without expectations, especially regarding orgasm. If it happens, fine, if not, fine. Some people never touch each other unless bound for orgasm. They don't want to start something they can't finish. Why not enjoy the start as much as the finish? In tantric lovemaking, you could gracefully stop at any point and feel complete.

Take Your Time.

Foreplay is wonderful when it lasts at least half an hour before penetration. Most women take that long to relax, to attune to their lover's energy, to get their juices flowing, to open themselves up to union. Find ways to please one another – sharing a bath, erotic dancing, creating a ceremony, massaging, kissing, stroking, fondling, oral stimulation or just being close and synchronizing breaths.

Non-tantric men are often preoccupied with sex. They are eager to get started and quick to finish. Their sexual history is based on hurrying to complete the act – before she changes her mind, before they get caught, before he loses his erection.

Sexual play is also short-lived because of a mandate planted in men's genetic code in earlier times when procreation was important. There is a strong instinctive urge to plant his seed in the most fertile field available as quickly as possible, so the egg can be fertilized. Once a woman has become aroused, the vaginal fluids begin to flow and the muscle movements in her vagina tend to push out. This compromises the sperms' chances of connecting with the egg.

Many men are conditioned to respond to their sexual arousal with an impulse to quickly relieve that tension by rushing into penetration and orgasm. Men in Tantra learn to take more time, to let their energy build. They relax into extended love play. Creative variations help maintain interest.

Stay Present with Feelings.

When sexual energy is aroused and sustained, there's a good chance that emotional "stuff" stored near the sexual energy will come into consciousness. Have you ever been making love and suddenly the woman bursts into tears? The man assumes he's done something wrong. Or suddenly one pulls away and you are in a big fight. It's probably old "stuff", not personal. If you or your partner begin to feel intense emotions, let the other stay present to the process without getting caught up in it. Be the Witness and hold the space for your partner's feelings to be expressed and released. With some practice they will quickly pass, and lovemaking can continue, if you wish.

Undulations.

It is essential in tantra to release muscular tension around the pelvic bowl. Most people are tight in the pelvis as a result of trauma, abuse or social conditioning. Imagine a piece of doweling inserted from one hip bone to the other with the pelvis swinging easily from that doweling. It feels wonderful. Pelvic undulations are particularly important for a woman to become aroused. That movement also helps awaken the sleeping Kundalini. If you can co-ordinate your breathing and pelvic contractions with the undulations, (as described in FireBreath), more energy and more oxygen-enriched blood will flow into the sex glands and organs.

Self-Stimulation.

By contracting and relaxing the anal sphincter muscles (Aswini Mudra) and the urethral sphincter (Vajroli Mudra) you can generate sexual energy. This enhances your manual stimulation.

Shakti Take Note.

Since many Tantra techniques were created to assist men, they have not always considered the differences in the way men and women activate energy. The anal contraction is a standard part of many Taoist and Yogic techniques. Those muscles stimulate a man's prostate gland (1st chakra), thereby stimulating his Kundalini reservoir.

The point in the female body comparable to the prostate is that 1st chakra area on the back wall of the vagina, near the cervix. Anal contractions don't stimulate that point nearly as well as deep vaginal contractions. When a woman makes this adjustment in a technique, the results will be much more intense.

Friction Sex or Energy Sex.

People in this culture usually practice friction sex – in and out, blow up the balloon until it pops, turn over and go to sleep. Most people reach orgasm by tightening their muscles and holding their breath, to keep the sexual energy confined to the genitals. That way a small amount of energy will produce a mini-orgasm of limited intensity and duration, limited to the genital area – a sexual sneeze.

In Tantra, you might enjoy friction sex for a while and then go beyond into energy sex, that is, moving subtle energy through your body, and through your partner. This spiritualizes your sexual energy so you are both nourished while making love. You learn to relax body tension in the midst of sexual arousal. You learn to contain more and more energy, using all of the body, rather than settling for instant genital discharge. The entire body becomes an erogenous zone. Orgasm becomes the full-body, long-lasting, mind-blowing experience you've been waiting for.

You lose energy through the eyes, tip of the tongue, nipples, fingers, toes, lingam and clitoris, and the anus. To keep the energy contained or circulating with your partner, explore these practices: either keep eyes closed or maintain eye contact; keep tongues either touching or in khechari mudra; have woman's nipples touching some part of man's body; have your hands touching your partner's body, let your feet touch your partner, or hold your soles together; close your partner's anal opening with a gentle finger on the anus or perform the root lock.

Oral Sex.

Oral sex plays an important part in tantric experiences. Oral-genital stimulation is probably the most intense sensation in preparing for tantric orgasm. It is suggested as a foreplay activity, since cosmic orgasm usually happens in union.

The 6-9 position, where his tongue is touching her clitoris (negative pole) and her tongue is touching his lingam (positive pole) sets up a closed energy circuit that can build up a high charge. Again you could climax in this position, but the woman is not getting the G-spot stimulation that allows a full body climax. The orgasm that results from clitoral stimulation alone is localized in the genitals, not transcendent.

In this position, if the man manually stimulates her G-Spot and the woman manually stimulates his perineum, they can share full-body orgasm. Each can ingest the nectars of the other, another way of sharing the essence of sexual secretions.

When you touch your tongue to the roof of your mouth (Khechari) you complete a circuit, allowing energy coming up the spine to enter your brain. When a woman is performing oral sex, and his lingam (positive pole) touches her hard palate, the woman's Kundalini (negative energy) is drawn up through Sushumna, into her brain. Polarities switch at the moment of orgasm, so the lingam becomes receptive to the woman's ascending energies The circulation is reversed from normal.

Due to the high incidence of AIDS and other sexual transmitted disease, oral-genital or any other kind of sexual contact isn't recommended unless you really know your partner and have made some commitment. Get tested for AIDS and other conditions so you can relax and enjoy each other.

Anal Stimulation/Internal Prostate Massage.

For many people stimulation of the anus is extremely pleasurable. It also provides another way to awaken Kundalini. But many people hold frozen emotions in the anal region, feelings that might surface during stimulation. This is why some people avoid anal activity.

Through anal massage woman can give her partner the experience of being penetrated, to share how the woman feels. This might help him contact his own Inner Woman. Agree in advance that you are going to do this the first few times. If his diet is good and his bowels operate well he can feel comfortable and presentable. If his system is sluggish he might want to spend a few days with colon cleansers or have a colonic or enema.

With nails clipped and filed, use a well-lubricated finger cot (a finger-sized condom) or latex gloves (both available at your local pharmacy). The woman slowly massages circles around the anus until it relaxes. She waits to be invited and then she gently inserts her middle finger, up to the middle joint, into the man's anus. The prostate is located just in front of the rectum and is easily stroked through the rectum wall. Doctors do this to palpate the prostate, often insensitively and painfully. Be extremely gentle and take it slow. The same applies for a man stimulating a woman.

Some people, men and women, have sodomy or other traumas to work through, including feelings of vulnerability, shame or embarrassment. Some are so tight that anal entry is painful. Others find it right away to be extremely pleasurable. You can create a vibration with the inserted finger. You could even insert a small vibrator and see how that feels. Just don't let it get away from you. It's so difficult to explain to the emergency room doctor. Nothing else should be inserted in the anus. The rectum wall is not a rugged membrane, not designed for aggressive activity.

Normal intercourse automatically stimulates a woman's 1st chakra. The G-spot is not the actual chakra point, but it is connected energetically and is a good point for stimulation. That's one reason why women experience a Kundalini rush during orgasm far more often than men do. Men do not normally receive this kind of stimulation. They can compensate for that by doing Aswini Mudra (anal contractions.)

Homosexual activity often includes anal intercourse, providing a more profound energy than is normally available to heterosexual men. By adjusting your loveplay, adding anal stimulation, heterosexuals can create this depth of experience, can help a man activate his Kundalini.

Anal intercourse for heterosexuals is not recommended for hygienic reasons.

Coming into Union

Penetration is most satisfying for a woman after she is fully aroused and her secretions start to flow. If a man enters before she is lubricated, it irritates her tissues and is uncomfortable. He might come to the opening, pause, and wait to be invited in. If she is not lubricating (peri-menopausal) use a water-based lubricant.

In Tantric union the man and woman share equally the top position. About half of the time the man is relaxed and the woman is more active, getting the juices flowing and energies vibrating. In the superior position she can control the motions and the depth and angle of penetration.

Once penetration has occurred, the couple should remain in union for at least fifteen minutes before he ejaculates, thirty minutes for a more complete tantric experience. In that time hormones have a chance to flow in abundance, producing a rejuvenation effect. If they delay and let the energy build, when they do finally climax it is far more intense.

When the man is active, he can enter slightly, come out, circling to better stimulate the woman. In most positions, it's not necessary to penetrate deeply into the yoni. Just touching the tip of the lingam to the clitoris or vulva allows energy to flow. All the nerve endings of the yoni are in the first one or two inches. After that there is little feeling. It is a cosmic womb, a vacuum.

Many women find the head of a soft lingam more erotic than a hard lingam because it feels like a tongue. The sensation for a man is most intense with the lingam 2/3 erect. There is a Tantric saying, "You go in soft and come out hard."

The head of the lingam is its most sensitive part. This is where the secretions and energies are exchanged. If you stay close to the surface when making love, you stimulate all the nerve endings that go to the sacrum. This stimulates healing and rejuvenation.

After a while, he can start going in deeper. Let her be the guide. She knows what penetration she wants. A great energy connection is possible when the lingam touches the 1st chakra area near the cervix, but she must guide this exploration. Men are encouraged to surrender control in these matters. Women are naturally wiser about sex and energy.

Some men think they have to go deep, but that is not really for women's benefit. Psychologically, these men want to conquer, and intercourse has a strong element of domination. They feel the deeper they can go, the better they can pin a woman down and hold her in sexual embrace. This is a patriarchal approach to sexuality, ready to be supplanted by a more balanced, honoring approach.

Deep penetration also stems from man's ongoing longing to return to the cosmic womb. That is basic to man's nature, just as it is woman's basic nature to be the Divine Mother.

When men go in deeply they are trying to touch the cervix. That pressure is a pleasurable sensation for the head of the man's lingam. Unfortunately, that rubbing irritates the cervix, and if the thrusting is too vigorous, eventually it can contribute to cervical cancer. It is more pleasurable for both for the lingam to go around the cervix in circular motions, not touching it directly.

With deep penetration, when the lingam withdraws it creates a vacuum within the yoni which is very pleasurable for a woman. Another pleasure also comes in stimulating the first two inches of the yoni where sensitivity is greater. To take advantage of both these pleasures, the Taoist system advises a man to do seven shallow strokes and two deep. Counting at such a moment is certainly not recommended. Just remember the principle of several shallow strokes, and an occasional deep stroke

If the man consistently goes deep, the woman doesn't get enough stimulation and will lose her secretions. That creates friction. When a man enters softly and gently two or three inches, that helps Shakti to stay lubricated. This way, the energy of the hormones that are being secreted continues to nourish you.

Variation is important. None of this technique needs to be rigid. When lovers are totally present, sensitive and meditative, Shiva and Shakti both come into full blossom naturally and harmoniously.

Secretions.

Fresh secretions during sexual activity contain hormones that enrich both partners. These hormones are the elixirs of youth, the secret nectar of longevity. When foreplay is extended, you allow time to get the hormones flowing. When lovers delay orgasm, they build up more and more energy, which stimulates secretion of more hormones. A man can further stimulate the production of hormones by bathing his testicles in cold water before beginning loveplay.

Some women produce an ejaculate that comes through the urethra. In Sanskrit it's called "Rasha," the fire essence. It is rich with hormones and nutrients to feed the body. In some sex workshops women take pride in their ability to shoot their juices across the room. What a misunderstanding of a great gift! Some teachers have cautioned women to use this fluid with great care and reverence. Frequent ejaculation is draining to the female body, and can cause premature aging as surely as it does the male body. The Rasha is precious fluid and of great value if ingested by the partner. This might be a special observance, happening seldom, perhaps in a private maithuna ritual.

Some women who don't naturally ejaculate can be stimulated to do so by G-spot massage. It's not clear that this would be to a woman's advantage. Solar energy descends through the crown chakra to produce this ejaculation. Opening the crown chakra prematurely makes it hard to stay in the body. It is much safer to bring in that energy through the medulla, as you learned in the Inner Smile.

In tantric lovemaking you learn to absorb each other's secretions and recycle the energy in your bodies to produce both a rejuvenation effect and an expansion of consciousness. While in union, a woman's juices are absorbed into the head of her lover's lingam. (Advanced tantric practices teach the man to draw in her juices.) When he ejaculates into the woman, she receives his essence.

If the woman transmutes at the moment the man ejaculates, that essence suffuses through her whole nervous system and glandular system. Absorbed through vaginal tissue, semen can lift a woman's spirit. Semen was considered sacred in ancient days, in alchemical works.

Women whose partners have chosen the Taoist limited-ejaculation method have reported feeling deprived. An energetic bonding comes from sharing that essence. A psycho-emotional bonding comes from exchanging fluids. There is also a chemical exchange. Women's juices are high in copper, which the male body needs. Male ejaculate is high in magnesium, which the woman's body needs.

Birth Control.

Some people have tried to use transmutation, seminal retention or pressing the perineum as birth control methods. There are a number of children on the planet as evidence that neither of these methods is adequate for family planning/avoiding pregnancy. Osho advocated vasectomy, assuring men there was no energy loss. Many women become so sensitive to their body cycles that they know when they are ovulating and can be especially cautious. Much has been written in conventional sources to help you make these decisions.

Sexual Positions.

You can practice Cobra Breath in a variety of sexual positions. Several positions are shown in *Jewel*. Many others are easily available in other books. Some tantric sexual positions (YabYum, Shiva Superior, Shakti Superior) put tension on the sacrum. This releases the spinal fluid, which is the Kundalini force, pumping the energy up the spine. This is nothing mystical. Through the tantric lovemaking act you learn to charge the fluid with electromagnetic energy pulsating in and out. Stimulating the vagina opens up Kundalini shakti energy – our life force – for spiritual awakening.

Tantric positions produce psychic pathways and circuits of energy flowing through the body. When the head is back, the prana suffuses into the brain to give enlightenment. If getting into some positions seems too hard, just do it in your mind. Visualization is a powerful tool and will produce the same effect.

Expanding Orgasm.

The key to tantric practice is: 1) coming to the brink of orgasm, and 2) transmuting the energy to delay climax. It's dancing on the razor's edge. This produces hydraulic pressure inside the body, which pumps the sexual energy up the spine and through the chakra (endocrine) system.

With some practice men can learn to delay their ejaculation. Frequent ejaculation depletes a man's spiritual energy. In Tantra, instead of using that creative energy for recreation or procreation, he circulates it through the body for longevity and rejuvenation.

Some men are concerned about getting "blue balls" if they don't have an ejaculation. This isn't very likely as long as energy is moving. The prostate swells, but in two or three minutes it shrinks back down to normal size. A gentle massage of scrotum and perineum helps to relieve that pressure. The man can do it himself, or enlist his partner's services.

When a tantric couple starts making love, they move in a very slow, meditative manner. Every time either one comes almost to a point of no return, they both do the Cobra Breath two or three times to transmute the orgasmic energy that has built up.

If your partner doesn't want to do this practice, you can do Cobra Breath by yourself. Make sure your partner knows what you are doing so they don't find it unnerving. Transmute subtly so it doesn't intrude.

Transmuting will stop the man from climaxing and he will lose about half of his erection. The woman will lose her sense of imminent climax. Build to near orgasm and transmute at least three times before letting the orgasm take over.

Transmuting is good for both women and men trying to increase their body's vitality. The more sexual energy you have, the healthier you are.

If a couple plans to produce "star children," it's good for the woman to keep building her energy. That allows her to produce an exceptional ovum and an ideal environment for conception.

When you do several transmutations, followed by orgasm, the orgasmic wave ripples throughout the entire nervous system. It is not just localized in the genitals.

Orgasmic Alchemy.

Using tantric methods, when two people share orgasm, the male/female duality disappears. Both come into neutrality which awakens the "Cosmic Fire" of Kundalini. If one goes into orgasm, both should do Cobra Breath building up an enormous energy charge. None of the energy is lost since it circulates from one to the other.

Consciously building your energies together might result in simultaneous orgasms. In the moment when this happens, you lose your identity as you expand into the universe, the realm of no thoughts, just total Bliss.

Don't get caught in goal orientation, working toward simultaneous orgasm. That brings you out of the moment and into your mind. Instead let your lovemaking be a spontaneous exploration and a playful experience, with an occasional delightful surprise.

Female Orgasm.

Most women take longer to orgasm than most men. Tantric methods assist a man in delaying his climax until his partner has reached her highest peak. A woman is encouraged to ask her partner for what she wants and needs from him. She also has resources within to stimulate and modulate her energies.

When a woman is aroused, her pelvic bowl is engorged with blood. If she doesn't reach orgasm, the blood takes days to dissipate. Non-tantric couples often get into a pattern where the man finishes quickly and the woman is left incomplete. If she thinks it's his responsibility to bring her to climax, she might feel irritable, hostile, or unavailable for further sex. She might want to avoid that frustrating, unfulfilling experience. If this pattern continues, it can even lead to disease in her reproductive organs. When a man feels a sense of duty or obligation, he could resent "servicing" his mate, especially if she is slow to climax. She can be active in keeping her energy primed, completing her own experience if that is what it takes.

When both partners share the creative possibilities of their sexual experience, each takes responsibility for their own fulfillment, and each takes delight in finding ways to pleasure his/her partner. Affectionate behavior not linked to sexual intercourse (spooning, lots of hugs and kisses, etc.) will help to keep her energy flowing.

Sex is so much more than an activity leading to orgasmic release. Let it be an unfolding, an expanding. As a man surrenders to his woman's orgasmic energy it pulls him into cosmic orgasm.

Ejaculation.

After at least thirty minutes of penetration, including at least three transmutations, the man may choose to ejaculate (providing that his partner is ready.) The timing is important. Ancient masters have mapped this out. After about thirty minutes of intercourse the electrical current between you and your mate switches. Everyone has both a male and female side. In orgasm the energy bodies switch polarities. She becomes masculine, he becomes feminine.

When you reach the point of no return and take the Cobra Breath up, you are recycling your own physical energy back into your body. If you wait the recommended time, you will not lose energy when you orgasm. Ejaculation will still be somewhat draining, but not nearly as much as it is in "normal" sex.

Internal Orgasm.

With a little practice, men are able to experience an internal orgasm, that is, orgasm without ejaculation. The energy rushes up the spine instead of out the lingam. Many men report that they have no desire to ejaculate at that point, feeling beautifully satisfied.

Maintaining deep relaxation, a man can have many orgasms vibrating through the body without ejaculation. The erection will not go down. The lingam is still engorged with blood even while the essence is going into the spine. A man can remain erect until his Shakti comes to her orgasmic flow and they can ride that energy wave together.

If a man loses his erection, that often indicates that his attention is wandering. To analyze or judge the situation would only draw him more into his mind and out of his body. He can best use that as a reminder to become present in the moment.

Cobra Breath.

Use the Cobra Breath to transmute energy several times while you make love. After about thirty minutes, when you are ready to come to climax, take that Cobra Breath up with your orgasm. On the exhale when you relax, see if you feel amplified tremors as you have a full body orgasm, expanding beyond genital orgasm. The energy diffuses as the whole body/mind lights up. This is the difference between spiritualized sex and "normal" sex. The key is the Cobra Breath.

Touching Tongues.

Energy discharges at the tongue tips. Touching of the tip of your tongue to your lover's tongue while you are in union completes an energy circuit. There is a psychic connection from your lingam or clitoris to the tip of your tongue. When genitals and tongues are in contact during orgasm you have a closed energy system.

Mystical Union.

When a couple's energies balance each other and wake up the kundalini, each orgasm sends this transformational energy directly into their brains. And then something wonderful happens. The two separate selves disappear into a divine cosmic union. The Egos are transcended and there is only the experience of ecstasy, just pure awareness, pure Bliss.

<u>Afterglow</u>

When your lovemaking feels complete, allow at least fifteen minutes, preferably more, to cuddle and be present in the afterglow. If you are really in your heart, you are beyond time and have no sense of its passing. In these moments you both are very vulnerable, very impressionable. Treat each other very sensitively. Conversation might take you out of the sublime state. Profound meditation is a better choice in these moments. You are already there.

ENTERING THE REALM
OF COSMIC CONSCIOUSNESS

(One student's experience of tantric union is recounted below in her own words. Her excursion into cosmic consciousness was the culmination of a period of purification, using the principles and practices of Ipsalu Tantra Kriya Yoga.

This verifies that the tantric arts, when fully embraced, provide us with keys to enlightenment, a doorway to cosmic consciousness. When the Ipsalu practices are pursued conscientiously in a spirit of love, devotion, reverence, and sacred honoring of the beloved, miracles can indeed occur.)

Bodhi has talked about the pervasiveness of cosmic consciousness. And while I had had brief glimpses of this expansive state in meditation, I had never really grasped the fullness of it until recently. I once heard Bodhi mention that all women have the innate desire to be one with the Divine Mother. I certainly did not have these feelings, I thought. I could not even fathom what this meant until one day when it magically occurred! I wish to share with you this magnificent experience.

As I entered into tantric union, I felt complete joy, ecstasy and boundlessness. My lover and I united, and became as one: one mind, one essence, one beingness. Then I was more! The lower dimensions began to slip away, and I felt myself expand into universality. I felt my own personal boundaries disappear as I became as one with infinite mind, eternal essence, and all pervasive being. A familiar image of the Divine Mother appeared before my inner eyes, and all of a sudden I knew that *I was That!*

I felt expansive beyond measure, as though I was everywhere at the same time. I was the energy of the cosmos, and one with every living thing in it. I was perfect peace. I was all knowing. I was serenity and harmony. I was complete fulfillment, for I needed nothing. All things were in me, and of me.

I was expansiveness of mind, and the essence of infinite intelligence and awareness. I could sense the feelings and emotions of all those that I loved. Knowing no energetic boundaries, my essence could extend and become as one with theirs. I could feel my lover and I washing back and forth between each other's shores, like the ebb and flow of the tides.

I looked through the eyes of God and saw that my creation was good. All was in divine order. Harmony and peace pervaded every cell of my body, for I was That. There was nothing beyond me. I was the font of creation, the Mother of the Universe. I held all the world in my hand, and all of love in my heart.

This was the world of stillness, beyond thought, beyond time and space. There was an infinite spaciousness to this non-dimensionality. I was Supreme Being, unified with The All.

This ability to expand has returned to me many times since that day, often accompanied by the beautiful image of Divine Mother that I experienced on that first morning. Initially I was not grounded enough to maintain the state, but it lasted for hours, fazing in and out through the day.

I was perfect femininity, perfect creative spirit. Creativity bloomed on that day, and inspiration has been a constant companion ever since. I keep coming back to who I am – fullness and completion. All women must surely desire to be one with their essence – to be this mighty, loving, compassionate, all-expansive being that holds all creation in her palm, that loves eternally and unconditionally, that nurtures, nourishes, and holds as a natural condition. Yes, who would not wish to be that!

I now consciously choose to join with All That Is, to be Divine Mother. And whenever I forget and am feeling less, I choose to remember the true reality. And in the remembering, I am free.

– *Nanji Cohran*

Going Deeper

---

1. Read *Jewel*, Lessons 9 through 11.

2. Experiment with the Couple Practices in Appendix A and the Maithuna in Chapter 12.

3. Try Trataka, page 277, for 15 minutes, gazing deeply into each other's eyes and souls.

Chapter Twelve

TANTRIC RITUAL

A Doorway to Bliss

Ceremony or ritual can create a bridge to the subtle world. It is a repeatable process whereby a person or group of people can remember the living connection with all things and can achieve a new state of awareness of the nature of existence.

The elements of ceremony – artifacts, words, symbols, activities – come to life when infused with your focused attention and LifeForce. By repetition you come to perform the ritual without mental effort, just as a spontaneous dance of events.

Ritual may find its power through rhythms and dancing, through song or chanting, through art or architecture, through psychotropic substance, through communion with nature, or through devotional ceremony. By engaging fully in the process you can move and attune energy and open your heart.

> Every culture that survives includes some
> form of ritual, personal and/or group,
> that brings participants into the state of Bliss,
> the coherent resonance, the mystical moment.

Sexual rituals have historically been a part of the tantric tradition. They evolved in many forms, incorporating the techniques of individual practices or couple practices into a group ceremony. They have sometimes been misunderstood and sensationalized.

Tantra offered liberation from the cycle of birth and death within a single lifetime, while enjoying all the sensual delights of life, without requiring the ascetic disciplines of the yogic path. Through sacred ritual, practitioners intended to fully embrace and transcend sexuality, using elevated sexual energies to access higher dimensions.

People wonder where in India they can go now to experience the original authentic forms of Tantra. Unfortunately, tantric ritual has such a suspicious reputation in India, all practices are private. Outsiders are seldom allowed to join in. Westerners would probably be disappointed if they could participate, finding themselves in a lengthy rite, mostly chanting mantras.

TRADITIONAL PRACTICE

There is extensive literature which forms the scriptural basis for tantra. Some of the tantric shastras (scriptures) were written at the beginning of the Christian era, or even earlier. Some appeared as late as the 19th century. They are usually in the form of a conversation between Shiva (or Vishnu or Buddha) and his consort or student. Some are rich with poetry and praise of the deities.

Although many matters are discussed in these works, the emphasis is more practical than philosophical. They protest the orthodox practices of both Hindus and Buddhists, and their long disputes over abstract matters.

For the tantrikas it was not enough to talk of God. They were primarily concerned with sadhana (daily practice) and rituals. The tantrikas claimed that sadhana alone produced results, proving itself experientially at every step. Shiva and Shakti were waiting to be discovered in every man and woman. This was, and is, the message of Tantra. A tantrika expected to join within his body the male and female principles, the unmoving and the moving, the pure consciousness (Shiva) and the world force (Shakti). The tantrika aspired to awaken and elevate Kundalini, to pierce the six chakras and realize Cosmic Consciousness.

Tantric Sadhana.

Personal practices varied from one tantric sect to another, but certain characteristics were usually present. It was assumed that an aspirant must have a guru, one who had achieved, at least partially, the tantric goal. In many places, the guru was a woman. The guru would: 1) advise the student which deity to honor, 2) prescribe specific practices to focus on (These varied according to the student's temperament.), and 3) perform an initiation.

1) Deities. Tantric practice traditionally included devotion to a personal deity. The worshipper would strive to embody the deity's qualities, even to become the deity. Here is a verse from an ancient shastra (scripture) praising Shiva.

> Ever gracious, ever blissful Lord whose compassion is like an ocean of nectar, whose body shines white as camphor and the jasmine flower, purest truth, robed in space, omnipresent, loving and beloved Lord of yogis, whose coiled and matted hair is drenched by spray from the torrents of Ganga; adorned with ashes, garlanded with snakes and human skulls, three-Eyed Lord of the triple-world: trident in one hand, in the other, blessing; embodiment of Gnosis, giver of Nirvana; everlasting; pure; flawless; amiable; benefactor to all that live, God of Gods.

> (Mahanirvana-tantra I.6-10)

In India people are very devotional. This ancient culture had many gods and goddesses to worship. From a modern perspective, you can see the deities as reflections or personifications of qualities and states of consciousness, finely discriminating the many nuances of human nature. Western world cultures have chosen to honor only one all-inclusive god and never a goddess. This restriction might limit westerners from valuing and exploring their full range of qualities.

You might assume that the deities don't exist, and it doesn't really matter. These images, which yogis saw in deep states of meditation, are very useful. The personal deity assigned to a student represented an archetype, an externalization of some aspect of the student's inner, unconscious world most in need of conscious attention and honor. Using that image as a focal point for concentration, the student could discover that dormant energy within himself and come to love and honor a banished part of himself.

Devotional practice has great value. Since things evolve more quickly now, it might be appropriate to move on to a new personal deity when the old aspect has been mastered, ultimately bringing all aspects of yourself into full consciousness.

2) Practice. The guru would give a mantra particularly appropriate for an individual to assist him/her in contacting the personal deity. Other techniques were prescribed, many of which have been mentioned in this book and *Jewel in the Lotus*, including mantras, yantras, mudras, pranayama and healing techniques The methods presented in these two books are valuable for anyone. Even without a guru's guidance you can experiment with the methods to find the combination that suits you best. Then stay with them long enough to get the benefits.

3) Initiation. In the past the guru would perform an initiation, thought to be essential to someone embarking on the path. The initiation puts one in direct connection with the guru's essence and the energy of all gurus in his/her lineage.

Ipsalu suggests that the age of gurus is over, that those drawn to tantra have matured spiritually enough to access their Divine Nature directly. "Guru" means "dispeller of darkness; one who brings forth the light of consciousness." Only you can dispel your own darkness. You can learn from various teachers that which is useful at the moment, but ultimately you will learn to trust your own inner guide.

Tantric Rituals.

• **Five Ms.** One form of ritual is based on the principles of bhutashuddhi, the highly developed science of the five "elements" from which the human body is composed: earth, water, fire, air, ether. Each "element" is honored and purified, along with its corresponding chakra.

Five substances are partaken, things normally forbidden in the Indian culture, but permitted in ritual since the tantrika has taken on the energy of the divinity being worshipped. These things are not for personal pleasure, but are consecrated and used only to promote spiritual awakening. The ritual of Five Ms refers to five Sanskrit words beginning with "M" (mamsa, matsya, mudra, madya and maithuna) which mean meat, fish, parched grain, wine and sex. Such a ritual meal has been described in *Jewel*. Since those items are not forbidden in modern times, their shock value is diminished.

The Dakshini (right-hand path) version of the Five Ms is symbolic and poetic.

> From the cellar of the mooladhara, the wine is taken up to the brahmarandhara (cave of Brahma, third ventricle of brain), where kundalini pours blissfully into the moonglass of pure consciousness. To taste the wine flowing from this ethereal lotus – ah – that is 'real wine-drinking.' Anything else is mere alcohol.

> To slaughter the beast of praise and blame with the sword of knowledge and merge one's consciousness with the absolute: this is 'real meat-eating.'

> Who controls the senses with his mind, and yokes them to the imperishable, is a 'real fish-eater.' All other are merely killers of creatures.

> In men of animal nature, Shakti sleeps, but in Tantrikas she is wide awake. He who honors Shakti is the 'real sexual worshipper.' Who knows the rapture of the soul's union with the Ultimate is a 'real adept of lovemaking.' All others are merely enjoyers of women.

> (Kularnava-tantra V 107-113)

• **Pujas.** For the sects within the Vama Marg path, the practices were sexually explicit. There are Shakti Pujas, usually held at the full moon, where one woman lies in the center of a circle of men. With great ceremony and use of mantra in praise of Shakti, each man in turn comes into union with the woman, or at least pays homage through oral sex.

There are Shiva Pujas where the Shivalingam is similarly honored, each man assuming the divine role, being honored by his partner or partners.

There are Chakra pujas where couples sit in a circle. First the men rotate around the circle, stimulating and copulating with each woman, always maintaining an attitude of worship, using mantra to hold their consciousness in a spiritual plane, while skillfully transmuting sexual energy.

When they have completed the circle, the men become receptive and the women become the initiators, moving from partner to partner. Each person has assumed the role of the divinity. There are no personalities involved, so there is no guilt about sexual behaviors that would usually be considered unacceptable. When two people come together sexually, it represents the union of Shiva and Shakti. Ideally the participants are intent on transcending sensual pleasure and achieving divine Bliss. In the tantric art the faces of couples engaged in sex appear detached and sublime, certainly not in the throes of lust.

Ritual involving multiple partners is not part of the Ipsalu practice.

• **Maithuna.**

The word Maithuna is the name of the constellation of Gemini in the Indian astrological tradition. It refers to the archetype of balancing opposite polarities signified by the symbol of "the twins." "Maithuna" also means "sex" in India. Often it is only through sex that the mind/body dance of polarities in a couple fuse into the Peace of Oneness.

The goal of the Maithuna Rite is to realize the profound extent of your true nature, Oneness, by dissolving the judgemental separate self and reconnecting to your Core Essence, the Light of your True Nature.

If you wish to explore a rather elaborate traditional, maithuna, you can obtain from Tantrika International a written guide to lead you through the steps. This was prepared by a good friend and colleague, Kirby Jacobson, who has gone more deeply into the study of traditional ritual than anyone in the Ipsalu family. The ritual described there can be performed by a couple or a group. (See Resources.)

The Challenge.

These group sexual rituals were traditionally performed with a sincere intent. Only advanced students were invited to participate, those who had developed great maturity and self-control. In spite of this, criticism of these practices has been intense and damaging. The critics usually had little insight into the attitudes underlying the ritual. What they perceived was an open invitation to licentiousness. In fact, some of the activity that passed for tantric ritual was so distorted and unspiritual that the bad reputation was well deserved. Few people can hold to their integrity in a sexually charged group situation.

Sexual ritual has been offered as the fastest way to enlightenment, but ritual certainly doesn't take the place of sadhana. In fact, sexual ritual represents the culmination of long personal practice and mastery of its individual elements. It is not a place for beginners. Not the least of the necessary accomplishments is your ability to remain present and focused for several hours. The ritual is much more intentional than normal sex, seeking transcendence rather than relief or pleasure.

Sexual experiences often lead spontaneously to an exalted and ecstatic state, a temporary blissfulness. Ritualized sex, even calling upon the deities, will not, in and of itself, draw you into the next dimension of consciousness. If, however, both you and your partner have been diligent with your personal sadhana (practice), purified the physical temple, processed the emotional blockage, learned to still the mind, mastered the flow of energy in your bodies and gained skill in sexual techniques, in short, explored everything suggested in the first eleven chapters of this book, (in addition to the three levels of Cobra Breath), then the sacred sexual ritual could very well awaken you into a more enlightened state.

To attempt such a ritual before you have prepared yourself could help you push through some barriers, but that could be accomplished just in your regular lovemaking. The attitudes and elements of Maithuna sadhana can become part of your normal sexual interaction. In ritual you simply gather together your many skills and dedication, fully surrendering to the most intense result possible.

There are groups, calling themselves tantric, that perform sexual rituals with relative novices in tantric practice. It usually involves drugs and deteriorates into an orgy. At best, if performed with sincere intention, their sex ritual might produce for some a period of samadhi, a moment of ecstasy or Bliss, an awareness

that such a state is possible. But the participants typically cannot hold that energy. There is no short cut, no way to bypass the purification work outlined in this book.

MODERN RITUAL

Ancient rituals, designed for another time and another culture, aren't as relevant today. It might better serve you to devise a simpler, more contemporary version for just you and your partner in privacy.

Once you understand the principles of moving energy, you can design your own ritual and experiment until you develop something useful. The suggestions here are a starting point, not a rigid formula. You are encouraged to experiment.

The suggestions given in Chapter 11 about tantric lovemaking bring the spirit of Maithuna into your everyday sexual activity You might choose to include lovemaking as part of your shared daily practice, the final step of the formula. Maithuna simply means sexual union within a sacred context. Every conscious sexual encounter is sacred and can be a meditation, a ritual.

The male's experience of expanding into a more enlightened state is often different from the female's. It's more abrupt. Suddenly it's present. Also it's a bit more on the mental plane. The female experience is often more gradual, with spirit intensifying over a period of several days. The woman goes first and her energy pulls her partner through in sexual ritual. A woman can transcend through union with a less enlightened man but the reverse is not usually true. This is because she embodies the Shakti force and is easily attuned to it throughout her body. This is why the tantric initiator has always been a woman.

The Kundalini is the deep primordial pulse emanating from the nucleus of the atom, to the core of the earth, to planets, suns and stars. During sexual climax, the Kundalini resonates and harmonizes with the original creative impulse (the Logos), the Universe. It is this resonance that opens the couple to the grand ecstatic experience of Tantra, the mystic feeling of cosmic unity.

Maithuna Sequence.

The Ritual described below could serve as a special evening or the culmination of a longer experience. Occasionally you might want to set aside a weekend, or even a whole week, to focus on your awakening without distraction, to build your sexual energies to full power. These are ways to celebrate a tantric marriage.

The week-long process produces more profound results if you are prepared that is, you have been practicing with a partner for some time, you are both comfortable with your old emotional issues and have been careful about diet for many months. To attempt such an intense program with a body and mind not yet flowing freely is inviting a heavy discharge, emotional and physical, which is a valuable experience, but different.

The daily exercises in this book and the experiential retreats are designed to maintain a tolerable level of continuous clearing over an extended period of a year or several years. Each level of Cobra Breath opens a deeper layer of processing. The more clear and free-flowing your internal body is, the higher charge it can contain. The power of the ritual comes from building higher and higher levels of energy in the body. Then the more intense practice can produce profoundly joyful results and quantum leaps in expanding consciousness.

An advanced version of Maithuna Ritual is an integral part of the Ipsalu third level course, Bliss in Cosmic Union. Here it is the culmination of Seven Nights of Tantra.

SEVEN NIGHTS OF TANTRA

Preparation.

Every morning for seven days, perform the Tibetan Alchemical Meditation (Appendix A) to build the Golden Body of Light. This fills every cell of your body with solar energy (Shiva). Every afternoon, perform the Rejuvenation Postures (Tibetan Five Rites from *Jewel*) and Lama Breaths (from Practicum or Level 3). Throughout the day, maintain your presence in the moment, speaking little, holding Khechari Mudra as much as possible, (tongue tip far back on roof of mouth.)

Every night, make love using stimulation and delay techniques without coming to climax. The sexual energy (Shakti) builds over the first six nights so that on the seventh night, during the Maithuna Ritual, when you allow the accumulated polarized energy to explode, your orgasm propels you into another dimension. Be available to visions, to sudden understandings and to infinite compassion as you open into the Unlimited Mind.

• **The First Five Nights.** Practice a different part of the ritual each night, particularly those that are unfamiliar. The final night shouldn't be clouded by uncertainty. Give yourself (or each other) a pedicure and manicure. Take along instructional videos that lead you through genital massage and other "super sex" techniques. This is not the place for erotic fantasy or porno stimulation. Leave behind the mental approach to sex and stay with the experiential.

Give each other lengthy erotic massages, one giving the first night, receiving the next night. Be playful as you experiment with each other's erogenous zones. Find out what your partner particularly likes. After the massage, make love, allowing the energy to build higher and higher without climaxing. Stimulate each other in any way that pleases you. As climax approaches, pull the energy up on the breath. As you exhale, whisper EE, vibrating your head, AH, in your chest, and OH, in your belly. This distributes energy throughout the body.

• **On the Sixth Night,** whenever climax approaches, use the Cobra (or Transmutation) Breath to distribute the energy. You will be highly charged by this point and greatly tempted to go to orgasm. Be determined to wait.

• **For the Seventh Night,** prepare a lavish and colorful atmosphere. Create a beautiful altar with candles, flowers, sandalwood incense. Have fruit and drink available. Make sure you will not be disturbed. Sacred Maithuna ritual is the culmination of Seven Nights of Tantra (or of a weekend or just a special evening)

Prepare CDs of the most romantic music you can find.

Illumination is important in a sensuous environment. An open fire is wonderful, as long as the temperatures are comfortable. Candles are a must. Use a cobalt blue light bulb to create the most spiritual atmosphere. That takes you into higher abstract spiritual realms as you make love.

Prepare the body. Feel totally clean. Give yourself an enema. Bathe luxuriously with candles and scented oils, individually or together. Jumping from warm water into a cold pool will stimulate your energy system.

Dress in robes made of natural fibers, preferably silk, in vibrant tantric colors (red and gold). Drawstring pants are good for the man. Choose clothing that is easily removed. Shakti can wear special jewelry as depicted in Tantric art.

The Ritual.

1) Invoke Babaji. Begin by kneeling at the altar. Light the candles and incense. Invoke the presence and guidance of Babaji through this ritual. Honor him as a living embodiment of a perfect balance of energy, a symbol of the balance you intend to create within yourself. You can use the mantra OM KRIYA BABAJI NAMAH AUM, or the advanced mantra (available in advanced courses). Use a string of mala beads and count off 108 repetitions. Enjoy the holy presence in a moment of gratitude and meditation.

2) Movement. Perform the Rishi Isometrics together, gazing into each other's eyes. This stretches and energizes the body.

To harmonize your energies, perform a slow mystic dance together, using sexercise-like movements. Do a mirror dance where Shakti mirrors every move Shiva makes. As the dance continues, <u>very slowly</u> undress each other.

3) Honor the Quintessential Male and Female. Forget personalities. In your nakedness, see yourself and your partner only as Shiva and Shakti, the Supreme Couple. Shakti honors her God for his clarity and Bliss; Shiva adores his Goddess as the most beautiful being in his life. In this honoring and the ministrations that follow, he calls forth in her the transformative aspect of Shakti, the Kali energy, the energy of awakened Kundalini. Shiva welcomes in his partner the energies she has never been encouraged to express, surrendering to her as his initiatress. He uses the Kali mantra to evoke that transformative power: OM KRING KALIKA NAMAHA.

4) Massage Shakti. She lies on a bed or on the floor (not a massage table.) Repeating the Kali mantra silently, Shiva gives Shakti an Erotic Massage, focusing on all the points specified below.

Shiva first caresses and adores each erogenous point using light strokes, then licks, kisses or sucks, then blows with a warm breath. He begins with the secondary points, then gives her a Kundalini massage as described in *Jewel*. Next he stimulates the tertiary points, leaving the primary points until the last fifteen minutes. He can include yoni massage if that is pleasing to Shakti. The massage could last about forty-five minutes (the length of one CD).

<u>Secondary points</u>	<u>Tertiary points</u>	<u>Primary points</u>
Earlobes	Edge of little finger	Lips and tongue
Nape of the neck	Palms of hand	Breasts, nipples
Sacral-lumbar junction	Navel	Genitals
Gluteal fold	Anus	
Inside of thighs	Nostril	
Back of knees	Ear orifice	
Soles of the feet		
Big toe		

He uses his skills of pranic healing, intending that the energy he gives will activate and excite each erogenous zone. Shakti is relaxed, receptive, and responsive, breathing deeply and fully present with the stimulation. She allows herself to be aroused. Shiva arouses himself doing Aswini Mudra while massaging.

5) Meditation. After the massage, Shiva lies behind Shakti. Do a Fusion Breath meditation together. (See Appendix A.) Lie still for about 10 minutes.

6) Massage Shiva. Shakti/Kali now becomes active, taking on the role of initiatress, embodying her full power to Shiva's emergence. She honors Shiva and chants to him the mantra OM NAMAH SHIVA (I disappear into Lord Shiva.) Continuing the mantra silently, she gives Shiva a massage, as described above. She may also use the mantra OM SHIVA HUM. (The energy of Shiva is embodied in this form.)

In the final phase of the massage, she worships the Shivalingam with her heart, her voice, her hands, her lips and tongue and throat. (See the video *Fire on the Mountain* for a repertoire of strokes.) She gently massages his testicles and stimulates his perineum. She is sensitive to his building energy and gives opportunity for him to transmute when climax approaches.

In the last few minutes, she massages and enters his anus. (See Lovemaking Guide.) Pressing her finger against the front wall of his rectum, she directly stimulates his prostate gland, his 1st chakra. After a few seconds the anus will probably go into spasms of pleasure. This is the climax to Shiva's massage.

She completes with long, connecting strokes, then holds one hand on his forehead, one on his heart, to connect and balance. She moves her hands so one is on his heart, one on his pubis, again to connect and balance the energy. Finally, she holds one hand on his forehead, one on his pubis.

7) Loveplay. Now Shiva and Shakti both become active, kissing and fondling each other in any way that brings pleasure.

8) Join Heaven and Earth. They go into genital union in yab yum position, reciting to each other vows to this effect: "Shiva brings to you the energy of the Heavens and offers it into your sacred Goddess body." "Shakti brings to you the energy of the Earth and offers it from my heart to your Divine Body." They begin the nipple-genital circuit, (Lesson 11 in *Jewel*. Gently rocking their pelvises, she exhales from her nipples as he inhales through his heart. He moves the energy down his spine and exhales through his lingam as she inhales through her yoni. She moves the energy up her spine to her heart.) They continue for about five minutes. Should orgasm approach, they delay it with several transmutations (First Cobra Breath/Tantric Kisses).

9) FireBreath. Still in yab yum, they begin the FireBreath and breathe together, thrusting pelvises together on the exhale. With seven breaths at each chakra, they draw the earth (Shakti) energy up to 6th chakra, touching the partner's back at each chakra point. If they have Second Level Cobra, they do it 7 times, then meditate for a few minutes.

10) Chant. Together they intone the mantra SAT CHIT ANANDA NAMAH. (May our minds be filled with Truth and may Bliss be experienced as the only Reality.) This attunes the physical temples to the Bliss (Shiva) vibration. They chant the mantra three times at each chakra, beginning at the crown and moving down.

11) Climax. Shakti stimulates Shiva again to bring his erection into full power. Shiva lies back and she mounts him, maneuvering so that his lingam touches as close as possible her 1st chakra near the cervix, on the back wall of her yoni. She contracts her vaginal muscles to massage the lingam to keep them both aroused. He sucks or fondles her nipples until she reaches climax. Several pillows under his back and head will make this more comfortable, as long as his spine is straight.

She will soon go into an extended orgasm, centered in the heart, and he will join her in that joyful, expansive state. They share seven Cobra Breaths while she is in orgasm. Together they move that orgasmic energy with alternating breath. As she exhales, he inhales, pulling her energy up his spine. As he exhales she inhales, pulling his energy up her spine. (Described in the last process of *Jewel*.)

12) Cosmic Orgasm. When the Cobra Breaths are complete, they lie close. Genitals are touching and legs inter-locked, maintaining connection but not in embrace. If Shiva and Shakti lie quietly in blissful meditation, they may notice after thirty-two minutes the Kundalini energy shooting up their spines. They might feel a tingle in the brain, a flush through the body when the energy moves. They might go into Samadhi, disappearing in the cosmic dimension where there are no longer lovers, there is only love.

Resources

Maithuna Ritual Sequence, Kirby Jacobson, available through
    Tantrika International.

EPILOGUE

New energies, never before available to the planet, now support mankind in completing the old way of being and moving into a new way. The materials presented in this book will allow you to complete this phase and prepare you for the next adventure. The time is now.

The Old Game.

A. Be constrained by rules because you fear severe punishment for disobeying.

B. Be motivated to do good works by a promise of future rewards.

The Current Game Plan.

A. Create the illusion of separation so you can work your way back to that elusive mystical union.

B. Build a reality on the basis of shame and unworthiness so you can come to appreciate the importance and sweetness of unconditional love.

C. Create a sub-conscious – a basement full of unexperienced feelings, limiting beliefs and compensating strategies so, as you bring this all into the light of consciousness, you can learn to enjoy emotion.

D. Be driven by a sense of duty and obligation, a host of "shoulds."

The Next Cosmic Game.

A. Secure in your connectedness with All That Is,

B. Honoring yourself and all around you,

C. Enjoying your feelings as they flow freely through,

D. Be drawn toward that which most fills your heart;
Play with your divine humanness. Follow your joy!

APPENDIX A
ENERGY PRACTICES

Conscious Breathing, (or psychic breathing), integrates the physical breath with awareness. Psychic breathing involves Khechari Mudra, with the tongue touching the soft palate and glottis in the throat contracted. The breath feels and sounds like a gentle snore deep in your throat.

Concentrate on the sound in the throat and make it sound the same while you inhale and exhale, a deep calm, relaxed breath. The tongue position increases production of saliva and prevents throat irritation. Once that is established, you can focus your attention on a particular part of the body (physical or subtle) that you want to move energy into, any channel you want to move energy through. Simply by visualizing that movement, and having the intention, that energy moves. You can breathe this way as long as you like. If you do it properly, you will experience greatly increased energy.

This technique has a powerful psychic effect. It also affects the relationship between mind and body and is beneficial to the nervous system.

Transmutation Breath:
To Diffuse Energy through the Body

1) Inhale through the nose as you slowly contract the anus.

2) With the breath pull sexual energy from the genitals up to the Third Eye. This transmutes the energy in the semen and vaginal fluids, devitalizing the semen so it can be ejaculated without loss of energy.

3) Think, or intone, the mantra EE-AH-OH as you exhale and relax the anus. The energy diffuses through the body.

Trataka: To Still the Mind

When the eyes are motionless, the thinking process stops and the mind becomes quiet. This exercise also helps awaken the Third Eye (Ajna).

1) Sit comfortably in a darkened room with no breeze.

2) Position a lighted candle at eyebrow level about two feet away from the face. The flame should be motionless.

3) Sit with the spine straight, close the eyes and relax. The body is motionless.

4) When you feel quiet, open your eyes and gaze steadily at the flame, with minimal blinking or moving of the eyes. Focus your attention on the flame.

5) The eyes may become tired after a few minutes. Let them close, but be aware of the candle after-image. When that image fades, open the eyes again and continue your concentrated gaze.

   The best time to practice is just before dawn or late at night, times when the atmosphere is still. Fifteen to twenty minutes is an ideal amount of time.

   Trataka can also be practiced concentrating on a dot, a full moon, a crystal, a yantra, a picture. You can focus on your own reflection in a mirror or on the eyes of another person. The images may start to shift, as layers fall away and different faces present themselves.

Uddiyana Bandha – Diaphragm Lock

Massages and stimulates the internal organs and Manipura, reservoir of pranic energies. Relaxes chronic tensions that separate sex energy from the heart.

1) Sit in the easy pose with palms on knees. Relax, close your eyes and focus on the navel chakra.

2) Exhale deeply. Perform a chin lock (Hold the breath, move the head back, drop the chin. Straighten your arms and lock the elbows, pulling shoulders up and forward.)

3) Contract abdominal muscles upward and inward. Hold as long as comfortable.

4) Relax muscles, raise head and then inhale.

5) When breathing is back to normal, you can repeat up to 10 times.

CAUTION: Practice only on an empty stomach. Do not practice if you have an ulcer or during pregnancy.

Golden Sphere Breathing – Individual or Couple

1. Sit in an easy cross-legged pose, facing your partner, eyes closed, tongue relaxed, your knees touching your partner's knees. Use Holding the Mind Mudra, making a circle with thumb and index finger of right hand and putting left thumb through this circle to touch the right palm, cradling the right hand in the left hand in your lap. Put your awareness at the crown center.

2. Take a deep breath up the spine and silently vibrate the mantram "Hing." Again inhaling, making it vibrate. "Hinnnnng." Once more.

3. In your mind's eye, imagine a small, cool, golden sphere sitting above the crown chakra. Be aware of the coolness. Put your full attention on this ball.

4. Gently inhale, drawing the energy of the golden ball down the spine to the root chakra. Very gently tighten the root, holding the energy there.

5. Gradually release, exhaling the energy up the front channel, just under the skin, relaxing the whole body. Feel the current coming up the body, to the tip of your tongue. Bring your awareness back to the crown chakra and the golden sphere of light.

6. Again, see the golden sphere of light dropping with your in-breath, all the way down your spine. When you get to Muladhara, tighten. This time, Shiva, try to make the head of the penis twitch.

7. Release the Root Lock, exhaling up the front channel. Let the energy come to the tip of the tongue. Return awareness to the crown chakra.

Golden Sphere Breathing with Stimulation – Couple

1. Release the mudra. Shiva, cup the testicles with your right hand. Shakti, insert your fire (middle) finger into your vagina and move it in circles for stimulation. Your awareness is at the crown chakra.

2. Inhale the golden ball of light down the spine and tighten the root. Shiva, gently squeeze the testicles and Shakti, gently massage the clitoris, to hold energy right at that point.

3. Exhale, releasing the root and the testicles or clitoris. Allow the energy to come up the front channel of the body. Totally relax in that current and let it come up and tickle the tongue. Place the tongue on the roof of your mouth. You might start tasting something.

4. Return to the crown chakra and repeat this breath cycle.

5. Now let your awareness slide back into the center of the head. Pause a few seconds, slowly relax the tongue and open your eyes, keeping your consciousness in the center of the head.

Hong Saw, Back to Back

As a preliminary, do the Rishi Isometrics to tune into subtle energy. Sit back to back with your partner, becoming very aware of their spine and sacrum, and begin a Hong Saw meditation. Coordinate your breathing. Within a few minutes your boundaries will become confused. You will not be able to tell where one body leaves off and the next begins. Your minds will be very quiet.

See if you can feel that hollow that creates a vacuum in the small of the back. See if you can feel a slight vibration there, a slight pressure. Let your heads touch. Lean back so you make body contact with your partner. Use the breath mantra so this energy can move up and down the spine, so you and your partner can feel a sense of oneness.

As you inhale, tighten the anus gently. Exhale, releasing the anus. (repeat two times) This time, as you inhale and tighten, mentally say the sound "hung." As you exhale and release the anus, mentally chant the sound "saw." Repeat many times. Inhale and pull up on the root lock. Exhale and relax.

Stay with your partner's breath rhythm. Follow the life current up and down the spine with Hung-Sau. If you feel tremors, relax and let them come. It's just energy moving through the body in a sacred way. See if you can feel the presence of your mate's life force moving up and down his or her spine. Now drop the mantra. Rotate in place on your buttocks, stimulating the sacrum. Go in first one direction, then the other. Stay with your partner's rhythm. We rotate like this so energy doesn't lodge in any one spot and can flow freely. Relax and stay in this space focused on your partner, totally still.

From this point you can begin to make love and find yourself in another dimension.

Attunement

Bring your vibrations into resonance with your partner's at all three levels: head, heart, and genital.

Head – Press your foreheads together (tantric kiss). This is far more intense as part of the Cobra Breath done together. If you are in yab yum position, when the chin comes down, the foreheads automatically come together.

Heart – Pressing your chests together, focus on each other's breath. Send an energy ball back and forth from one heart to the other, as one inhales (sending the energy) while the other exhales (receiving the energy) and vice versa.

Genitals – Intercourse in any position will produce resonance, as long as this part of the body is your mutual point of focus. You can do it without being in union by practicing Vajroli Mudra with the genitals in close proximity.

Spinal Spiral

This energy circuit is the advanced Microcosmic Orbit of Taoist practice inhaling down the back, exhaling up the front. The front channel is just beneath the skin. The back channel, just behind the spine. This is not a rigid process. Variations are possible. Once you have the general flow, feel free to experiment.

1. Shiva: Place your right hand on your partner's spine behind her heart. Using your left hand, start massaging the base of your partner's sacrum with circular strokes. The tips of the tongues are touching. Shakti: Help direct the energy using breath and visualization.

2. Now Shiva, very gently allow those circular strokes become a spiral, as you pull energy up from her sacrum to her heart. Return your hand directly to the sacrum, without spiraling. Again spiral energy up into her heart.

3. Shiva, put your right hand over your partner's crown chakra. With the left hand, make several spirals from her heart to her crown.

4. Touch the tongue tips. Shiva, inhale as you raise both hands. Exhaling, bring your hands down, following the contours of her body. Bathe your goddess with this energy Bathe her life force field, creating a layer of protection for her. Spread the energy out on the floor around her. Repeat once more.

5. Release the tongue contact very gently and very slowly. Swallow the energy you have exchanged into Manipura.

6. Synchronize your breath, following the woman's lead, each inhaling down the spine, up the front of the body. Inhaling down the spine, tighten the root chakra; with your mind, engorge the penis and the vaginal lips with blood, exhale up the front. Make tongue contact. You can feel a pulsation coming out of the tongues. Take several more breaths this way, very gently thrusting your pelvises together on the exhale, pulling back on the inhale.

7. Now release tongue contact and reverse roles spiraling energy. Shakti, put your left hand on his sacrum, your right hand behind his heart. Start bringing his energy up from the coccyx in a

spiralling, massaging motion, only to the heart. Letting the energy collect there provides a safety valve. Let the lower energies be transformed by the heart before proceeding up to the crown. Drop your left hand back down to his sacrum, and run his energies up again several more times. Now move your left hand to your mate's crown chakra. With your right hand, spiral his energy up from his heart to his crown chakra.

8. Now touch tongues, Shakti inhale, raising your hands, and exhale, bathing your man with this energy. Repeat. Slowly release your tongues and swallow. Just relax. Notice what's going on in your body. Feel what's going on in your emotions. If you feel something coming up to the heart, notice it and let it go. Be aware of what is coming into the mind, and release it.

Fusion Breath

1. Lie with your partner, both of you on your left sides, facing the same direction, with the man behind the woman. He enfolds his goddess with his free arm. Both bend your legs a little, so you look like two spoons nestled together. Be nude and have as much skin contact as possible.

2. Coordinate your breathing so both are inhaling and exhaling at the same time. Just lie very still and watch the breath. It will probably be fairly shallow. Focus on the expansion and relaxation of both your chest and your partner's. Let your total awareness be on the movement of your breath and your partner's. At this point there is no movement, nothing that would stimulate sexual arousal. Just be totally present.

3. After a few minutes, the woman can signal a change in breath pattern by breathing much deeper and slower, doing a very relaxed Complete Breath, filling first the belly, then the chest, then emptying the chest and belly. Be totally aware of each other's breath as though it were a single breath.

4. Begin to see the breath entering the Third Eye, traveling through the center of the skull, and down the spine on the inhale. Perform one contraction and relaxation of the anal or cervical muscles. Exhale, watching the breath go back up the spine, through the head and out the Third Eye. See both of your breaths moving together, a perfectly matched team. Each brings the tip of their tongue to the roof of their mouth.

5. Hear the etheric sound of the breath, the mantram "So Hum." On the inhale, hear the sound "So," on the exhale, the sound "Hum." Continue for a few minutes until your mind is totally quiet and you feel absolutely present, absolutely at one. Then release the mantra. You might just decide to drift into sleep at this point, or you might be turned on and want to make love. Be sure to transmute the energy using Cobra Breath.

Continuation

1. Perform Fusion Breath, above.

2. If you feel to go on, the man continues to pull energy down on the inhale, but on the exhale, sends that energy out the root chakra to his partner's root chakra with a very gentle thrusting of the pelvis. When she feels his body begin to move, her breath changes. She receives the energy he is exhaling with an inhalation. Her pelvis moves together with his. Now one inhales while the other exhales, the pelvises rocking together gently.

7. After a few minutes, he begins sending energy to her 2nd chakra. He takes the breath all the way down to the root, and does the anal contraction, then exhales back up the spine just to the 2nd chakra (a very short distance) and gives the energy from the lingam. His hand lies lightly over her pubis. She continues to breathe in from the 1st chakra, pulling it up to the second, receiving the incoming energy. She exhales gently, retaining the energy in the first two chakras.

8. When those chakras feel activated, he moves his hand to her belly, and begins to send energy to Manipura. She continues to breathe up from the root to the chakra being energized, but also receives his energy directly from behind. When it feels right, he moves his hand to her breast, and gives energy from and to the heart chakra.

9. You could then turn over and reverse roles, with the woman drawing energy directly from the root to the higher chakras on her inhale and giving it on the exhale, working up from the root to the heart. Her left hand would stimulate her partner at the area being energized – perineum, testicles/penis, navel, breast.

10. This whole attunement and nurturing process could take about an hour (but don't watch the clock). At that point you are ready to make love more exquisitely than you ever dreamed possible. Remember to delay your orgasms with the Cobra Breath and let the energy take you into Bliss.

TIBETAN ALCHEMICAL MEDITATION:
Golden Body of Light

This secret meditation will show you how to recycle sexual energy through what is known as the "Backward Flow Method." This technique will intensify the Universal Life Force flowing through your body and connect you with the Cosmic Prana outside for vitality and pranic healing.

This meditation takes two hours in a monastic setting in Nepal. We have shortened the process to thirty minutes for the restless Western mind, but still maintained the energy and intensity of the Tibetan Tantric Rasa tradition.

Perform this meditation every morning during the Seven Nights of Tantra.

1. Sit with your eyes closed and back straight. Rest your tongue against the roof of the mouth, just behind the top front teeth, touching the teeth slightly. Breathe through your nose.

2. In your mind's eye, see yourself sitting on a blue lotus. The petals come up around your hips. Now see this blue lotus lift you. You are as light as a bubble as the lotus lifts you into an endless blue sky. Higher and higher you climb, effortlessly, lifted as if by a giant hand.

3. Right above, you now see a giant beam of warm, shimmering light. The light is a radiant gold, like the sun. As you move closer to the beam of liquid light, you feel the warmth from the waterfall. Now move even closer. Move right into the beam of golden light. You can feel the cascade of golden light flooding over your head. You float higher and higher into the beam and the golden liquid is an avalanche of light flowing down and over the top of your skull. See this golden light enter your skull in a place behind your eyes.

4. Now this warm radiant light is flowing down to your nose; now your mouth; now your chin. The warm golden light flows down your neck to your shoulders and chest. Every cell of your body is warmed and excited by the touch of this golden light. Now it trickles down from your chest to your belly and finally to manipura chakra, the storehouse of this golden life energy. Now see it separate to spill down the outside of both legs at the same time.

5. The warm golden light has now reached the soles of your feet. You can feel how warm the light is and how it thrills every cell of your body it touches. Gradually, the warm golden current flows up the inside of both legs at the same time. Slowly it reaches your knees. Eventually it enters the sex center and moves to the coccyx (tailbone) where once again it is a single flow.

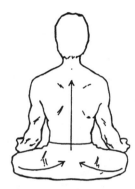

6. Now this warm golden current is at the small of your back. Then from the small of your back it flows up the center of your spine to the middle back.

7. It moves between your shoulder blades and down the insides of your arms and then back up the outside of your arms. Now it moves back to the spine between the shoulder blades and up to your shoulders, your neck and to the base of your skull. Allow the beam of energy to cascade up through the top of your head. Your skull and brain are washed by this warm, golden force.

8. Now repeat this cycle three times. On the fourth cycle, when you get to the Manipura chakra, which is the storehouse of this warm, golden Life Energy Current, let it rest there for several minutes. Strive to feel the force there with great intensity. Just sit in full awareness of the light in your Manipura chakra. Just feel, without thinking. Just feel this golden warmth and force resting in your special place of power.

9. After this period of quiet meditation in Manipura chakra, take the light down the legs and up the back, through the arms. This time, as you go up the back, slowly inhale and take the breath with the light up to the top of your head.

Tighten the Root Center as you inhale and coordinate moving your eyes up as the breath and light moves up. Your eyelids remain closed. When the light reaches the top of your head, hold the breath with your eyes raised up for a few seconds and allow all of the skull to be radiated with this light.

10. The light now goes slowly forward, pouring over the top of your head. You begin to exhale and slowly release the Root Lock and move the eyes back down slowly. When your breath is completely exhaled and your eyes are completely lowered, that's when the warm, golden light has reached your Manipura chakra. Holding the exhale, you sit silently, feeling the light there, not thinking, just feeling.

Important Points.

A. The Golden Light Circle can be started from the base of your spine (Muladhara). If you start it from the Root Center, first draw it from the Manipura chakra through the space between the legs to the base of the spine, for Manipura chakra is where the life force makes its home.

B. The beginning part (when you approach and enter the beam of golden light) can be repeated each time you begin the golden circle at the top of the head. So you would approach and enter the cascade of golden light in your imagination each time the light has gone up the back and neck and head and is ready to pour down over the top of your head again.

C. Make sure that the light moves very slowly. Try to feel that each cell of your body is bathing in the warmth and radiance of this warm golden light as the light passes through on its journey through your body. This warm golden light is the concentrated life energy (pranic energy) known in Tibet as "Lung"

D. Emphasize the pouring of the warm golden light over the top of your head and the sitting with the feeling of the light in the Manipura chakra. Always conclude the meditation by resting in Manipura chakra. This ensures that the energy does not get blocked or scattered. Remember, Manipura chakra is the energy storage battery of the body.

E. Begin practicing the Golden Circle for 5 minutes each morning. You could eventually try for as many as 18 cycles.

F. This meditation will increase and balance your sexual drive and will bring healing to any part of the body that needs it.

G. You will find that you develop the ability to heal others as a by-product of practicing this meditation. Other experiences of a psychic or occult nature may occur to you as well. Resist the temptation to explore or exploit these and instead pursue the absolute, the only true source of happiness and peace of mind, which is beyond time and space.

APPENDIX B
YOGA NIDRA
Conscious Sleep

Yoga Nidra, derived from the most ancient tantric scriptures, is a powerful technique teaching complete relaxation of the body while maintaining awareness. The body goes to sleep, but the mind stays awake.

BENEFITS

This safe and simple practice provides many benefits, including:
- Deep relaxation of mind, body and personality.
- Entry into a state of meditation.
- Bringing to consciousness repressed psychological material.
- Healing of psychosomatic ailments.
- Removing insomnia, aiding in deep sleep.
- Rejuvenation of the whole organism at all levels – physical, mental, pranic.
- Opening the potential of the mind, awakening the faculty of intuition.
- Increasing memory, learning capacity, awareness of inner knowledge.

In the threshold between sleep and wakefulness, contact with the powerful subconscious and unconscious dimensions occurs spontaneously. When consciousness is dissociated from the senses (pratyahara) and focused inward, the mind is extremely receptive. As the body sleeps, habits can be reprogrammed and knowledge can be infused. You can perform such tasks as developing memory, rapid learning, increasing creativity and transcending limitations. This higher consciousness leads to samadhi.

Psychology has termed this impressionable state "hypnagogic," but yoga nidra goes far beyond suggestibility. It also allows you to receive information from the unconscious mind. It is the fountain of artistic and poetic inspiration, as well as the source of scientific discoveries. All truly creative geniuses have learned to tap this inner well of knowledge.

The intuitions received in yoga nidra enable you to find within yourself the answers to all problems. Your true nature manifests, pervaded with divine consciousness, far beyond the conditioned neurotic personality.

Releasing Tensions.

In yoga nidra you learn to totally relax. What most people think of as relaxation (TV, sports, vacations, etc.) are simply unconscious diversions, ways to ignore the existing tensions.

Most of the diseases that plague modern man are created by stress. Cancer, heart disease, diabetes, hypertension, migraine, asthma, ulcers, digestive disorders, skin diseases, all arise from tensions held in the body. All emotional imbalances involve tension in the mind.

Each day we collect more tensions – physical, mental, emotional. These tensions cut us off from our own divine inner guidance. Normal sleep is not sufficient to release us. The mind and feelings continue their turbulent struggles as the body sleeps. Billions of tranquilizers are taken every year, but they only treat symptoms and don't address the root problems. If our daily practice does not include a time to deeply relax, tension accumulates until it finally overwhelms us.

Yoga nidra is a far more efficient way to rest and rejuvenate mind and body than ordinary sleep. One hour of yoga nidra – half hour as you wake up and again as you go to sleep – is worth four hours of normal sleep without awareness. You can get by with three hours less sleep. This is one way to find enough time in your busy life for spiritual practice.

Layers of Consciousness.

Yoga nidra allows you to explore all the layers of the psyche – conscious, subconscious, unconscious, superconscious – as the deeper layers are brought into awareness.

Conscious mind is a waking state where you process perceptions of the outside world and entertain thoughts. It corresponds to physical reality.

Subconscious mind is the dream state, the home of individual memory. It corresponds to the pranic body. The brain stores millions of impressions that record everything we experience in life. Memories of events where consciousness was not fully present, karma, are in storage. During this practice the mind becomes subtle, and experiences are almost on the same level as in dreams, except that they are much more vivid and clear.

When awareness penetrates subconscious realms, it is temporarily detached from the body. Then you can experience this karma, residue from this life or previous lives. Maintaining consciousness, you draw these impressions into the conscious level, reducing your stock of unexperienced impressions.

Unconscious mind is deep, dreamless sleep. Here memories are engraved and processed, but they remain latent, without any manifestation. Instinctive desires are competing with rational choices for expression. When entered consciously, the unconscious allows total memory. It corresponds to the causal dimension.

The four states of consciousness are identifiable by the frequency of the brainwaves produced.

- BETA (13 to 30 Hz) – In our waking state of external awareness, the fast beta waves predominate. The senses are fully active. Here we can focus our attention and solve problems. Here we also find anxiety and apprehension.
- ALPHA (8 to 13 Hz) – In this alert but very relaxed hypnagogic state, the slower alpha waves predominate. Here you feel tranquil and floating and are highly suggestible.
- THETA (4 to 8 Hz) – In dreams, the state when the subconscious is working out deep problems, the theta waves predominate.
- DELTA (0 to 4 Hz) – In deep, dreamless sleep the unconscious manifests. Here the delta waves predominate.

The Menninger Foundation monitored Swami Rama as he progressively relaxed body, mind and emotions through yoga nidra. He entered the state of "deep sleep," as verified by the delta wave patterns recorded on an EEG. However, he remained perfectly aware and later recalled everything that occurred while he was "asleep." This startling discovery simply shows what is possible with training and practice.

Theta Threshold.

Yoga nidra occurs at the threshold between alpha and theta, between sense consciousness and sleep (7 to 8 Hz). This is the state of true meditation. It is a transcendental state of consciousness. Each morning as you awaken, each night as you drift into sleep, you go through this threshold. Normally we remain there only a few seconds, but with intention and some practice you can stay in that space for longer periods. This is the moment when you can remember your dreams. It is the state where magic happens. Some rituals of witchcraft and shamanism are designed to induce this state. The thoughts you entertain here are strongly inclined to manifest. It's interesting to note that the frequency 7.8 Hz is the natural resonance of planet earth's electro-magnetic field (the Schumann resonance). We are in the state of being most complete, most able to create, when we are attuned to Mother Earth. The Schumann resonance frequency has increased in the last several years, showing that portals to the unconscious are opening into conscious states.

That last thought you have before transitioning into sleep occurs in this special moment when you are at your most suggestible. What you think in that moment will manifest the next day. As children we were encouraged to say our prayers just before sleep. We've all been told not to go to sleep on a quarrel. It's frightening to think how many people are in the habit of falling asleep in front of the TV, with violence and insanity penetrating this tender place. That could, in part, explain the senseless brutality of our times. In those moments, review any upsets of the day, follow them back to their source, and release the energy on them. Let your first and last thought each day reflect your determination to live in divine light. Attune to your higher nature.

During the practice of yoga nidra, your awareness travels through these layers of consciousness, sometimes going very deep to produce more fantastic and explosive experiences. Sometimes it stays near the surface, producing pleasant relaxation. Sometimes experiences come up directly, but usually they manifest symbolically. The language of the subconscious is symbols, colors and sounds. These are the archetypes which emerge during yoga nidra. The subconscious is an efficient storehouse because a single image can convey an experience which a thousand words cannot adequately express.

Everything in the cosmos is contained within the mind in archetypal form. The mind is a hologram of the entire universe. During yoga nidra the symbols you are asked to visualize draw out the various latent archetypes. The symbols are mandalas or pictorial conceptions – a rose, a temple, a boat. Mandalas are composed of yantras. These are fundamental geometrical arrangements, all permutations and combinations of a line, a point, and a circle. Yantras and mandalas are the most powerful way of releasing the stored archetypes into conscious awareness.

Super-Consciousness.

When we reach the core of the unconscious, we can manifest the latent faculties of certain cerebral circuits in the brain, the centers of extra-sensory perception. These circuits sometimes explode in yoga nidra, producing visual effects. They are not objective, but are certainly not hallucinations.

These centers are not related to karma. This facility for extrasensory perception is inherent in every human, but only a few yogis and madmen have attained those experiences. Indeed, madness is often a spiritual experience which man has not been able to handle. Through practice of yoga nidra, the yogi has learned to manage this extrasensory input. He can go comfortably into that deep state where he is completely united with his inner being.

(Extract from *Theta Threshold*, an audio course with manual, much more detailed information, and CDs to guide your exploration. Available from Tantrika International.)

APPENDIX C
FIREBREATH
Seven-Chakra Orgasm

FireBreath is one of the most powerful methods of transmuting energy in the body. It is not the fire breath as taught in Kundalini Yoga. It is a bellows breath, a Kriya breath that consciously pulls sexual, earth energy into the body and directs it through the chakra system.

Some of this information appears in various chapters of this book. It is repeated here for completeness.

The Cobra Breath provides you with experience in running Shakti energy through spinal paths. The FireBreath process is more connected to the emotional body. Doing this practice you will come up against karmic energies you have been able to bypass thus far.

Source. FireBreath was originally practiced in Egyptian temples and variations are found in the East Indian and Taoist traditions. A form of it is practiced by Tibetan Buddhist nuns, allowing them to utilize their sexual energies while remaining celibate. A similar practice is found in the Cherokee Indian tradition, incorporating their way of working with energies from Mother Earth. This was popularized in America by the medicine man, Harley Swiftdeer. We will begin with a version similar to the well-known process, and take it to the next level.

BENEFITS FROM PRACTICE

Health Value. The Seven-Chakra Orgasm is a natural way to stimulate your endocrine glands. When they produce more hormones than you need for maintenance, the excess will be directed toward rejuvenation.

When lovemaking is prolonged past twenty minutes, through self-stimulation or with a partner, the hormonal balance in the body starts to change, activating the rejuvenation process. The longer you can stay in an aroused state, the more hormones are produced, and therefore the more health benefits.

After practicing the FireBreath, you go into a very beautiful after-glow. It will be much more intense when the FireBreath is coupled with the Cobra Breath. You will see how they work together.

Psychological Value. This is a wonderful technique for women who have never experienced orgasm. You don't need a partner and are free from the pressure of involving another person or invoking debilitating memories. Many pre-orgasmic women have been violated, victims of rape or incest. The pelvis has become locked up in order to numb the pain of this humiliation. These women can learn to once again allow their natural energies to flow, to heal the trauma, and enjoy orgasmic fulfillment.

The FireBreath is one of the most powerful processes to bring repressed psychological trauma into consciousness. The rush of sexual energy cleanses the nadis and opens up the chakras, one by one, releasing the memories stored there. Given the proper support and tools to deal with this material, one can easily have breakthrough experiences.

Psychic Development. This is a great practice to do by yourself for learning to feel your energy. People who have had trouble feeling prana or sensing the aura will definitely feel it in this process. The pranic energy becomes very thick for three or four inches around you and a foot above. You may need to practice several times before you have a real energetic experience. If you are open and have done a lot of pranayam and consciousness-expanding work, it will happen more quickly. If you are a beginner, be patient with yourself, and it will come. Eventually you will feel the tingling in your body and an ecstatic state of mind.

Sexual-Spiritual Enhancement. When your partner wants to make love but you feel tired or not turned on, five minutes of FireBreathing will leave you totally aroused, even without your partner's help. This is a good demonstration to show that you can be orgasmic at any time. In Tantra, we don't wait for "the right moment" for sexual expression. We make the moment happen.

In the FireBreath, orgasm becomes a distribution of energy throughout the whole body, the whole being, not just a localized genital experience. Women naturally experience a full-body orgasm, due to the nature of their nervous system. Most men, however, have never known anything other than an isolated genital release. This practice could provide your first full-body orgasmic experience.

You can do this process: 1) in the psychic way with the breath, 2) through self-pleasuring, or 3) with a partner. If you are making love with a partner, the FireBreath orgasm can be ecstatic as the vibration takes over the whole body. The process works with self pleasure too. You may immediately get to the peak, or might stretch it out for a long time, reaching higher states of orgasmic energy, over and over and over again. This is a beautiful way for a man to have multiple orgasms.

Students have reported including FireBreath in their lovemaking, and subsequently experiencing an orgasm that climbed from one chakra to the next until the entire system was in full orgasm.

Once you get to a highly aroused state, if you have a mate, come right into the yab yum position and continue pulling energy up into the heart. When you feel orgasm getting ready to explode, take the Cobra Breath up, touch foreheads (during the chin lock) in the tantric kiss, lean back and exhale down. You will have an illuminating experience. You will feel the presence of your souls merging in space – the Cosmic Orgasm.

Emotional Release. You will find that moving energy through the chakras brings up emotions. When you do strong breathing, it breaks through repression. Every time you do the FireBreath you will feel different feelings. Sometimes you might cry and feel sad. Sometimes anger may surface. That is to be expected. Simply experience the emotion, hold the Witness and keep the breath and movement going. You are purifying and clearing the chakras.

Initially you will be working through heavy emotional material that surfaces from the lower levels. Eventually you will work all the way up to the crown chakra where the feelings are sublime. You will come to know the breadth of emotions available to you.

Physical Sensations might manifest. You might feel a kind of buzzing all over the body. Your body might feel paralyzed in some places. It might feel like you are lifting off into weightlessness with no effort involved. There might be a buzz, starting in the genitals, that keeps amplifying and moving up, going back and forth. You might feel like your head is opening up. The FireBreath can take you into kriyas (involuntary shaking or twitching). That simply means that energy blocks are being released. Occasionally, tetany might occur, caused by too much carbon dioxide in the system. You might experience the hands drawing up into claws and feeling immobilized. Simply continue the breath, with more attention to the exhalation. The tetany will eventually pass.

CAUTIONS

Contra-Indications. 1) If you have high blood pressure, don't do this practice. 2) If you have a headache don't do this technique. That indicates there is already too much energy in the body. 3) Women: During the menstrual cycle, and a few days before, it's not advisable to practice. At that time there is an engorgement of blood in the pelvic bowl. The FireBreath might upset the cycle and increase your blood loss.

Pleasure Overload. It's possible to have such ecstatic experiences in FireBreath that you get fascinated with the lower chakras. Be sure to move that energy into the higher centers by doing Cobra Breath at the end. Your higher centers are activated only through the spinal channel.

Energy Loss. When you're ready to have the orgasm, you should exhale the energy back down through the spine, do root lock and take the energy up through the spinal channel with the Cobra Breath. In this way you won't lose your energy.

Emotional Overload. One danger inherent in doing the FireBreath, especially for beginners, is opening up the chakras prematurely. Each chakra is a virtual Pandora's box. It's very important in Kriya Yoga that we magnetize the spine first and activate the Third Eye, the Witness, before we ever touch the chakras. Make sure that energy is flowing up and down the spinal canal in a gentle, flowing manner. A few months of Cobra Breath is the best way to accomplish this.

Emotional release only happens on a permanent basis if done with consciousness. Total Shakti energy is just hysteria. Rebirthing, Primal and Reichean therapies often deteriorate into that. You can scream and yell week after week and not let anything go. The only time that you can release that emotional charge is when your non-attached consciousness is watching the process. It is only when the Witness Consciousness is active and the emotional expression is going on at the same time that you can actually accomplish a healing.

Opening up too fast could cause a psychotic break. There are therapists whose whole practice involves repairing damage done in cathartic meditation. And yet catharsis often has to happen. Analysis by itself will never release neurosis. Objectivity and subjectivity must happen simultaneously.

This is advanced work. Don't attempt it by yourself if you have not reached the Second Level.

Energy Overload. If you overdo the FireBreath, you might actually damage your nervous system from running energy that's too hot. The practice might become addictive because it is so exciting and wonderful. Use this powerful tool with respect and only occasionally. Once a week is plenty.

Lost in the Astral. You are strongly advised NOT to take this breath all the way to the crown chakra. Students who have tried this have reported opening their eyes and being surrounded by demons and strange creatures. Moving this energy to the crown, you can blow yourself into the lower astral dimension, which is populated by entities you would rather not know.

303

There are several body channels you can use to move energy, depending on what you wish to accomplish. If you are going to stay inside the body and circulate the energy, use the spinal channels. When you work with the spinal channel, you get all of the physical and emotional sensations. You are still connected to the physical body.

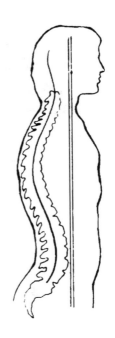

If you are looking for transcendent states, the central channel, Uma, could take you there. Uma doesn't exist in the body. It is created by your mind. But once created, it is more powerful than the spinal channel because when you move through Uma you can go up and out of the body into the pure abstract space of nothingness. That can be frightening.

The Tibetans say that all of this world is illusion. Moving your energy up the central channel allows you to see reality as it really is. Tibetan practitioners hope to blast through the crown chakra into the Void. The East Indians prefer to work with the spinal channel first, until you are ready to go into the Void.

If the spirit is not pure enough, it will fall short of the Void, and find itself in the lower astral where negative thought forms appear as demons. The Tibetans realize this danger. Their sacred art is full of demon images. They carry rattles and have procedures to deal with these entities. Such an encounter doesn't serve you, and it's potentially dangerous.

FireBreath can slip into the central channel if done incorrectly. You are well advised to stay in your spine. In your practice, take the FireBreath only to the 6th chakra! You are not ready to "travel." We use the breath, visualization, and mudras with the intention of pumping the energy up. You will then push the energy down on an exhale and pull it up the spine on the Cobra Breath inhalation.

FIREBREATH FOR INDIVIDUALS

Before doing the FireBreath, arouse yourself sexually, either through self-pleasure or with a partner, building up an intense erotic energy in the body. The anal contractions (Aswini Mudra) keep the energy pumping so the process is more dynamic.

Notice how it feels to do the process clear to orgasm compared to stopping short of an orgasm. Men, see what happens if you have transmuted the energy before you have an ejaculation. Women, see how your orgasm feels if you have taken the time to transmute the energy.

There is a controversy between various schools of Tantra about ejaculation. We have observed that if a man can maintain sexual energy in the body and delay orgasm for an hour, he can ejaculate without losing energy. He will stay in a high vibratory state. You are learning to build more energy in the body, and then suffuse it through the body, before having an orgasm.

When you first start, it is important to go slowly. Move at your own pace, according to your body strength. Don't overdo it. Get into the rhythm and build up the energy. It might take several sessions before you begin to feel a total body vibration. Be pleasantly surprised if it happens sooner. Just get the mechanics of the process at first. Achieving an ecstatic state will happen sooner or later, depending on how open you are. As you move the energy, you are cleansing and purifying your chakras. Only when the channels are open can the energy rush come through.

• **Position.** Find a space to lie down comfortably. Your head should not be on a pillow. You should be lying flat on a blanket. Moving on a carpet can irritate the skin. After some practice, the FireBreath can also be done sitting on a cushion.

• **Chakra Breathing.** Begin by breathing in and out through the mouth, but visualizing the energy moving directly in and out of each chakra. Breathe five times at each chakra, beginning at the base and working up. Allow a soft, gentle opening of the chakras.

- **Nauli.** Roll the stomach for about one minute.

- **Undulation.** Lie with the knees bent, feet flat on the floor, so you can get a smooth rocking motion in the pelvis. Begin pelvic undulations, tilting the pelvic bowl, thrusting tailbone forward (upward) as your back flattens onto the floor and then rocking the pelvis backward while arching the back. Set up a rhythmic wave.

Many people are frozen in the pelvis. This rocking releases those chronically contracted muscles. Soon the body will start its own undulating movement without your control. It might be helpful to imagine the wave-like motion of the dolphins. Feel your head and neck moving back and forth while you are rocking. If you don't move your neck, energy will get stuck there.

This undulating motion is an essential part of generating sexual energy. Practicing this movement while making love will greatly enhance your arousal.

- **FireBreathing.** As soon as you feel comfortable with the undulations, coordinate your breathing with the pelvic movement; inhaling through the nose, exhaling through the mouth in a breathy "hoo" sound, with lips pursed as if to whistle. Inhale as the tailbone rocks back, exhale as the tailbone thrusts forward. There is no gap between the exhale and inhale. As you inhale, expand your belly. As you exhale, pull in the belly. Start slowly, about one second to inhale, one second to exhale. The pace quickens as your arousal intensifies.

- **Contractions.** When the breathing is coordinated with the undulations, add a root lock (perineal or vaginal contractions) to stimulate the earthy, sexual energy. Inhaling, visualize the balloon expanding, exhaling, visualize closing the balloon's mouth by contracting the muscles of the perineum. Relax the contraction with the next inhalation, contract with the next exhalation. You don't have to hold the contraction for a long period. You will eventually be able to distinguish between the three types of pelvic contractions – aswini, root lock, and vajroli (anus, perineal/vaginal, urethral). Initially everything contracts together.

You may come across another version of this process instructing you to contract on the inhale instead of the exhale. The two variations produce very different results. When you contract on the exhale, the energy diffuses through the chakras. When you contract on the inhale, the kundalini is more likely to shoot up the spine out of control. This is not recommended.

• **Pulling Energy.** Inhaling through the nose, draw energy in through the perineum or vaginal lips. Exhaling through the mouth as you contract those muscles condenses the energy and creates a vacuum. Continue until the first chakra feels activated. Then begin to visualize earth energy from the root chakra moving up to the sex center. Start building a circle connecting those two chakras.

Contracting your pelvic muscles draws sexual, earthy energy into the body. Many people are not connected to their lower energy centers and only experience sexuality on the mental level. By doing these contractions you start bringing blood and prana into the pelvic area, and with that prana, increased consciousness.

• **Hand Movements.** It is helpful to use your hands as you are spinning the energy. It helps you remember where you are in your chakra rolling. With each undulation, make a circle with your hands, following the energy movement. Hands move up on the inhale, down on the exhale, in line with the spine.

Alternatively, you can use stimulation points at each chakra. Put the right hand on the lower of the two chakras to help send the energy and left hand on the higher chakra to receive the energy. The pressure points are:

1st chakra – perineum or Sacred Spot (G-spot);

2nd chakra – top of the pubic bone or genitals (scrotum or clitoris);

3rd chakra – navel;

4th chakra – sternum, between the nipples;

5th chakra – throat indentation; and

6th Chakra – Third Eye.

• **Connecting Chakras.** When you feel that chakras one and two are full of energy and connected, go from the first chakra up to the third until that connection is made. Then circle down to two and start the connection between two and three. Move up to the fourth (heart), connecting two and four, then three and four, and so forth up to the sixth. If emotional release is triggered, stay at that chakra until it is clear. Follow each energy circle with your hands.

• **Restart.** If you lose touch with the energy, you can go back to the beginning. Continue the breathing pattern and the rocking motion. Continue with your visualization as you move the energy up the body in loops.

• **Surrender.** At this point, don't be too concerned with how you are breathing. As the breath continues, the mechanical movements will disappear and your body will be taken over by its own undulating rhythm. You will be gasping and you won't have control anyway.

If you are practicing with a partner, one of you could call out chakra numbers. If you really want to bring the fire up, you can keep going back to one and picking up more energy.

Once you reach the sixth chakra, exhale, pushing the energy down. Then perform the Cobra Breath three times.

Relax for a few minutes, then begin another cycle.

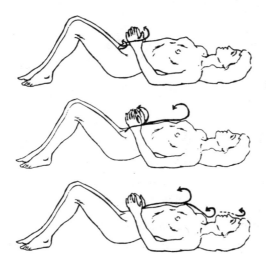

Make a loop connecting 1,2,1,2. When you feel that area is warm and full, connect 1,3,1,3.

Connect 2,3,2,3. When that is full, move to 4,2,4,2,4.

Then make smaller circles, 3 to 4, 3 to 4, until that is full. Then 3 to 5, 3 to 5. Big circles, small circles, then on to the next connection. Continue all the way to the 6th chakra.

• **Mantric Sounds.** At the 1st chakra, intone the sound "UH" on the exhale; 2nd chakra "U" (oo); at the 3rd, "O" (oh); the 4th, "A" (ah); the 5th "E" (eh); and the 6th "I" (ee). This helps to activate the respective chakras.

• **Duration.** Practice the breath for twenty minutes initially, working up to sixty, but don't go beyond that.

• **Cosmic Orgasm.** The FireBreath is a preliminary technique to get the energy moving up the spinal channel. Once energy is moving, once you reach those high levels of excitation, you can use the Cobra Breath to take that energy up the spinal canal into the higher chakras in the brain, the source of true spiritual experience, to have a Cosmic Orgasm. You cannot reach the higher chakras through the central channel. The central channel is a psychic channel. The spine is a physical channel. The physical glands in the brain must be stimulated to achieve the Cosmic Orgasm.

Without the Cobra Breath, this process will probably culminate in a conventional orgasm, more intense than usual, but still just at the physical level. In the Cosmic Orgasm, all of the chakras, including those in the brain, open up simultaneously, not one by one. You create a dynamo of exalted energy, vibrating through the body.

For Men. Men might want to perform an extra step before climbing the chakra ladder. Men and women are of opposite polarity. Women draw Shakti energy directly up from the earth through the soles of their feet and up the inner thigh. Men pull Shiva energy down from the sky. "Shiva" is that hot, solar energy which men roll down into the body to prepare the chakras for opening with Shakti energy. There are two ways to accomplish this.

1) Men begin by pulling energy through the crown chakra all the way down the back channel to the root chakra in a single inhalation. Visualize energy coming in through your crown as you inhale, moving all the way down to the perineum. Then tighten the anus and push the energy up to the sex center as you exhale. Repeat this twelve times, or until you experience the energy building up at

Muladhara. When you come down to Muladhara chakra, the polarity reverses so that men can feel the Shakti force. That balances the Shiva/Shakti energy so you start to become androgynous.

When the root chakra feels full, begin rolling the energy back up the chakras, as described above.

2) Another option is to pull the energy down from the crown, on the breath, chakra by chakra, until it reaches Muladhara. Some men find that putting the soles of their feet together assists the energy. Experiment with your own system to see if this works more effectively for you.

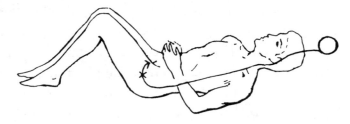

FIREBREATH FOR COUPLES

Practice the FireBreath technique individually until you attain some mastery of it. When you and your partner both feel ready, you can share the more advanced couple practices.

If the orgasmic energy dislodges an emotional block and some old feelings come up for process for one of the partners, let the other one be there in support to hold space for that process. Be present, hold witness, don't personalize anything that comes up. It is old and has nothing to do with you.

Once that wave has passed through, the next orgasm can go to places you never felt orgasmic before, places that had been blocked and are now clear.

Nauli

1. Still in the Yab Yum embrace, exhale fully, then begin making small circles with the abdomen – navel up, out, down, in. When you need to, breathe in deeply, exhale completely, and resume making circles. Continue, very gently for about a minute. Then push all the air down into the pelvis and hold it in.

2. Inhale all the way up the spine. Press foreheads together, connecting your third eyes in the Tantric Kiss. Touch tongues, and exhale down the front of the body.

3. Again, inhale all the way up the spine, tantric kiss, exhale down the front, just letting the energy descend.

4. Start again, inhaling up the back, tighten the Root Lock, tips of tongues touch, and exhale down the front. Repeat the entire process if you wish.

Meeting at the Heart

1. Begin the FireBreath, slowly breathing in through the nose, out through the mouth, synchronizing your undulations and breath, following Shakti's lead. Penetration is preferred, but not necessary.

311

Thrust together on the exhale, pull apart on the inhale. Create a sexual bond between you gently, slowly.

Shakti is rolling the energy up, chakra by chakra, and Shiva is pulling the energy down, chakra by chakra, each only coming to the heart. When you both reach the heart, pass energy back and forth from one heart to the other. Alternate your breathing so she inhales while he exhales.

2. Roll the energy a second time. She comes all the way up to the heart and he comes down to the heart. Exchange on the breath. Again. Breathe deeply in through your nose and out through your mouth.

3. Inhale up the spine and touch tongues together and exhale down the front. The last time, inhale up the spine, exhale down the front. Go deeply within and sense the oceanic feelings.

Full FireBreath

1. You could be in Yab Yum, or each sitting in easy pose. You can choose to be in union, or with the penis just touching the clitoris, or sit several inches apart with tailbone tucked under to put a little pressure on the sacrum.

2. Begin the FireBreath, both pulling energy from the root chakra, synchronizing your breath and undulations. Let one call out the chakras, so you move up together. In through the nose, out through the mouth.

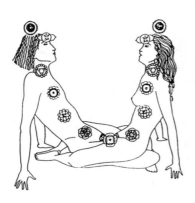

3. When you reach the 6th chakra, let the energy wash back down the spine on a hissing "I" (ee) sound. Begin another cycle.

4. Bring the energy up on the FireBreath. At the top, hold your breath, touch foreheads together in the Tantric Kiss, and exhale down the spine, thrusting into

sexual union. Inhale up the spine and touch tongues together for an energy discharge.

5. Continue until climax. Just before orgasm, during the Tantric Kiss you will feel illumination, the merging of two souls. Go deep within and sense the oceanic feelings.

Shiva Shakti Marriage

Still in union, both now lie back and relax. Grasp each others' big toes and massage the sides of the toes between the base and the joint with circular strokes. You will each feel energy come all the way up from the toes and go into your Third Eye. Shiva doesn't have to penetrate deeply into the yoni. If the head of the penis is just touching the clitoris and the vaginal opening, it is enough for the energy to flow.

By massaging these two points on the big toe, you are stimulating the pituitary and the pineal glands, creating friction inside, deep in the brain. The pituitary gland is analogous to the vagina, the pineal to the penis. The friction can create an electrical arc inside the brain, which vibrates the hypothalamus for a second or two. This connects the pineal and pituitary glands, starting the lights and whirls of colors flashing – the Tantric marriage of Shiva and Shakti.

The connection will only happen if your Shiva and Shakti energies are well balanced and your system is purified. If it doesn't happen for you, then you know you still have work to do.

If this transcendent moment does occur for one of you, come together and hold each other. Share that rapture for a long time. Let your separating be gentle and sensitive. You will be in a very precious and delicate space.

This is the culminating experience of the tantric practice for couples, the moment when you as an individual disappear into the Cosmic Whole, when you are totally at one with all creation.

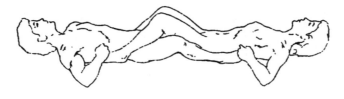

APPENDIX D
NETWORK SPINAL ANALYSIS

Emotional blockage results from the inability to stay present. An experience -physical or emotional trauma, mental worry or fear, or biochemical stress - was outside our context of what we were able to assimilate. We did not have the awareness, flexibility, tools, support, time, or it wasn't safe, to integrate the experience so it was stored, to be assimilated later. The vibration of the unresolved experience is "held" in our energy, pranic body, which steps down into the physical body and is expressed as muscular armoring which is related to the emotional sub-system.

The subconscious patterns in the spinal cord, the control subsystem, are in the subconscious mind, where the automatic, habitual patterns function without cortical involvement. These subconscious patterns filter our environment, like looking through a veil, distorting the information our body is sensing as it ascends to the cortex. Our cortex (conscious mind) takes this distorted information and responds, sending orders to the body that also get distorted in a subluxated (less light-ed) spine. There are also spinal reflex archs that respond to our environment at the spinal level without any cortical input. In a distorted spine these responses are in that same distortion. We respond to the world as we perceive it through the patterns of our unresolved trauma.

Network Spinal Analysis is a gentle way to bring awareness to the distortions, the holding patterns we have in our spine and para-spinal muscles. As we bring awareness to these patterns we develop new strategies to resolve the old holding patterns.

In the first level of care we connect to the trauma and find ways to release our hold; our breath increases and the vertebral segment begins to rock, freeing itself. People begin to see how they are holding on to old patterns in their body and in their life. They may feel "stuck."

As we become less invested in the old patterns we move into level 2 of care and use this stuck energy of the old pattern as fuel to connect to other areas in the spine. This transforms the old patterns and refines the relationship between different areas of the spine as segments begin to entrain with each other, synchronizing their movement in time and space. In the second level of care people have an increased awareness of the inter-connectedness of life.

An NSA chiropractor follows your body as it retraces and unwinds, similar to a telephone cord unwinding the kinks in it. During an entrainment session your doctor uses gentle contacts to help you become aware of specific points of holding so you can re-choose, bringing that holding from the past into the current time. As your awareness is present to the holding, healing happens and an integration occurs. What was separate and locked away in us is assimilated back into the whole, the holy, the healed.

Abundant Health Associates, Lexi Fisher D.C.
(760) 327-4041
758 S. Vella Rd., Palm Springs, CA 92264

INDEX OF TECHNIQUES

Chapter 1
Babaji Mantra................18
Bated Breath................32
Kriya Energization 12-part....33
Witness Thoughts............33

Chapter 2
Watching the Breath.........55
Breath Mantra, Hong Saw.....56
Khechari Mudra..............56
Complete Breath.............56
Rishi Isometrics............57

Chapter 3
BodyFlow (latihan)..........70
Ganesh mantra and yantra....71
Sex Magic...................72
Aswini Mudra................76

Chapter 4
Inner Smile.................83
Nadi Kriyas.................99

Chapter 6
AUM Mantra..................146

Chapter 7
Alternate Nostril Breath....169
Vajroli Mudra...............171
Sahajoli Mudra..............171
Solar/Lunar Breath..........171

Chapter 8
Moola Bandha................193
Sushumna Activation.........194

Chapter 9
Stomach Rubs................214
Nauli.......................215

Chapter 12
Kali Mantra.................272
Erotic Massage..............272
Shiva Mantra................273
Sat Chit Ananda
Namah Mantra................274

Appendix A
Individual Techniques
Conscious Breathing.........279
Transmutaion Breath.........279
Trataka.....................279
Uddiyana Bandha
(Diaphragm Lock)............280

Couple Techniques
Golden Sphere Breathing.....281
Hong Saw Back to Back.......282
Attunement..................283
Spinal Spiral...............283
Fusion Breath...............286
Tibetan Alchemical Meditation
(Golden Body of Light)......288

Appendix C
FireBreath for individual...305
FireBreath for couples......311
Full FireBreath.............312
Shiva Shakti Marriage.......313

FROM COURSE PARTICIPANTS

"Bodhi Avinasha has brought to men and women of the western world a spiritual truth about our sexuality and our divinity. Her path is about loving our human-ness, loving ourselves and opening our hearts to all of mankind."

"Bodhi's clarity of vision and gentle humor combine with her unflinching desire to help me take the next step I need. She's truly a gift."

"Bodhi is a rare human being and I'm so grateful for the work she does."

"Awesome! Bodhi comes from such a state of non-inflation. She is truly a guide and teacher."

"Bodhi is the most compassionate loving pure teacher I've come across. Her love for humanity is clearly expressed. I'm honored to have been taught by her."

"Bodhi has the amazing gift of being able to integrate the wisdom teachings of multiple traditions into a coherent whole that, if used, will lead us to bliss."

"A teacher in whose eyes and smile I see profound joy and in whose heart I feel deep love."

"Bodhi is a totally dedicated instrument, vehicle and voice for this technology. She is an embodiment of the earth's energy and commitment to us all"

"Bodhi is the love in light and the light in love – pure compassion in human form brought down from the heavens to gift this world."

ABOUT THE AUTHOR

Bodhi Avinasha has been a lifelong spiritual seeker and student, experiencing the gamut of human development offerings in the Western world. As a sannyasin with Osho (Bhagwan Shree Rajnesh), a foremost tantric master, she went through a metamorphosis while training in his unique blend of psychology and mysticism.

She has spent three decades creating and refining Ipsalu Tantra Kriya Yoga while sharing it with thousands around the world.

Bodhi facilitates workshops of extra-ordinary depth and transformation. She is skilled at leading people to an experiential discovery of higher states they may not have known before. She has a solid, down-to-earth presence that cuts right to the core with insight, wisdom, humor and compassion.

Her first book, *Jewel in the Lotus*, has become a classic tantric text.

Being an accomplished classical pianist and choral director, she accesses the power of sound in mantra, song and dance.

The founder of Tantrika International, Bodhi currently offers courses in Ipsalu Tantra Kriya Yoga at various locations around the country and is available for private consultation via phone or in person. To learn of scheduled courses or consider creating a course in your area, contact Bodhi Avinasha at:

IPSALU TANTRA

12115 Magnolia Blvd. #143
Valley Village, CA 91607

info@IpsaluTantra.com

(800) 451-3704

319

PARTICIPANTS SPEAK OF THEIR EXPERIENCE

"The Level One and Two Ipsalu Tantra Workshops have changed me deeply, and I <u>never</u> thought I could change. They have shown me the Bliss possible in life and given me tools that <u>work</u> to come to that Bliss."

– Myles Maloney (Edmonton, Alberta, Canada)

"Level Two is an ascension to the divine. My soul, my essence resonated, and my heart beat with a universal beat. I saw the world through a new vision. I'm alive in all ways."

– Karla Rowe (Chicago, IL)

"It is a journey into the unknown which opens the Heart and takes me places I've only dreamed of. To embrace a group of souls and feel loved is such a gift."

– Jeff Osztian (Calgary, Alberta, Canada)

THE TANTRIKA INTERNATIONAL COMMUNITY

This work is supported by Tantrika International, a non-profit organization dedicated to transforming people's lives, offering to the world a real possibility of living in Bliss. To accomplish this, T.I. makes available the comprehensive system of Ipsalu Tantric Kriya Yoga:

- A Technology – powerful tools to reorganize the subtle energies that determine our health, our well-being, our level of awareness.

- A Paradigm – a way of looking at life that allows for dramatic changes.

- Materials – to support the process of rapid awakening.

- Life-Altering Courses – to introduce three levels of spiritual development, as well as additional courses for couples, special groups, related materials, etc.

- A Support System – to guide people through the process.

- Communities in Various Cities – new ones coming together every year, where people can gather to create and share a magical space.

- Year-Long Groups – Facilitator Training for those who would lead groups, and Bliss in Service for those who want to go deeper in their process and to serve in ways other than facilitating.

- Biannual Multi-University/Festival – to go more deeply into the practices, to learn more of related matters, to celebrate in the company of like-minded souls.

Tantrika International has been blessed with volunteer efforts of many talented people and donations from those who wish to give financial support. The opportunity continues for anyone inclined to contribute to the growth of this work.

For more information on scheduled activities or available materials, contact: **TANTRIKA INTERNATIONAL**

P.O. Box 516
Loveland, OH 45140

www.TantraBliss.com
info@TantraBliss.com

Toll Free: (888) TANTRIKA
826-8745